SWEAT EQUITY

Since 1996, Bloomberg Press has published books for financial professionals, as well as books of general interest in investing, economics, current affairs, and policy affecting investors and business people. Titles are written by well-known practitioners, BLOOMBERG NEWS® reporters and columnists, and other leading authorities and journalists. Bloomberg Press books have been translated into more than 20 languages.

For a list of available titles, please visit our Web site at www.wiley.com/go/bloombergpress.

SWEAT EQUITY

Inside the New Economy
of Mind and Body

Jason Kelly

BLOOMBERG PRESS

An Imprint of

WILEY

Published by John Wiley & Sons, Inc., Hoboken, New Jersey.
Published simultaneously in Canada.

For general information on our other products and services or for technical support, please contact our Customer Care Department within the United States at (800) 762-2974, outside the United States at (317) 572-3993, or fax (317) 572-4002.

Wiley publishes in a variety of print and electronic formats and by print-on-demand. Some material included with standard print versions of this book may not be included in e-books or in print-on-demand. If this book refers to media such as a CD or DVD that is not included in the version you purchased, you may download this material at http://booksupport.wiley.com. For more information about Wiley products, visit www.wiley.com.

Library of Congress Cataloging-in-Publication Data:

Names: Kelly, Jason, 1973- author.
Title: Sweat equity : marathons, yoga, and the business of the modern,
    wealthy body / Jason Kelly.
Description: Hoboken : Bloomberg Press, 2016. | Series: Bloomberg | Includes
    bibliographical references and index.
Identifiers: LCCN 2016011018 (print) | LCCN 2016011198 (ebook) | ISBN
    978-1-118-91459-5 (hardback) | ISBN 978-1-118-91461-8 (ePDF) | ISBN 978-1-118-91460-1 (ePub)
Subjects: LCSH: Businesspeople. | Leadership. | Success in business. | BISAC:
    BUSINESS & ECONOMICS / Consumer Behavior.
Classification: LCC HB615 .K3955 2016 (print) | LCC HB615 (ebook) | DDC
    338.7/616130973—dc23
LC record available at http://lccn.loc.gov/2016011018

Printed in the United States of America.

10 9 8 7 6 5 4 3 2

MIX
Paper from
responsible sources
FSC
www.fsc.org
FSC® C101537

For Owen

Contents

Acknowledgments   ix

Introduction: Take Your Gym to Work   xiii

CHAPTER 1
Money Moves   1

CHAPTER 2
On Location   13

CHAPTER 3
Barry and the Art of Boutique Fitness   29

CHAPTER 4
Mob Rules   43

CHAPTER 5
Dress the Part   61

CHAPTER 6
Looking for Meaning   77

CHAPTER 7
Charity Case   93

CHAPTER 8
Work and Working Out   109

CHAPTER 9
Mary's Merry Marathons   127

CHAPTER 10
Money on the Run   143

CHAPTER 11
  The Man Makes the Shoe   **157**

CHAPTER 12
  The Money in Color   **169**

CHAPTER 13
  The Guts   **183**

Conclusion   **197**

About the Author   **201**

Index   **203**

Acknowledgments

It's a rare and wonderful thing when things you love collide in a single project and I'm deeply grateful to the many, many people who helped me along the way.

None of this would be possible without the support of Bloomberg, my journalistic home since 2002. Working there has provided me opportunities, challenges, and adventures I never imagined and I owe more than I can express to Bloomberg's leadership, starting with Mike Bloomberg and Peter Grauer. I've been able to work for two amazing editors-in-chief, including *Bloomberg News* founder Matt Winkler, who hired me and has supported me for more than a dozen years. More recently, I've learned much from and been inspired by John Micklethwait.

John McCorry hired me almost 14 years ago and it's an honor and pleasure to work closely with him these many years later. Reto Gregori has encouraged and challenged me, as has Chris Collins. Jennifer Sondag is my Bloomberg conscience and de facto life coach.

Evan Burton and Tula Batanchiev at Wiley understood the idea from the beginning, stuck with me, and helped me find the book in this big topic, adding their personal fitness experiences into the mix. James Belcher, a fellow endurance athlete, provided a burst of enthusiastic support that got me over this particular finish line.

Bob Bierman gave early encouragement and space to get this book going, and advice based on his triathlete adventures. Laura Chapman, work neighbor, friend, and yogi, endured the tortured final months of the manuscript. Kristi Huller, Tatiana Mishin, and Jay Hass all provided key introductions to characters in this book.

I'm grateful to friends and colleagues inside Bloomberg and beyond, especially those who, sometimes unwittingly, spurred me forward with a simple, "How's that book coming along?" as well as insights from their own fitness lives. I'm indebted to Liz Hester, Duncan King, Allison Bennett, Laura Marcinek, Shelby Siegel, Katherine Sayers, Laura Zelenko, Karen Toulon,

Tom Contiliano, Stephanie Ruhle, Erik Schatzker, David Westin, Kevin Sheekey, Meridith Webster, Lee Cochran, Ty Trippet, Jill Watanabe, Ashley Bahnken, Craig Gordon, Cory Johnson, Ken Karpay, Betty Liu, Kristen Hensley, Lisa Kassenaar, Barbara Morgan, Clyde Eltzroth, Holly Doran, Dennis O'Brien, Ashley Merryman, Stephanie Mehta, Stacy Kennedy, Adam Levy, Noam Neusner, Randy Whitestone, Chris Ullman, David Marchick, Deirdre Bolton, Mike Buteau, Rob Urban, Tallin Braun, Christine Ong, Robin Wood Sailer, Sally Armbruster, Suzanne Fleming, Jonathan Keehner, Derick Schaudies, Herbie and Ellen Calves, Jennifer Meyers, Beth and Steve Loffredo, Jim and Allie Baller, Denise and Bill Scaglione, Margaret and Dave Yawman, Burns and Ruth Patterson, and many others in Sleepy Hollow. I'm grateful for my association with the Hudson Valley Writers' Center, whose work I deeply believe in.

Wendy Naugle is a brilliant editor and writer, and a dedicated, crazy-fast runner to boot, making her invaluable to me over the course of this project, on the trails, and on the road to races that appear throughout this book. She's also among a group of diehard fun runners that show up to run through Rockefeller State Park every weekend. The day that my neighbor Todd Ruppel, the unofficial mayor of the group, invited me to join that merry band changed me as a runner and person. Ben Cheever taught me a lot about writing and life on those trails.

My modern life as a runner began in 1999, when I watched my friend Billy Robins run a marathon at Disney World. Within months, he'd hooked me into his gang of runners. Through hundreds of phone calls, e-mails, and texts, he encouraged and cajoled me through a dozen marathons. He's a coach and role model beyond compare. His wife, Kendra, by virtue of her unyielding support, knows more about marathons than most people who run them.

As the years go by, I'm increasingly grateful to early influences that set me on a rewarding path, including my teachers at Christ the King School in Atlanta, as well as St. Michael's Elementary School and St. Thomas High School in Houston. It was at the latter, as a member of the cross country team and editor of *The Eagle* newspaper, that I first fell in love with both running and writing. My time at Georgetown University not only introduced me to my future wife, but taught me that I might actually make a living as a journalist. I learned both in the classroom, from professor/practitioners like Ted Gup, and in the hothouse of a college newspaper—the Georgetown *Voice*—where I found through writing and editing (and, most important, being edited) that there is no greater place than a newsroom.

My parents, Dennis and Debby Kelly, have made me the son, father, and writer I am, along with my brothers Wynne and Sam, architects of a perpetual, sometimes multi-continental "brother chat." I'm grateful to my in-laws, Alice and Jack Kane, for their constant, unwavering support (and for being devoted viewers of Bloomberg TV).

My sons, Henry, William, and Owen, are nothing short of my soul. My wife, Jen, has made countless sacrifices and concessions to my craziness as both exercise fanatic and neurotic writer. I remain in awe of her grace and intelligence.

—JK

Introduction: Take Your Gym to Work

Aarti Kapoor was an investment banking cliché in 2008. She was a study in stress, owing to the hours she was logging at Citigroup as the financial crisis deepened, along with a dash of existential crisis thrown in. She and her peers were scrambling to stay relevant and employed. Top executives at her bank and others were defending themselves to regulators, clients, and their own employees. The promise of a rewarding career on Wall Street seemed increasingly elusive.

Growing up in Princeton, New Jersey, Kapoor had been an especially active adolescent, wide-ranging in her extracurricular interests—ballet, voice and piano lessons, swimming, editor of the school newspaper, admissions tour guide. Tennis became her sport of choice and she ended up the captain of her high school varsity team. At Harvard, she stayed fit, then hit Wall Street, where an extra 10 pounds was practically guaranteed by the demands of a long-hours banking job, with ordered-in dinners and little sleep.

In a moment of quasi-panic about being out of shape, she joined the closest gym to the office, an Equinox gym in downtown Manhattan. She went all in, hell-bent on getting in shape. "I was militant about it," she says. "And then I was addicted." Exercise was a refuge and a release, a way to calm her mind while taking care of her body.

The exercise obsession followed her when she changed jobs after witnessing several rounds of job cuts at Citi. Landing at a boutique firm called Moelis & Co., she endured the same hours, but was generally happier, working for a firm a step removed from the aggressive anti-banking headlines.

With Equinox too far from her new office, she reluctantly gave up her membership there and joined a 24-Hour Fitness near Moelis, where she took full advantage of its always-open promise. Some nights she'd leave the office at 2 a.m., run on the treadmill for two hours, go home and sleep, and be back in the office by 9 a.m. "I didn't like any days that didn't have fitness in them," she says, conceding she got addicted to the post-workout high. "I'd gotten out of shape once, and I didn't want to be in that place again."

Fully immersed, Kapoor reverted to her adolescent tendency to try lots of different things, an M.O. shared by many of her Millennial generation. Then a new concept landed in New York's Flatiron district, a downtown hub of high-end apartments, technology start-ups, cool restaurants, and increasingly, fitness studios.

Flywheel, a then-new indoor cycling concept, opened its flagship location across the street from Kapoor's apartment and, while intrigued, she balked at the price of $30 for a single, 45-minute class. "I thought, who in their right mind would spend that?" she says. Flywheel offered a promotion to building residents for their patience during construction of the studio. She showed up.

Flywheel was tailor-made for Kapoor. While indoor cycling isn't new—Spinning was created in the early 1990s—Flywheel's twist is to pump up the competitive element. In addition to the sinewy, barking instructor, Flywheel adds a way to keep score—called the TorqBoard—that ranks every member of the class, in real time. Riders watch while they pull ahead, or fall behind, their classmates. Members keep track of their progress.

As she had with the Equinox workouts, Kapoor went big. "Another class turned into a 5-pack of classes, then a 10-pack, then an unlimited monthly membership," the last of which runs $375. Her weekday routine included a long run followed by a Flywheel class. Kapoor the banker watched Kapoor the consumer make radical changes to her spending. She asked her parents for Flywheel credits instead of handbags or shoes for Christmas.

At the studio each week, she watched classes fill up and waiting lists form. Over brunch with friends, she heard not just about Flywheel and Equinox, but SoulCycle, Pure Barre, Physique 57, as well as yoga, half marathons, marathons, and triathlons. At the Moelis office, she began to craft a pitch.

The first audience was her mentor, a senior banker named Roger Hoit who specializes in consumer and retail companies. The pitch included sending Hoit, an avid golfer, to a couple Flywheel workouts.

Hoit and his fellow Moelis senior managers gave Kapoor the go-ahead to test her thesis that health and fitness were bankable businesses—an industry comprising companies growing in a way that they'd be taking on investors, seeking investors, getting sold, and going public. In other words, all the things bankers earn money arranging and giving advice on.

Kapoor tacked it on to her regular job: "I did my normal work until 11 p.m. and then worked on my fitness research." She cold-called companies to meet with their top executives, with Flywheel at the top of the list. It wasn't long before Kapoor's side project became her full-time gig. Within two years, she represented Flywheel in a sale of a majority stake, one in a series of companies drawing billions from PE, venture, and public investors. Kapoor now spends all her time banking health, wellness, and fitness companies; she is one of small handful of bankers making their living in the space. The happy collision of her banking and fitness lives included Kapoor's ability to work out and call it work. "My diligence trips have gotten a lot more interesting," she says.

Kapoor operates, personally and professionally, in a new sphere and a new economy—one revolving around the mind and body. She has a 94-page presentation (pitch book in banking parlance) stuffed with statistics and charts and graphs. Her bio within that book touts her fitness bona fides, including that she runs roughly 2,000 miles a year, is both gluten- and dairy-free, and is a "serial juicer."

Her credibility resides not only in her informed view of the market dynamics but also from the fact that she's the target audience for the companies she's pitching to represent. Her age—30—is crucial to understanding the state of the fitness business and where it's going. Like her peers, Kapoor lives in a place, geographically and demographically, where health and wellness are a given, where almost every choice throughout the day—when you get up, what you eat, what you wear, what you do, and who you hang out with—points back to that lifestyle.

That shift, from activity to lifestyle, makes Kapoor's job possible. The breadth and depth of the need for products and services has created a new economy of mind and body, drawing investors to back the entrepreneurs and big, established companies clamoring to fill that need.

The market is massive. By one estimate, health and fitness—gyms and studios, clothes, and various equipment, comprise a market worth almost half a trillion dollars.[1] Add in food you're talking more than $1 trillion. Wellness overall —the spas, wellness tourism, workplace wellness, and the like—is pegged at $3.4 trillion.

How in the world did this happen?

To hear Kapoor and many others tell it, the birth of this economy came from a collision of elements including a multigenerational move to healthier living and an historical technology boom that enabled an entirely different lifestyle and changed our relationship to our family and our employers, as well as gave birth to an enormous swath of affluence. An increasing amount of that affluence is directed toward health and well-being.

---

[1] Alexandra Plessier, "Wellness Is Now a $3.4 Trillion Global Industry—Three Times Bigger Than the Worldwide Pharmaceutical Industry!"   http://blog.globalwellnesssummit .com/2014/10/wellness-is-now-a-3-4-trillion-global-industry-three-times-bigger-than-the-worldwide-pharmaceutical-industry.

Baby Boomers (born 1945 to 1964) helped kicked it off, becoming the first generation to favor sweating over smoking, opting for Jane Fonda workouts and Arnold Schwarzenegger movies. And while they held onto those habits into their retirement years, their influence on their children, and how those kids have lived those lessons, is what really accelerated the fitness boom. As Generation X came into the workforce, fitness manifested itself largely in the pursuit of slightly more extreme activities. A chunk of Generation X (born roughly between 1965 and 1979) took up running and cycling, pushing endurance sports from the fringe into popular culture. Marathons and triathlons especially have become a borderline-cliché badge of honor for forty- and fiftysomethings who came into adulthood in the 1990s.

Those generations especially helped propel running, which saw a surge in the past twenty years that moved running, notably in long-distance races, from the fringe to the mainstream. The number of people who finished races in 1990 quadrupled to more than 19 million in 2013. During that same period, the number of women increased more than nine-fold, to the point where there were about 30 percent more women finishers than men. Back in 1990, men had nearly a three-to-one advantage.[2]

What Baby Boomers created and Generation X accelerated, Millennials—especially Millennial women—have codified into their everyday work and social lives. This demographic, born in the two decades between 1980 and 2000, have pushed fitness into a defining personal characteristic, both through activities like running and especially in their enthusiasm for boutique fitness. And that's where it gets really interesting for anyone who cares about business and economics. The massive social shift toward fitness has created a multifaceted, global, economic juggernaut, with entrepreneurs, investors, and the world's biggest companies scrambling for a piece of the growing market worth hundreds of billions of dollars.

As both observer and participant (I've run more than a dozen marathons and numerous other races, and taken the odd yoga or fitness class along the way), I went in search of the people defining this new economy. I found entrepreneurs and investors who manage to make a living—and in some cases, millions or even billions of dollars—feeding our obsessions with races, classes, clothes, and equipment.

This book is a snapshot of sorts, a glimpse inside an ever-changing series of overlapping businesses. I emphasize "ever-changing" because some of these companies may flame out or slowly fade. Kapoor says she's constantly on the lookout for what's real and what's fleeting, what will play for a few months

---

[2] Running Event Finishers, 1990–2013. Running USA, www.runningusa.org/statistics.

among the maniacally fit cognoscenti in certain New York or Los Angeles neighborhoods, and what will translate into an actual business that can take root in places between the coasts, transcend a fad status, and be a sustainable activity for employees and consumers, and profitable.

Kapoor's among those with a deep conviction that while the players are dynamic, the underlying fitness economy is solid, and growing. There's a lot of money in sweat.

CHAPTER 1

Money Moves

Despite all the evidence for this new economy of mind and body—the races, the studios, the endless conversations at work and on weekends about someone's latest and greatest workout or personal best triathlon—I wasn't convinced it was real. Until I found the bankers.

Bankers and journalists, sometimes much to our mutual chagrin, pursue our jobs by similar means: We follow the money. And it's clear that Aarti Kapoor, and her increasing number of competitors, are finding lots of it to chase. The money's seemingly everywhere. It starts by leaving our wallets as disposable income, directed at fitness, and our bodies, as never before. We're spending billions on race entries, memberships, and class fees, plus all the stuff it takes to get us outfitted.

And it's not just our own dollars. Consumers' money is often augmented, directly and indirectly, by employers, many of whom see a healthier workforce as happier, more productive, and cheaper. Those health initiatives often come from highly placed, high-octane fitness nuts who made it to the corner office, and want to push health down through the ranks.

What we're buying has also changed. Technology, as always, acts as jet fuel for the most radical changes in how we live, work, and spend time and money. Technology is pushing our homes and offices ever closer to a *Jetsons*-like existence. Software programs, gadgets, and an Internet-connected world have all changed our perspective on our minds and bodies. We have unprecedented access to data about ourselves, our habits, and our lives.

Technology plays a dual role, connecting and alienating us at the same time. On the one hand, it enables us to run faster and work out smarter, with new machines and techniques and means to measure every calorie, watt, and step. It allows us to share our achievements in real time and congratulate and

1

encourage each other. On the other hand, our broad technology addiction is pushing us to seek meaning away from the growing din of the information age. We're drawn in that search for meaning to what the sociologist Ray Oldenburg called "third places"—the first two being home and work—where we socialize and connect. That reaction is adding another dimension to this economy and an opportunity—one that's based on physical, not virtual, space.

All of these colliding elements draw money, and, in turn, the people in the business of moving money around—venture capital and private equity investors eager to capitalize on growth industries, entrepreneurs with a big idea, and savvy executives looking to reinvent their companies. From food purveyors to workout equipment manufacturers to fitness centers and race series, smart money is moving in. Now some of those investors are starting to reap financial rewards as companies like Lululemon, Fitbit, SoulCycle, and Mind Body pursue initial public offerings, a key milestone in creating an enduring enterprise—enterprises supported by consumers and businesses that, when successful, ultimately reward their creators and investors.

And where there's money to be made, there will be investment bankers—the well-educated, well-heeled set who make their living connecting buyers and sellers. Yet given the relatively early nature of this economy, those bankers aren't legion. They're tucked into smaller investment banks, firms outside of Wall Street's bulge-bracket banks like Goldman Sachs, Morgan Stanley, and JPMorgan Chase.

Piper Jaffray's Brian Smith is one of them. He grew up in Northern California, and, armed with an economics degree from Claremont McKenna, he went to work for Bain & Co., the management consulting firm that a few decades ago begat private equity stalwart Bain Capital. After two years at Bain, he got an offer from a shop in Connecticut called North Castle Partners, which had a distinct focus on sports, health, and wellness. "They were doing some interesting investing," he says. "They were investing in brands that I loved." He was on staff there when the PE firm owned Equinox, the high-end gym operator.

After a stint in the nutritional supplements industry, he reunited with a North Castle partner, Brent Knudsen, who was opening a merchant bank—a type of firm that both arranges deals and raises money from investors for those transactions. It was 2006, and while fitness was coming on strong, it lacked anything cohesive in terms of financial advice. "There was no banker, no one working this segment of the market," Smith says.

The new firm, Partnership Capital Growth, set up shop in San Francisco, drawn to the city's long-standing commitment to a lifestyle steeped in health-consciousness. Smith, now married to a California girl, was back in his home state and the firm worked with companies like Anytime Fitness, KIND Healthy Snacks, and Muscle Milk, and managed $200 million in assets. At the end of 2013, Partnership Capital linked up with Piper Jaffray, creating a relationship with the 120-year-old Minneapolis-based bank. There, Smith has worked on the sale of Pure Barre to Catterton and the purchase of California Family Fitness by Perpetual Capital, as well as an investment in Orangetheory Fitness.

Down the coast in Los Angeles, Brian Wood at Imperial Capital is using a similar playbook. He's been in the investment banking business longer than Kapoor and Smith, graduating from Notre Dame in the mid-1990s and earning an MBA from Georgetown at the start of his banking career.

His first job out of business school took him to Houston and a then-exciting opportunity at Enron. When the company imploded amid an accounting scandal a year and a half after he arrived, Wood headed back west and took a job in the investment banking group of The Seidler Companies, an L.A.-based investment firm. The private equity side of the business took a stake in LA Fitness, a successful chain of gyms. On the banking side, wellness deals were mostly focused on nutrition, healthy food, and natural products, a harbinger of the broader move to healthy living.

Now at Imperial, he says the past two years have seen his work shift hard to the fitness space, where competition is fierce and there's a lot of business to be had. He and his colleagues make a practice of attending a class of the company in question the morning of the meeting, because understanding how it works is critical given that need for differentiation. And the consumer is voracious, and ever changing, in her appetite for these services. "You need to make sure you have the flexibility to move with the consumer," Wood says.

Even outside of work, Wood's not just poring over spreadsheets and balance sheets. He's signing up for races and classes—when we talked for the first time, he was about to participate in a 24-hour relay race run by Ragnar—to understand the texture of this new economy. There was also a social component; his team comprised a dozen fellow parents from his neighborhood, aged 35 to 55, banding together to complete the 200-mile relay. Even with the personal interest, Wood and Kapoor's respective bosses aren't just indulging them so they can be fit and healthy. Investment banks exist only when there's money moving, an ecosystem of investors—private and public pools of money—and companies for them to buy and sell.

The private pools have become especially important during the past two decades, and a critical accelerant for the fitness economy. Kapoor in her deck identified no less than 45 financial firms who'd already somehow participated in the fitness and wellness sector. The list comprises specialty firms, as well as brand-name investment shops like KKR, Apollo, Warburg Pincus, and TPG.

A note on private equity is relevant here, especially since it was a catalyst for me to undertake this project. I wrote a book in 2012 called *The New Tycoons: Inside the Trillion Dollar Private Equity Industry that Owns Everything*, the product of five years leading Bloomberg's coverage in that area. The genesis of that book was the realization of private equity firms' entrenchment in the global economy that was largely unnoticed but massive in its scope.

Kapoor's work validated the anecdotal evidence I gathered, namely that private equity money was increasingly interested in this area from various angles—from the underlying technology, to apparel, to studios, to races. In some cases the investors' pursuits are personal, just like for Kapoor and Wood—and me. Another catalyst for this project was consistently running across private equity executives I got to know in the course of my work who were spending early mornings and lunch hours training, and weekends racing.

This thread ties into another element—the overlap between high-achieving executives and participation in endurance sports. Bankers and investors have increasingly traded their fancy Rolexes for Timex Ironman and Garmin watches, in part as a not-so-subtle indicator that they spend their free time working out and staying fit. It's only natural then that many of the men and women making deals would seek out companies in businesses they're personally fond of, and in which they believe.

The evolution of the fitness industry has tracked the growth and expansion of private equity, which now accounts for more than $3 trillion in assets around the world, after existing as an industry for less than 30 years. Private equity firms in their early incarnation were known as leveraged buyout (LBO) firms, a nod to their reliance on debt, or leverage. Early profits came mostly from financial engineering—buying cheap, with lots of borrowed money, and selling quickly, without a lot of work on the company itself. Clever and lucrative, yes, but with little lasting impact.

The past decade has seen an evolution of private equity firms, who wisely shifted to that gentler nomenclature over the course of the 1990s and early 2000s. (Even private equity now feels outdated, given that KKR and Blackstone, to name just two, are publicly listed on the New York Stock Exchange). Buyout firms spent the first decade of this century chasing, and catching, ever-bigger targets. Fueled by available and inexpensive debt, firms by 2007 were spending $15 to $20 billion or more on the biggest deals, buying the likes of Hilton and Dunkin Donuts.

The financial crisis that began in 2008 chastened dealmakers and checked private equity ambitions. Purchase prices became more reasonable. More important, investors and companies became more demanding of their private equity partners, pressing for more details about their plans and strategy for targets. A still-competitive market, with a lot more firms chasing deals, also made it much more difficult to buy low and sell high, with little actual action in between. Firms started talking lots more about growth and operational improvement.

Doing that demands a higher level of expertise, well beyond analyzing balance sheets and income statements. The successful firms, especially those smaller than the giants like Blackstone, KKR, and Carlyle, began to tout specialties. A history of winning chemical, manufacturing, health care, or technology deals became much more attractive to both investors and targets.

That was good news for the handful of firms that quietly grew up focused on health and wellness, especially as those types of companies became more and more successful, and began looking for additional capital. These firms were by definition smaller, because the companies they'd bought stakes in weren't very large, especially through the late 1990s and into the early 2000s. Most targets had well under $200 million in annual revenue, putting them outside the screens of big-cap PE firms.

Investing in wellness and fitness seems obvious now, but two decades ago—even around the turn of the century—it felt niche, probably too niche to make any real money. But the guys who were living it every day, outside the office, saw a huge opportunity. That's what happened to Jesse Du Bey.

Du Bey grew up in Seattle watching his father run, and it came naturally to him, too. "I remember being able to run faster and further than other kids," he says. "And I remember liking the suffering."

At age 12, he ran a 5:30 mile, which placed him among the fastest in the nation, as measured by the Presidential Fitness Test. He voiced a sentiment I'd often heard, and felt—that running provided a chance to excel where other athletics didn't. "I liked the feeling of it. I was unremarkable at the 'main sports' like basketball and football."

Du Bey didn't run track or cross country in college at the University of Washington, but did continue to work out and became more muscular. He arrived in New York in 1999 to work on Wall Street, putting in the 100 hours a week that's common for a young analyst. He began his career advising companies and investing money for the late Bruce Wasserstein, a legendary dealmaker.

In 2005, a friend of his in the investment business, Fernando Vigil of Bain Capital Ventures, introduced Du Bey to an entrepreneur named Chris

Hessler, who was already an accomplished triathlete. Hessler convinced the two investors to enter a triathlon. They rented mountain bikes and, Du Bey says, "swam for the first time since I was 8." Even after finishing close to last, he found it "amazingly fun."

He was hooked. Du Bey signed up for several more local triathlons. Something inside him changed. "I'd been a working drone on Wall Street for seven years, solely focused on work," he says. "I think a lot of people throw themselves into careers and get numb, a kind of lack of inspiration and passion for life. Triathlon helped me find that; I think maybe it really changed my life."

He identified the Ironman as the ultimate triathlon test and signed up for the Lake Placid version. He joined a team called Full Throttle Endurance at Chelsea Piers and discovered an entire subset of the population he wasn't aware of. "It's a whole world, all these Type A people who like to solve problems," he says.

The Ironman stands as an extraordinary physical test, and essentially began as a Hawaiian daydream, part of an ongoing friendly debate about which of three local events—the Honolulu Marathon, the Waikiki Rough Water Swim, or the Around Oahu Bike Ride—was the most difficult, and thereby produced the best athlete. A U.S. Navy officer named John Collins and his wife Judy decided to combine the three as the ultimate endurance test. In 1978, 15 participants took on a 2.4 mile swim, followed by a 112-mile bike ride, capped with a marathon (26.2 miles).

The winner was to be called Ironman; Navy officer Gordon Haller was the first, crossing the finish line in 11 hours, 46 minutes, and 58 seconds. Eleven others completed the race, and Ironman entered the lexicon. Word spread, fueled in part by a *Sports Illustrated* writer who happened upon the race while in town to cover a golf tournament in 1979. His 10-page story drew interest, and more competitors. In 1980, ABC's own icon—*Wide World of Sports*—televised parts of the race. Long before viral videos, most Americans had only a handful channels to watch. The Ironman became must-see TV, especially when what became the championship moved from Collins' original course to Kona, where the stark lava fields cyclists pedaled through added an element of visual drama.

The drama that helped cement the event's reputation came in 1982, when 23-year-old Julie Moss, a graduate student competing to complete a thesis, led for much of the race and then collapsed yards from the finish line. Her minutes-long lead evaporated and she was passed by the eventual winner, Kathleen McCartney, also competing for the first time at the Ironman distance. Moss' determination to finish—she literally crawled to the finish line—was broadcast on national television.

The world record, set in 2011, is 8 hours, 3 minutes, and 56 seconds. That's more than three-and-a-half hours faster than Haller's inaugural time. (Haller himself posted a 10:58 during the second Ironman, knocking 47 minutes off his first attempt.[1])

His first time in the race, Du Bey posted a more-than-respectable 10 hours, 15 minutes. "As soon as I finished, I thought, 'I've got to get faster,'" he says. "You're in it like an addiction."

Meanwhile, he'd gone to work for Providence Equity Partners, a Rhode Island–based private equity firm specializing in media and telecommunications deals. Its New York office sits in the iconic 9 West 57th building, also home to the buyout firms KKR and Apollo. Providence's investments include Univision and Warner Music; the firm has assets under management in excess of $40 billion.

As Du Bey got deeper into the world of Ironman, he set different aspects of his daily life on a happy collision course. Du Bey rightly identified Ironman as an iconic brand, a modern marvel of branding, and, it turns out, intellectual property management. What other company inspires customers to tattoo themselves with its logo?

That logo is known as the M-Dot because it resembles an *M* (meant to resemble a body) and a circle representing the head. World Triathlon Corp., the parent company, trademarked the logo, the word Ironman, and even the combined mileage in an Ironman (140.6) and a half-Ironman (70.3). Both Ironman finishers, tattooed and otherwise, fiercely protect the brand. And so do WTC's lawyers. That was part of the appeal for Jesse Du Bey, investor.

Du Bey was able to complement his investment pedigree with a stellar Ironman resume. He first qualified for the Ironman World Championships, held annually in Hawaii, in 2007. That race was, he says, "so difficult I was literally hallucinating, which is not uncommon." He vowed to return to the island of Kona, which is a one-word Holy Grail, like "Boston" for marathon runners. He made it back in both 2008 and 2009, after training "like a professional," dropping weight, and reducing his time. In 2009, he posted a 9:28, making him the seventh-fastest American Ironman and placing him in the top 100 overall, including professionals.

His initial approach toward buying Ironman was subtle; he knew it would be a long game. He flew to its headquarters in Tampa armed only with five PowerPoint slides laying out what he proposed to do, returning half a dozen

---

[1] Blake Whitney, "Ironman's First Champ, Gordon Haller, Looks Back 25 Years," *Active*, October 20, 2003, www.active.com/triathlon/articles/ironman-s-first-champ-gordon-haller-looks-back-25-years.

times to bolster his internal pitch. His bosses at Providence "got it fast," he says. "They all ride bikes and do competitive stuff." Like Du Bey, the broader push toward competitive endurance sports wasn't a theoretical trend to the other investors. They were living it themselves.

In 2008, Ironman was in an era of rapid growth, along with triathlons in general. From 1998 to 2014, membership in USA Triathlon, a requirement to participate in any sanctioned triathlon, grew more than fivefold, to 550,000 from 100,000.[2] Du Bey discovered the popularity didn't wane in the economic crisis, supporting the theory that tough financial times may actually bolster participation as we look beyond the stress of the office for satisfaction.

Triathlons also were reaping the rewards of a populace that had grown up running and trudging to the gym and was bored and dissatisfied. Cyclists, too, were hemmed in to some extent by the constant one-upsmanship of the latest and greatest bike. Cycling clubs can be cliquey.

By grabbing the public imagination, Ironman made the concept of swimming, biking, and running together appealing. As shorter distances became more popular and prevalent, people who might not otherwise have tried it took the chance, goaded by friends and family. Some raised money for charity, others just wanted to challenge themselves. There's also a return-to-childhood element for many of us who grew up riding bikes around the neighborhood and spending summers at pools, lakes, or the beach. Add in running—among the most basic human pursuits—and it has a strong appeal.

Du Bey contends the triathlon's appeal rests largely on a simple but not necessarily obvious element: No one is good at all three sports, certainly in the beginning, and even after a number of races. The need to ask for, and give, help lends an air of collegiality to the triathlon that doesn't exist in large measure in the sports individually. The sum of the parts makes the triathlon an endeavor you simply can't do alone, at least happily.

"Everyone needs to learn something because no one comes from a complete running, swimming, and biking background," Du Bey says. "Even if they did, they need to learn training, nutrition, and transitions. This creates a culture of learning and sharing. The nicest vibe you'll ever get in competitive sports is in the start corral at a triathlon. And the difficulty of the event and the primal thing about the suffering—it creates a tribal community. Respect is earned through the effort, the personal breakthroughs, the pain, the positivity. That's what you need for a viral trend: real humanity."

---

[2] Kate Lewis, "Is Rapid Growth Endangering the Ironman and Endurance Sports?" Glideslope *Runway Blog*, October 14, 2014, www.theglideslope.com/runway/is-rapid-growth-endangering-the-ironman-and-endurance-sports/.

Providence aggressively expanded Ironman, from a handful of races to 200 annually, and growing its staff more than tenfold, to 250 from 21. Part of the expansion was in variety, specifically in the so-called 70.3 distance, half of the traditional Ironman across the swim, bike, and run. Seven years after its purchase, Providence entertained offers and the winning bid emerged from a country that had never staged an Ironman.

In August 2015, Providence sold World Triathlon Corp. to China's Dalian Wanda Group for $650 million plus the assumption of debt, reportedly valuing the entire company at roughly $900 million.[3] At that price, Providence quadrupled its money over seven years, according to published reports, a spectacular return even in the high-flying world of private equity.

The Wanda Group bought the company with an eye toward even more aggressive international expansion, especially in its home country. A Wanda executive said at the time of the purchase that only about 100 Chinese had ever participated in an Ironman to date.

Du Bey, as an investor, has remained focused on businesses that broadly have the same characteristics as World Triathlon. In 2013, he left Providence (but remained on the World Triathlon board) to start his own private equity firm, Orkila Capital. Orkila seeks out investments where experience and media can coexist and accelerate the other, a concept Du Bey saw play out vividly as an Ironman, and an Ironman investor. He watched the power of the brand manifest itself in actual people doing something physically together, and the business opportunities that come from that collective interest. He's invested in the Webby Awards (the Oscars of the Internet) and music festivals, among other things—all of the assets focus on, Du Bey says, "investments focusing on experiences, content and products that inspire real passion and joy."

Triathlons, and the Ironman deal, clearly changed Du Bey, deepening him, he says. He started the Du Bey Family Foundation, which supports sick children with money he raises through races. "I think this is true for lots of endurance athletes—the sport brings them to an emotional place where they want to be better and help others. This is a key cause marketing factor driving the industry."

And in the wake of the World Triathlon sale, he's introspective and nostalgic in a way that's surprising in the world of deal making. "The best thing about identifying and leading the Ironman deal was that it felt important, like it might be the project of a lifetime," he says. "That is also the worst

[3] Kevin Helliker, "Ironman to Be Acquired by China's Dalian Wanda," *Wall Street Journal*, August 27, 2015, www.wsj.com/articles/ironman-to-be-acquired-by-chinas-dalian-wanda-1440642571.

thing about it—I don't know how I'll ever find a deal I care so deeply about again."

Du Bey is part of a small but seemingly growing number of investors, even entire investment firms, aiming to capitalize on fitness and wellness. There's Falconhead Capital, a New York-based firm that back in the 1990s decided to focus squarely on several aspects of health and wellness. Falconhead's original thesis, and one that remains today, is that content plays a vital role in the sports and fitness economy, says founder David Moross. One of Falconhead's first deals was for the European version of ESPN Classic Sports, a channel that shows games that have already happened, often years or decades earlier. It was a surprising success.

Falconhead's perhaps best known for its investment in what became Competitor Group, creator of the Rock 'n' Roll series of marathons and half marathons. Moross saw a content play there, as well, given that Competitor's connection to its customers was in part fueled and fed by niche publications for the participants in its running races and triathlons. (For more on Competitor, see Chapter 10.)

Moross, in partnership with the sports and talent management giant IMG, started what became Falconhead in 1998 under the name Sports Capital Partners. His initial pitch was met with skepticism, he says, because sports was seen as a closed, limited opportunity, in the form of teams and maybe some team equipment. What the doubters missed, Moross says, is that "sports" is just a name—"a term that describes activity and competition. It drives to a very profound thesis of passion," he says.

Moross says the passion for sport—broadly defined to include not only your home team, but also what you do in and around your home for your own body—has only become more important culturally. He recalls a recent conversation where a fellow investor reminded him that passion for sports these days is more deeply and broadly felt than passion for religion: "You can make money by looking at what drives the passion, what allows it to be fueled on an ongoing basis."

Another group that's dedicated investments toward fitness and wellness for the better part of two decades is North Castle, the Connecticut-based private equity firm where Brian Smith worked as a young analyst. Like other investment firms that collect former CEOs and top executives for their manufacturing expertise, North Castle has a stable of fitness and wellness experts it uses for due diligence. The firm's investors work the big industry trade shows, like the Natural Products Expo, to identify the nascent companies that may someday need a financial backer. Jon Canarick, a North Castle managing director, says the firm's focus sets it apart, especially when courting would-be portfolio companies.

"You'll never find a smokeless tobacco company or an unhealthy restaurant chain in our portfolio, which matters to some entrepreneurs," he says. That extends to the firm's executives, who need to walk the proverbial walk of a wellness-oriented investment shop: "It would be very hard to sell yourselves as the right partner for a boutique fitness company, walking into a meeting with the owners weighing 250 pounds and eating a bag of chips," he says. "There's a passion and involvement."

The firm in 2015 bought a controlling stake in Barry's Bootcamp at a reported valuation of more than $100 million. (For more on Barry's, see Chapter 3.) The Barry's deal came to North Castle in part because of its familiarity with the nuances of the gym and studio business One of its most successful deals was what became a key player in the high-end gym business: Equinox. That chain, now owned by real estate giant Related Companies, sits amid a fiercely competitive set of gyms and studios slugging it out to be the favorite destination for the affluent and sweaty.

Those people are everywhere—from a small town in Boston on a rainy April morning to studios in strip malls and high rises. And lots of money is chasing them.

CHAPTER 2

On Location

If running is the basic unit of exercise, the gym is the fitness industry's local headquarters. Walk a few blocks in any city, or drive a few miles in any suburb, and it's virtually guaranteed you'll see some sort of fitness chain nestled in a strip mall.

The ubiquity speaks to the gyms' importance in this fitness economy—for us as consumers, and for those looking to make money in our space. Fitness is front and center, and unashamedly so. Gyms aren't hidden from you. On the contrary, fitness centers are in the same complexes as supermarkets, shoe stores, dry cleaners, and pizza joints. They're a key part of our consumer habits.

That's what excites investors. Just as Moelis's Kapoor found herself directing more of her discretionary income to her Flywheel habit, even average people are devoting an increasing slice of their cash to sweating. Have any doubts about the competition for that money? Check your mailbox—or email box.

Numbers are somewhat elusive, and largely estimated, given the fragmented nature of fitness clubs; there are so many of them, and few dominant companies to give a cohesive sense of the market. Kapoor estimates that in 2015, clubs will pull in about $27 billion in revenues, a figure that grows steadily these days at around 3 percent a year.

Then there's the number of memberships, which she estimates at about 55 million, growing at about 2 percent a year. Putting the figures together, that would mean folks spending roughly $500 a year on memberships alone. This triangulates a bit with another oft-cited figure—the average monthly membership is about $55/month, or $660 a year—indicating we're in the right ballpark.

The traditional gym business did not explode in this most recent boom around fitness and wellness. Many of the current trends and fads have their foundation in the fitness clubs of the previous decades. It's a business that's seen its share of booms and busts and constant competition for the consumer. Where it stands today is an emblem of both the fitness economy and the way modern businesses fight for identity and profits.

Kapoor and her fellow bankers watch the gym space closely because it's, for lack of a better term, investable. The business is relatively simple to model in term of costs, margins, and profits, once the basic elements (geography, products and services, pricing) are established. The gym business in that sense isn't so different from any other retail concern.

The birth of what we know as the modern gym is generally pegged to the early 1980s, driven in part by a few pop-culture moments. In addition to Jane Fonda's videos, there was *10*, the 1979 Bo Derek movie that inspired many women, and men, to get in shape.

By 1980, according to history compiled by *Club Industry*, about half the adult population claimed to exercise, up from about 24 percent in 1960.[1] Tennis was popular, as was racquetball, and racquet clubs with both kinds of courts proliferated, especially in suburban areas. Over the early part of the 1980s, those clubs expanded their offerings, adding some equipment and classes to broaden their appeal and their membership. In 1981, there were about 5,000 fitness clubs across the United States; by 2012, that number swelled to more than 30,000.[2]

Clubs like Bally, one of the early stalwarts, advertised heavily, relying on some of the biggest stars of the late 1970s and 1980s, including singer Cher. The ads, available for grainy viewing on YouTube, are fun to watch. A very young Cher, in various combinations of leotards and wigs, strides through a busy fitness center, delivering a message meant to underscore that gyms aren't just for meatheads anymore. In one ad, released around the holidays in 1985, she starts out saying, "Some people worry about getting muscles. I worry about getting fat. Dieting doesn't keep me in shape. Exercise does."

After Cher's exhortations, the ad lays out the business model that Bally's helped create and persists among its legion successors in some form today: the monthly plan. Back in 1985, Bally's would sign you up for $18 a month, assuming you agreed to a two-year contract. That wasn't exactly dirt cheap—it's almost $40 in 2015 dollars. The subsequent years have seen all kinds of price

---

[1] Pamela Kufahl, "Club Industry Features Clubs of the 1980s," *Club Industry*, December 1, 2008, http://clubindustry.com/25th-anniversary/club-industry-features-clubs-1980s.

[2] International Health, Racquet, & Sportsclub Association, www.ihrsa.org/about-the-industry/.

wars that have pitted gyms against each other. In the New York area, where nothing is inexpensive, a chain of gyms offers a no-commitment monthly fee of $19.95. Other chains, including discount leader Planet Fitness, charge as little as $10 a month.

Bally's was onto something and competitors proliferated, creating a sector that stood firmly at the center of the burgeoning fitness economy, for a time.

Fitness centers are a sector of the business where private equity has long played, owing largely to the business model advertised by Cher and her cohorts, from the 1980s on. At its core, the business has a lot of what an investor is looking for, especially one of the private equity variety. The key is predictable cash flow.

A gym that signs its members up for long-term contracts has a clear picture of its business. Its costs—rent, salaries for staff and instructors, equipment, and maintenance—are effectively fixed. With those contracts in hand, the gym operator also knows the revenue side, with very little downside risk. Once a contract is signed, the member is obligated to pay the monthly fee, or face a stiff penalty that's designed to recoup enough of the money owed to make it hurt the member. Plus, that penalty can be easily modeled into the gym's business plan.

Big gyms sprung up in cities and suburbs and were the only real game in town for the person who knew they wanted to be in better shape and were willing to take the first step. Fitness clubs were a slightly more posh alternative to the local YMCA and they were accessible. The chains installed rows upon rows of machines—treadmills and Stairmasters and rowing machines and stationary bikes. Some had pools, racquetball courts, and a basketball court for pick-up games.

These clubs introduced a component that became even more important as the decades wore on, and one that today's clubs embrace. Shelly McKenzie, in her excellent study *Getting Physical: The Rise of Fitness Culture in America*, writes: "As a social center, the gym became a new kind of urban or suburban country club. Friendships and social connections were enabled because members believed that their fellow exercisers shared common interests and *were likely to have a similar economic status and lifestyle*."[3]

The italics are mine because this is precisely how cohorts of like-minded people have formed over time, first physically on location in health clubs and gyms, and later in races. Today, many of those communities are a blend

---

[3] Shelly McKenzie, *Getting Physical: The Rise of Fitness Culture in America* (Lawrence, KS: University Press of Kansas, 2013), 168.

of both actual and virtual. That is, technology helps create the scenarios by which people find each other and/or deepen existing relationships formed around fitness.

And the lifestyle piece has evolved as well. Now more than ever, fitness *is* the lifestyle, or at least an even bigger part than it was back when folks were just starting to head to the gym after work or on a weekend.

It was a profitable business, with a perverse (in an economic sense) twist. The gyms wanted you to be just motivated enough to sign up, and then show up as little as possible. After all, they had your money. The less you actually worked out, the fewer towels you sweated on, the less water you showered in, the less wear and tear you inflicted on the machines (meaning the less often they had to repair and replace the equipment).

All of these financial elements made the gyms attractive to the handful of private equity firms paying attention to the burgeoning fitness megatrend.

Created in 1984 as a single club in Covina, California, LA Fitness tracked much of the growth of the broader fitness club business.

It remained a California company and expanded modestly, with a total of 11 locations by the end of the 1980s; it wasn't until 1993 that the chain expanded beyond California, through a purchase of a smaller chain in Arizona. Growth accelerated then, and by 1998 the company raised money from the city's Seidler family and others for expansion beyond its 36 clubs and 1,600 employees.[4]

LA Fitness leveraged that cash into an increasingly meaningful piece of the gym market and took on additional private equity, including from Madison Dearborn, a well-known Chicago investor. In 2011, LA Fitness acquired a slug of gyms owned by Bally, bringing its total locations to almost 550 across the country.[5]

Among the most notable forays by private equity into the gym business was the 2015 purchase of Lifetime Fitness by TPG Capital and Leonard Green & Co., a pair of well-known buyout firms. The two investors, both with their primary offices in California, collaborated before on consumer-oriented deals, including the purchase of retailer J. Crew. The firms also invested in Petco together.

The Lifetime deal came after the gym operator had gone it alone for 13 years, operating somewhat quietly from its suburban Minneapolis

---

[4] Debora Vrana, "L.A. Fitness Prepares to Pump Up," *Los Angeles Times*, April 1, 1998, http://articles.latimes.com/1998/apr/01/business/fi-34744.

[5] Stuart Goldman, "Bally, LA Fitness Complete Sale of 171 Clubs," *Club Industry*, November 30, 2011, http://clubindustry.com/forprofits/bally-lafitness-complete-sale-171-clubs-20111130.

headquarters. The company, created by CEO Bahram Akradi, operated 114 fitness centers at the time of the acquisition, and owned a line of supplements. The company also had snapped up a series of races, including triathlons and well-known ultra-endurance contests like the Leadville 100. The company also purchased CEO Challenges, a series of races within races limited to top executives (see Chapter 8, "Work and Working Out").

What TPG and Leonard Green saw was a company that managed to figure out how to navigate the harshly competitive world of so-called big box gyms, according to Imperial Capital's Wood.

One of Lifetime's competitors is surprisingly close by. Anytime Fitness is also based Minnesota and demonstrates another model that also attracted investors. Chuck Runyon, Dave Mortensen, and Jeff Klinger created the company in 2002, after working in and around the gym business, mostly giving advice on sales and marketing. Seeing the popularity of fitness centers surging, they decided to start their own.

Anytime's twist is one that relies heavily on scale and technology. The company has more than 3,000 locations, owned and operated by franchisees. The technology element comes into play by living up to the name—the gyms are always open and members essentially let themselves in and out of the facility, with little need for staff.

And yet even without a high-touch approach, Anytime is among the fitness companies that amps up its personality as a differentiator. Consider the seven-page *AFI Investor Manifesto* that Runyon and Mortensen send to prospective franchisees. It describes the founders in personal terms—native Minnesotans, they have nine kids between them—and takes pains to lay out the culture of the company. Eschewing the notion that the customer is king, they list their stakeholders in the following order of importance: employees, franchisees, members, vendors, and investors/board members.

They describe a company whose success will be judged by its ROEI—return on emotional investment. Any good business school student or graduate can rattle off the Four Ps of marketing (place, price, product, and promotion). Anytime has its own four—people, purpose, profits, and play.

It's apparently working as a motivating force. In the vein of inking the Ironman M dot on your leg, the manifesto notes that the Anytime approach led more than 1,000 people to tattoo the company's Runningman logo on themselves. And it goes beyond enthusiasm. Anytime was number one on *Entrepreneur* magazine's Franchisee 500 list in 2014. That same year, it sold an undisclosed minority stake to Roark Capital, an Atlanta-based private equity firm.

Even with that serious endorsement, Anytime talks a lot about play, in its offices and in its gyms. "Aside from alleviating stress and making the workplace more enjoyable, a playful culture stimulates creativity and minimizes the friction that builds between departments in a fast-moving company," Runyon writes in the manifesto.

Runyon remains focused on technology as a way to stay relevant in an increasingly competitive landscape. A series of very simple PowerPoint slides he shares with investors and franchisees shows, in classic business quadrants, the evolution of the fitness industry in three chunks—2000 to 2008, 2008 to 2013, and 2013 and beyond.

Big box (New York Sports Clubs, Lifetime Fitness) and convenience (Anytime and 24-Hour Fitness) are stable. By his reckoning, the positions once occupied by "free-weight gyms, YMCA, and community centers" and Curves for Women were replaced after 2008, respectively, by low cost (like Planet Fitness) and studio gyms (SoulCycle, Barry's Bootcamp). Moving ahead, there's an overlay of what he calls digital growth, whereby each one of the four quadrants feels some pinch, or opportunity, from leveraging technology to gain and keep members.

Runyon's initial technology breakthrough was the now seemingly simple use of a key fob to allow his members to gain access whenever they wanted. Now he's got to figure out a way to use technology to serve them, even when they can't or don't want to show up to the gym.

In late 2015, Anytime bought Pump One, a New York-based company that provides personal training through mobile devices in the form of videos and workout programs. In announcing the deal, Runyon underscored his point about the importance of the mobile device in fitness: "It's in the pocket of nearly every consumer. They lift it more often than a fork and, at a minimum, it's used 50 times more often than a treadmill."

All of this speaks to the deepening competitive environment for the fitness dollar, in the studios and beyond. While the creation, popularity, and growth of gyms from the 1980s, through the 1990s, and into the 2000s helped fuel the fitness economy, the last five years have seen a reckoning of sorts.

It's a classic business conundrum, where among the worst places to be is the middle. Business school classes might study it as a barbell, where the bulk of the viable companies are on either end (budget offerings on one side and high-touch, high-cost products and services on the other) and a tough slog for those who are a little bit of both.

What's emerged is a war to differentiate, fought on two fronts. The first is price. At the low end, gyms are duking it out where they have for several decades, offering a bare-bones experience. Here, Planet Fitness has emerged as one of the clear winners.

The company and its locations revel in the no-frills approach. Planet Fitness eschews pricey real estate (its Manhattan locations, for instance, are on the far west side of town, where rents are cheaper than in the center of the island) and staffs at minimal levels in order to keep costs down. There are no classes, which take up space and require costly instructors. There are only machines, and sometimes bagels or pizza the staff brings in—a far cry from the high-priced juice bars embedded in boutique gyms.

Planet Fitness has to play a relentless ground game, market by market, sometimes neighborhood by neighborhood. The majority of its members are mostly not the affluent, fitness-obsessed crowd, but rather the gym newbies who are joining a gym as a relatively low risk (i.e., cheap) effort to get a bit healthier. This crowd is totally content to show up, get on a treadmill or bike, do their thing, and leave. This isn't a part of their social life and few are Instagramming their workout. Attrition can be high, as members either quit or graduate to a higher-touch gym.

There's a smaller part of the Planet Fitness population that's more affluent. For them, the cheap membership is only a part of their total monthly fitness outlay. The cheap gym membership—at $10 a month, it's a fraction of a single SoulCyle or yoga class—is an inexpensive way to get one's basic work-out needs, a treadmill or some weights, satisfied.

While that ritzier crowd is nice to have, the Planet Fitness business model rests on the former group, the new-to-fitness crowd that so far forms a wide funnel of potential members. Even if those folks drop away at high rates every year, there are more behind them. Being the gateway to the broader fitness fix is pretty good business.

The ethos of Planet Fitness also is a careful balance between embracing the current wellness boom while rolling its eyes and allowing people to chill out a little amid the growing class of aggressively fit people. Its mission, planted right on the website: "We strive to create a workout environment where you can relax and go at your own pace without ever being judged." There's some action behind that pretty talk: each gym has a lunk alarm—a button activating flashing lights and sounds if anyone violates the stated prohibition on grunting, posing, or dramatically dropping weights.

Kapoor says Planet Fitness owes its success to a combination of timing and clarity of mission, wrapped in clear branding (bright purple and gold), and effective gimmicks (lunk alert, free pizza on Mondays). It was the first to unabashedly stake out a claim for the low end.

Chris Rondeau became the Planet Fitness CEO in early 2013, when Planet Fitness sold a majority stake to TSG Consumer Partners, a private equity firm. He came up through the ranks, arriving two decades earlier while in his early twenties, eventually heading operations and becoming a partner in the business in 2003.

Rondeau in 2013 launched an ad campaign around the slogan "No Gymtimidation" and provided the business case for the approach. "The stat is 80 percent of the population doesn't belong to a health club and we really feel that [the] rest of the industry's kind of fighting over the 20 percent, but we're just going after that 85 percent," he says. "So creating that atmosphere really brings them in. And when you throw a $10 price point on there, it really opens the market up."

Going after that 80 percent also allows Planet Fitness to embrace the notion that—despite the happy exhortations of the exercise evangelists out there—showing up at the gym, especially when you're starting, can be sort of a drag. "I always look at working out as a bit of a chore, not really a hobby in my eyes," Rondeau says. "It's much like mowing your lawn, right? You know you have to do it. You don't want to do it. So the light-hearted approach with the purple, yellow colors, with the lunk alarm on the wall, it makes it a little bit more fun [inaudible] to come in."[6]

By June 2015, Planet Fitness was in a groove, and sought to capitalize on its own success and a clear appetite among investors for fitness-related companies by filing to go public. In its papers, it revealed it had 7.1 million members in the United States and just fewer than 1,000 locations. On the basis of members, it claimed to be the biggest company of its kind.

Revenues for the previous year were $279.8 million, up 32 percent from 2013, quite a healthy increase. The bottom line showed that even the business of sweating on the cheap was profitable. The filing showed adjusted income for 2014 of just over $100 million, versus $71 million the previous year, a 40 percent gain.

The second way to differentiate favors quality over price, aiming to capture a customer who's willing to pay more for something special. This is where Equinox sits. Members pay multiple times, sometimes ten times, what a Planet Fitness or other discount-oriented gym commands. In New York, Equinox charges upwards of $150 a month, versus rates as low as $10 a month for the low-end centers.

At the high end, it's an arms race for the best new classes, the best instructors, the best equipment, and the coolest facilities. In big cities—and Equinox is only in big cities—the high-end gym evokes a cachet normally associated with expensive cars or resorts. Their ads, some of which cover several stories of a building, evoke a sexy, mischievous lifestyle. Gorgeous, fit people in states of undress, confessing, "Equinox made me do it."

Equinox has emerged as an emblem of urban, affluent fitness by virtue of its price tag and its location. And location is the key word in understanding what Equinox is all about.

---

[6] "How Planet Fitness Plans to Beat 'Gymtimidation,'" Bloomberg TV, March 5, 2014, www.bloomberg.com/news/videos/b/6d1f6bca-7ae9-474e-b042-8b5adfaa5a20.

It's yet another gym concept with private equity roots. North Castle bought the then-nascent New York City company in 2000. With 11 locations in and around Manhattan, Equinox had a loyal but limited following. Unlike bargain gyms, which can open relatively quickly in a strip mall, each Equinox facility requires substantial planning and investment. Under North Castle's ownership, Equinox increased its footprint, nearly tripling the number of clubs and doubling membership. Expansion took Equinox to other wealthy urban areas, including Chicago, L.A., San Francisco, and South Florida.

That put Equinox squarely in view of consumers and investors who were noticing the increase in interest in fitness. Well-educated high earners were flocking to a healthier lifestyle and in the most influential corridors of the trend-setting U.S. cities, Equinox popped up.

Five years later, what might have seemed like an unlikely buyer emerged. Related Companies, the real estate developer famous for buildings like the iconic Time Warner Center at the southwest corner of Manhattan's Central Park, picked up Equinox for $505 million, providing North Castle and its investors with a return of more than double its original investment, according to published reports.[7]

The deal came as Related's ambitions were accelerating. Billionaire founder Stephen Ross (also the owner of the NFL's Miami Dolphins) made his name and his money largely in New York but also by thinking more globally. Ross came to know Equinox intimately initially as a board member after being introduced to the company's CEO Harvey Spevak through, naturally, a personal trainer who worked with both men. The trainer knew of their shared history at, and love for, the University of Michigan, where the business school bears Ross' name.

What Ross and Jeff Blau, his protégé and successor as Related CEO, saw was an ability to marry their property expertise with the fitness megatrend. "The biggest constraint to growth is real estate," Blau says. "There are no 40,000 square-foot boxes lying around. You either provide the real estate or you have to go get it."

The Related-owned Time Warner Center and some of its other properties in cities like Los Angeles featured high-end shops and restaurants. Here was a chance to place one of the highest-end exercise offerings in its commercial and residential buildings. "Our markets overlap exactly," Blau says of Equinox. "That's not a coincidence. The demographics are the same." With Equinox, Ross and Blau created the ultimate amenity for its residents. Surveys

---

[7] Shasha Dai, "Gym Clubs: The Latest Gold Rush for Private Equity," wsj.com, January 16, 2013, http://blogs.wsj.com/privateequity/2013/01/16/gym-clubs-the-latest-gold-rush-for-private-equity.

of residents showed the number-one amenity they were willing to pay for was high-quality fitness. "No one really likes to work out in private," Blau says. "A room with two treadmills is not attractive." The same desires apply to well-heeled workers in its buildings and visitors, who often lived in one Equinox city (the chain expanded to Toronto and London) and took business or leisure trips to another.

With that in mind, Equinox said in early 2015 it was creating a line of branded hotels, the first of which would open in New York in 2019 (with Los Angeles scheduled for a year later). The New York Equinox hotel would be a part of Related's massive Hudson Yards development on Manhattan's west side. The hotel is meant to house Equinox's largest-ever facility (at some 60,000 square feet), built from the ground up. The rooms and restaurant will cater to the Equinox lifestyle—which favors food that's either healthy, or, if not, smartly sourced and assembled (chocolate cake with organic ingredients).[8]

Equinox CEO Spevak said at the time of the announcement that 95 percent of his members surveyed said they'd stay at an Equinox hotel, a demonstration of their affection for the brand—and their desire to be associated with it in other aspects of their life. "We are appealing to the discriminating consumer who lives an active lifestyle and wants to have that as a hotel experience," Spevak said.[9]

From the beginning, Equinox catered to a clientele who increasingly saw working out as more lifestyle than activity, and felt good identifying themselves with what emerged as a luxury brand for fitness.

One of its seminal moments—and a reflection of just how much fitness had solidified its place in the modern lifestyle—came at the depths of the global recession in 2008 and 2009, Spevak notes. Observers worried aloud, and competitors hoped, that Equinox's pricey membership would be a luxury that the skittish affluent would ditch amid belt-tightening. It didn't happen.

"Everyone in the market was playing to survive," Spevak says, "And our average usage went up. We saw our members staying with us. They consciously cut back spending when the recession hit, but health and wellness still remained a financial priority in their lives."

With Related's blessing, Equinox secured new leases to take advantage of the soft real estate market. Inside the clubs, managers made sure not to skimp on maintenance or cut classes, even as slightly lower revenue squeezed

---

[8] Craig Karmin, "Equinox Fitness Clubs Expand to Hotels," *Wall Street Journal*, April 21, 2015, www.wsj.com/articles/equinox-fitness-clubs-expand-to-hotels-1429627895.
[9] Ibid.

margins. Equinox struck a deal with Kiehl's to offer high-end soaps and lotions in the locker rooms.

Part of the appeal is a combination of personalization and innovation. Equinox offers personal training, as well as group fitness. For the latter, it's constantly trying out new concepts, creating a boutique feel that gives members a first look of sorts at what might be the next cool exercise concept at any given time. (One such concept, known as Speedball, is discussed in Chapter 4).

Equinox saw the boutique fitness craze coming early, and its management and owners realized that not every concept could be simply tucked in as a class. So when a singular indoor cycling program went up for sale, Equinox bought it. (One of the advantages of Equinox's position and success is that any banker thinking about selling a fitness asset puts Spevak or a member of his team on the call list for a pitch.)

To the passerby, SoulCycle and Equinox aren't obviously related, but an eagle-eyed urbanite might notice that a lot of Equinox locations have a Soul-Cycle studio *right next door.* It's not a coincidence. The whole building's probably owned by Related.

SoulCycle began as a cult-like following of women on Manhattan's Upper West Side back in 2006 in a small single studio with a couple dozen bikes. By the time Equinox came calling, SoulCycle's pair of founders had expanded to six studios in Manhattan, Westchester, and even in the Hamptons—the summer playground on Long Island for many of SoulCycle's New York City-based devotees.

Keeping SoulCycle's brand distinct has proved wise. (Equinox's purchase of SoulCycle followed a similar deal for Pure Yoga, which also kept its separate brand identity and similarly co locates at numerous Related properties.) Even with increased competition from boutique fitness offerings, SoulCycle has a rabidly loyal customer base.

SoulCycle is like Planet Fitness—it's clear in what it wants to be, and for whom. SoulCycle classes are meant as sweaty meditations, complete with candles and mood music (even if the mood is sometimes best expressed through a mix of only Taylor Swift songs in honor of a regular's birthday). Despite its appeal to a customer who tends toward the hypercompetitive in many aspects of her life, SoulCycle strives to eschew judgment.

Keeping it separate also allowed Equinox and Related to exploit SoulCycle's brand and profits, notably through an initial public offering announced in mid-2015.

The filing put hard numbers on what any SoulCycler already knew based on her own spending—SoulCycle is a cash machine. Despite being in the Equinox family, SoulCycle doesn't sell memberships, opting for the more lucrative per-session model. That means it pulls in an average of $34 per 45-minute session. Per rider.

By the time it filed for its IPO, the company had expanded to 38 studios, with about 300,000 unique riders. That translated to revenue of $112 million in 2014, up from $75 million in 2013 and profit of $25 million, versus $18 million the year earlier.

While the workout is the thing, SoulCycle also plays to its riders' affinity for high-end apparel—there's a tank top that will set you back $52— and bottles of water and cycling shoes. Dedicated riders bring their own shoes; others opt to use loaners, making it feel a little like a post-modern, fancy, sweaty bowling alley.

But dingy it is not. One morning, I arrive for a ride at a studio in a Manhattan neighborhood wedged between Union Square and Times Square. I'm a guest of CEO Melanie Whelan, then the recently promoted CEO, who has offered to ride and then chat. The lobby is gleaming white, evoking a South Beach hotel reception area, and heavily populated with fit, mostly female staff, who get me checked in and toured around. There's a unisex locker area, with well-stocked gender-specific showers and changing areas in either direction.

Inside the room, there's a distinctly New Age vibe, right down to the candles. Instructors attend Soul University and are wont to sprinkle their sessions with talk of destiny and tips and tricks for becoming a better you. While it's a lot about the body—in addition to the cardio, each session features some upper-body work—SoulCycle's among the modern exercises trained on the mind, as well. Our instructor, Lauren, tells us this will be the hardest thing we do all day, pushing us to stay in the moment, moving around the room to adjust the form of newbies like me and to cajole the regulars she knows by name.

This cocktail of sweating and ad hoc life coaching won SoulCycle a rabid following and, like Equinox, it actually gained traction with its audience through the recession, spending on upgrades and expansion even as business slowed. Whelan says, "It was interesting to see Harvey invest in that moment, and SoulCycle did the same thing," Whelan says. "With SoulCycle, there was a real sense that there was more than fitness—some said it was therapy combined with the sense of community."

Whelan worked for Barry Sternlicht as an analyst (on the Starwood Hotels corporate development team) and then for Richard Branson, on the launch of Virgin America. Moving to Equinox in a business development role for Spevak, she was an architect of the SoulCycle acquisition. She jumped to the company to lead, build, and run SoulCycle's operations, and was promoted to CEO in mid-2015.

Echoing Jesse Du Bey talking about Ironman and music festivals, Whelan says SoulCycle is deeply focused on what happens to the rider from the moment she enters the studio. "We create experiences, every hour, on the hour," she says. "We create evangelists, not just riders."

SoulCycle's ultimate success may lie in its ability to keep that experience not just fresh, but relevant to a consumer who's proven to be fickle. That's where the notion of not just service, but community, comes in. "We're about the pack, the tribe, the posse," she says. Her opportunity—and challenge—is to keep growing that very lucrative tribe.

All of this accrues to some extent to Equinox's mission—and bottom line—given that it stood to make money on the IPO. It's clear that the upper end of the fitness spectrum is a profitable place to play. Equinox also sees opportunity on the other end. The company started the Blink brand of gyms in 2011 because Spevak saw a need for "a traditional gym that's not intimidating and not expensive," he says. "Blink gave us that value-based offering, but still had top-of-the-line equipment and a clean environment."

As any MBA student worth their tuition will tell you, the middle is often the toughest slog. With Planet Fitness at the low end and Equinox at the high, those in the middle are stuck in a state of in-between. Unable to compete successfully on either price or quality, they end up fighting on both fronts, often with middling results.

That's been the case of Town Sports International, which operates clubs under their city names (New York Sports Club, Washington Sports Club, et al.). The stock symbol (CLUB on the Nasdaq) speaks to its status as among the first to identify the trend. But it's clear from the stock price that while concepts like SoulCycle and Planet Fitness are ascendant, the in-between is proving tricky.

"The middle tier is suffering," says Kapoor, who has followed the recent history of Town Sports closely, in part to gauge how it and its peers play against either side of the barbell. "Planet Fitness had made it hard for everyone else."

That's largely because for many years Town Sports had a nice business with higher rates, up around $70 a month, and little competition from below. They were willing to cede the ritzy customers to Equinox but not the more cost-conscious. As competition increased, Town Sports suffered in the eyes of investors.

From a high of $14.71 in late 2013, Town Sports was bottoming by late 2015, trading at around $1.18 a share. Its market capitalization was a mere $29 million at that price. Activist investors, stockholders who buy stock and then agitate publicly for a change in management and strategy, were swarming. One such investor, Patrick Walsh, stepped in as executive chairman after forcing the CEO out.

Town Sports' new strategy is to essentially abandon the middle and go simultaneously for each end of the barbell. The company converted about 100 of its 125 clubs to offer a budget, no-contract membership for as low as $19.95. For that you get use of the facilities and barely a towel (for a time, towels weren't included in the lowest-end membership, causing a mini-uproar).

On the other end, Town Sports launched a line of boutiques called BFX, starting with locations in the Financial District and Chelsea neighborhoods of Manhattan, and then expanding to Boston's fancy Back Bay. The boutiques are focused on group fitness almost completely. All the machinations lead Kapoor to say: "Even they're saying, 'There's no room for the middle tier.'"

Then there's the more radical approach, which rejects some of the underlying premises of a gym all together.

One of the recent, persistent, and controversial voices in fitness belongs to a crowd that intentionally seeks to undermine the traditional gym business at every turn. Bring up the notion of fitness fanatics and you're more likely than not to hear the name CrossFit.

That's in part owing to the upstart method's relative ubiquity and rapid growth. As of mid-2015, there were upwards of 7,000 CrossFit affiliates, from only a couple dozen a decade earlier. There are the CrossFit Games, where regular people—or as regular as you can be and still compete in a national fitness tournament—vie for the honor of being crowned Fittest on Earth.

For the uninitiated, CrossFit has the characteristics of a religious movement, right down to the fervent believers who are alternately evangelistic, defensive, and dismissive. More than most fitness crazes, CrossFit has spawned both disciples and critics. It's created a mini-economy of its own.

CrossFit isn't a chain, but a method, and one that's essentially franchised through training. Box operators buy a license to use the name, then go through a series of workshops that qualify them to run sessions at their location. *Essentially* is a key word here. A 2013 story in *Inc.* magazine captured it this way: "It's neither a wholly owned chain of gyms nor a franchise, but the nucleus of a sprawling worldwide network of entrepreneurs."[10]

While other brands maniacally control their logo, CrossFit is fairly loose with most everything beyond its name and its brand, which it defends fiercely. (Its mascot/logo is affectionately known as Uncle Pukie.) The brand protection

---

[10] Burt Helm, "Do Not Cross CrossFit," *Inc.*, www.inc.com/magazine/201307/burt-helm/crossfit-empire.html.

has its roots in the cost of ubiquity. The lawyers are paid to ensure that CrossFit never goes lowercase, like escalator (a name coined by the elevator company Otis), or ping-pong, or, to use an example in the fitness world, spinning. If CrossFit ever becomes crossfit, the sprawling worldwide enterprise is largely doomed, at least from a revenue and profit-making perspective.

Pay attention on a trip through your town or on a road trip and you'll see CrossFit boxes wedged into strip malls and in stand-alone buildings. The bare bones nature makes it easy to turn most any open space into a box. All this simplicity comes at a cost, and lest you think CrossFit is a discount operation, some boxes charge upwards of $300 a month for unlimited use, making them more expensive than high-end gyms like Equinox.

The relative freedom the box operators enjoy extends to their pricing. That's largely because CrossFit gets paid the same, regardless of how big your box is, or how many people you attract. A box near Wall Street in lower Manhattan that limits its session sizes to eight participants charges on the high end; a box across the East River in Brooklyn in a more modest space and with less restrictions on class sizes charges about $150 per month.

CrossFit created a system whereby they make their money up front, through training and licensing fees and then turn their affiliates loose to create their own business arrangements.

Devotion to CrossFit runs deep, and lots of CrossFitters pull their average visit cost down through frequent sessions, with hard-core aficionados going daily. As with other activities and studios, CrossFit encourages and cultivates community, with regulars showing up at the same sessions.

Many of them choose CrossFit because it's the anti-gym and take it a step further—they see it as a condemnation of a fitness system headed for extinction. They point to the race-to-the-bottom price wars as the best evidence.

What's implicit in the economic one-upmanship is that some sizable portion of the gym-going population is pocketbook-driven and will ultimately view the local big-box scene as commoditized. Whatever loyalty remains is based on either an actual contract—signed to ensure the lowest possible price—or geographic convenience. Absent or diminished is loyalty based on the instruction or the instructors themselves.

That's where CrossFit wins, on multiple fronts. It's created something that has both an increasingly recognizable international brand, with the critical element of locally facilitated personalization and community. CrossFitters are buying in to both the overarching methodology and their own special twist on said methodology. To use a more a traditional analogy, they have fealty to both the religion and the parish.

Detractors, and even some supporters, refer to CrossFit as a cult and the workout as a spiritual experience. That's a common theme across much of the fitness landscape (hello SoulCycle). Fitness also has crept into a personal and social space once occupied by organized religion, and it's not just yoga studios and meditation clubs. It's got a lot to do with the Millennial crowd, which is abandoning or never even showing up to churches and temples in unprecedented numbers.

It's important first to understand where some of the most dedicated souls congregate, and that's in the boutique studios that collectively are the most dynamic and fascinating corners of the new fitness economy.

CHAPTER 3

Barry and the Art of Boutique Fitness

Barry Jay remembers the day that changed his life, because for years he carried the membership card in his wallet. The date was August 4, 1988. The card is from a Los Angeles gym called Sports Connection.

Five years of hard living in L.A. had taken its toll. Then-25-year-old Barry started going to the gym, and soon he started working at their front desk. Next he was an instructor. Then he was a sought-after instructor.

Now, he's the man behind an eponymous chain of boutique fitness outlets, with locations on the American coasts, London, and Oslo. His company is worth upwards of $100 million, about 20 years after its creation, and won a coveted private equity investment in 2015.

The décor at Barry's Bootcamp in the Tribeca neighborhood in New York is downtown workout-hip. In a nod to the loft spaces in that part of Manhattan, the ceilings are high, the floors concrete. The walls are painted in gray shades of camouflage, featuring the Barry's Bootcamp logo, complete with the sergeant's chevron.

"I think I'm going to die," a twenty-something woman groans to her boyfriend as they walk out. Barry appears a minute later, having taught the class that brought her to that point. She's gone, but I relay the comment. He brightens. "I love it when people say that," he says. "The worst would be if someone say, 'That was it?'"

We walk over to the Fuel Bar, past the refrigerator with $3 bottles of water (with Barry's Bootcamp labels). Offered a protein shake, I follow his lead. He orders a vegan version of the PB Special, a concoction blending peanut butter, bananas, unsweetened almond milk, some protein powder, and, in my nonvegan case, some whey. His version uses rice instead.

Barry dropped 15 pounds by going back to veganism. He'd been vegetarian for seven years, vegan for three, and then experimented with paleo for a while. He used that diet to get to 150 pounds in honor of his fiftieth birthday, in 2013. He gained it back in the intervening year. In the summer of 2014, he was back to 150.

He picks up my shake tab, only to find that his was already paid for by a student. We stop to thank his patron, who it turns out is currently playing Jean Valjean in the Broadway revival of *Les Misérables*. Barry makes plans to see the actor, Ramin Karimloo, sing that night at Birdland, the noted New York City jazz club. "He's the second Valjean we've had," Barry tells me later. Hugh Jackman, who starred in the film adaptation the musical, was the first.

Broadway celebrities are Barry's favorite kind. Karimloo became a client after Barry visited the cast backstage, at the invitation of Nikki M. James, who plays Eponine in the current cast. The week after we first talked, Barry had plans to see *Wicked*—for the eighth time.

He discovered Broadway as a kid growing up in Rockland County, a clutch of New York suburbs north of Manhattan, on the west side of the Hudson River. After seeing *Annie* (starring Sarah Jessica Parker in the title role), he became obsessed with his parents' Broadway albums. Soon he was taking buses to New York and buying $10 standing-room-only tickets, watching for a seat that stayed empty through the first act, then grabbing it after intermission.

Three months of community college back in Rockland County didn't take and he pursued a more vocational route to acting through an acting school in New York City. Upon graduating, he landed a role in the chorus in a Broadway show; he quit when the show went on tour, to Alaska. Los Angeles sounded better.

He ditched acting in favor of writing songs, scraping by for a few years. Barry's devotion to Broadway is matched only, if incongruously, by his passion for horror movies. That led him to interview for a tour guide job at Universal, by his wits the top studio in the horror genre. He didn't get the job. The next five years were a mid-1980s Los Angeles blur of late nights, booze, bad food, and more. Which brought him to that fateful day in 1988.

"I thought to myself, 'I don't want to die,'" he says.

The intervening decade found Barry moving up the gym instructor ladder. He gathered a following as he honed his teaching style, an approach that borrows heavily from his theatrical history. In person, he's lively and intensely engaged, a personality that shows through in his classes.

He's also, in his own friendly way, sort of mean. The bootcamp name came from the mouth of a weary client after a class he was teaching at a local box gym who said, "This isn't body sculpting, it's a bootcamp!" (In Barry's telling, the story includes an expletive adjective.) When Barry told that story to his eventual business partner Rachel Mumford, she jumped on the name, and added "Barry" to it.

The opportunity to start what became Barry's Bootcamp came in 1998, when the boutique gym where he worked—and where Rachel and her husband John were members, as well as his personal training clients—abruptly shut down. At his last class, Barry gathered up his students' phone numbers, the foundation of his first, unofficial client database of sorts. Then, and for years, it was decidedly low-tech. "Twitter didn't exist," he says. "There was no Facebook. Our first check-in system was index cards."

The business model they settled on was different from the typical gym. Monthly fees provided little actual incentive for customers to show up, especially for the gyms themselves. "I pay every month and go once a week," he says. "It's a dream for the gym."

Barry's idea was different. He created "The Academy," where members would sign up at the beginning of the month, pay $200, and register for a series of classes. If they were going to miss class, they had to call. Not notifying risked a call, usually from Barry, asking where the student was. In one case, he sent two students—running—to the absent student's house to fetch her.

Once they settled on bootcamp, they embraced it. Early customers were issued dog tags. If you threw up during class, you got a T-shirt. Barry went grocery shopping with some students and asked them to clean out their refrigerators of food they weren't going to eat any more and bring it to class, where he'd donate it.

One day, a student sold out a couple of fellow bootcampers, who he'd spotted at Sprinkles cupcake store. When they arrived at class, Barry had them run to Sprinkles, take a picture of themselves there, run back and show it to him. "I heard you liked to go there, so I figured I'd help you out," he told them. "They also burned off the cupcakes they'd eaten over the weekend," he tells me.

Such antics, plus the workout, helped him develop a cult following at the first studio. The original Barry's Bootcamp sits at a busy corner in West Hollywood, wedged in the center of a V-shaped two-story strip mall. There's a parking lot underneath, a 7-Eleven next door, and a gas station across the street. The eclectic West Hollywood neighborhood—a cocktail of hip and sleazy shops, dive bars, and hard-to-get-into restaurants—unfurls down the hill.

On a sunny October afternoon (is there any other kind of afternoon in L.A.?), the music is thumping and half a dozen bootcampers are in class, behind glass in a darkened room. Outside the studio, there's barely enough room for the check-in desk and a rack of apparel.

Barry's sits in a complex that now offers varying flavors of fitness and wellness. There's a Brazilian jiujitsu studio on one side, a gym geared toward kid's fitness on the other. Upstairs, you can get a massage. A new juice bar announces its grand opening. It's just the sort of normal-but-Hollywood milieu that gives rise to those "Stars: They're Just Like Us!" photos in the weekly entertainment magazines we all pretend not to read.

This is where Barry's was born, and his legend grew. One of the desk attendants verifies the running-to-the-cupcake-store story. She adds that one time, in a partner workout, one of the Spice Girls refused to keep going. Barry made her—and her furious partner—run up and down the nearby, congested La Cienega Avenue. Just outside the door, there are the stairs Barry used on early students who showed up late for class. "I wanted to create a new format where being on time was imperative, that every minute of the workout matters—where we were reminded self-discipline IS self-love," he writes me in an email after our initial conversation.

The location, and word of mouth, also began to draw the occasional celebrity. On its website, Barry's has references to and from notables including Kim Kardashian and Katie Couric, people familiar to almost everyone, but not always to Barry himself. Beyond Broadway and horror, he has the pop culture literacy of a recently arrived alien. When introduced to Jessica Biel, he knew her from the *Texas Chainsaw Massacre* reboot, not from her numerous TV or movie appearances (or her husband Justin Timberlake, also an early Barry's client).

What keeps them coming back, Barry says, is the workout and its wicked (some would say brutal) efficiency. Each workout comprises a single hour, and involves a combination of heavy weights and cardio, the latter using a treadmill. Each instructor—one of Barry's executives refers to them as entertainers—has his or her own method, every class. Some split the class into 30-minute segments; others go for four 15-minute intervals of weights and cardio.

Barry and the others don't tell students ahead of time exactly what the workout will be that day (other than saying it's an "arm day," for instance), until they're actually in the room. The element of surprise is part of the appeal, another way to break the drudgery many associate with the soulless routine—and isolation—of the treadmill or elliptical machine at the local gym. "There's a whole sense of 'I'm bored doing this alone,'" he says. "People like the camaraderie and the personal attention. It's like we've livened up the party."

That piece, the sweating-as-friendship-foundation, is critical, Barry says, echoing many in the boutique fitness space. "You know that you can come with your friends, or that you're going to at least get to know the people in the class," Barry says. "Then the trainer starts knowing your name and what's going on in your life. We give out our cell phone numbers."

This all-in-this-together approach is driving the broader boutique fitness movement, where the successful outlets give their clients a sense of community. Even if one is too busy trying not to barf during the actual class, the ability to commiserate after is deeply appealing. There's a basic human comfort to seeing the same people at the same place.

It's a phenomenon that cuts across a number of modern fitness phenomena, including clubs devoted to running, cycling, or swimming (or all three). We do, as the *Cheers* song says, want to go where everybody (or at least somebody) knows our name. Or, to name check a more recent production, the Disney tween hit *High School Musical*, we're all in this together.

At Pure Barre, a Spartanburg, South Carolina–based fitness chain, that's part of the appeal, says Jaime Wall, one of Pure Barre's investors who became a regular after her firm, WJ Partners, acquired Pure Barre in 2012.

Pure Barre's model, like Barry's, is made to feel personal. Signing up for a class means the instructor can see a roster of that class before it happens. In the moments before the session begins, she can walk around and greet people by name, armed with bits of knowledge like the last time each student took the class.

"There's a level of accountability associated with Pure Barre," Wall says. "No one wants to go by themselves and run on the treadmill anymore. It's a personal experience. You see the same women every time, and there's an instant connection when you walk in."

Barre classes involve a series of exercises inspired by ballet movements— the "barre" is the bar attached to the mirror in a typical studio.

Barre studios are geared almost exclusively toward women, promising a dancer-like body through a series of exercises mimicking ballet workouts. Depending on the approach—and there are many distinct programs—classes may mix in elements of yoga, Pilates, or other schools of fitness thought.

While the approaches vary, there's often an element of women helping women, with a healthy dose of everyday spirituality thrown in. From Pure Barre's description of itself: "Pure Barre is more than just a workout; it's a lifestyle. At Pure Barre, women share a sense of community, in which they are inspired and empowered by each other's fitness and lifestyle goals."[1]

---

[1] Pure Barre, http://purebarre.com/story/.

Pure Barre was the brainchild of Carrie Rezabek Dorr who, in 2001, opened a basement studio in Birmingham, Michigan. After growing it organically for eight years by moving from city to city and opening studios herself, she pursued franchisees starting in 2009.

During her itinerant period she was visiting her Denver studio and met her now husband, Frank Dorr. They married in 2011 and she moved the company's headquarters to Denver, where the couple now lives with their son and twin girls. After the WJ Partners acquisition, the company moved its headquarters to Spartanburg, South Carolina (where WJ Partners is also based) and expanded to more than 200 studios by mid-2014.

WJ Partners is the private equity firm created and managed by Benjamin Wall and George Johnson Jr. The latter is the former CEO of Extended Stay America, who went on to create Johnson Development Associates, a real estate firm, along with the investment firm. After the WJ Partners investment in Pure Barre, the investors and Rezabek Dorr agreed to install Sloan Evans, who'd served as chief financial officer at Johnson Development, as the Pure Barre CEO.

After growing to more than 300 studios, the company took on an additional private equity investor to expand even further. Catterton, a retail and consumer-focused firm, took an undisclosed stake in May 2015; WJ Partners remained an investor. Catterton increasingly is positioning itself in the midst of the fitness economy, with investments in companies including CorePower Yoga and Flywheel. In the nonfitness world, the firm has backed P.F. Chang's and Outback Steakhouse.

Pure Barre is only one player in the barre craze. The practice dates back to 1970, when a German dancer named Lotte Berk created a new form of exercise. The Lotte Berk Method created many disciples, a growing number of whom have created their own studios, or chains of studios, with their variations.

Other barre-oriented boutiques popped up around the globe, some spurred by the loss of Lotte Berk's locations. The Bar Method was among the new entrants, as was Bar Bee Fit. Local and national gyms began to teach barre classes and the indoor-cycle juggernaut Flywheel offers FlyBarre at many of its locations to draw a new crowd.

Boutique fitness is difficult to define, and is probably easiest to describe for what it's not. While some have multiple locations, boutiques distinguish themselves from the big box fitness chains like Planet Fitness and Town Sports International Clubs in the same way new retail concepts separate themselves from Best Buy or Wal-Mart. For fans of the movie *Dodgeball*, think Regular Joe's versus GloboGym.

What's more important is the business model. Monthly memberships at gyms actually work best when members *don't* show up. After all, the money is rolling in and machines that aren't used require less maintenance and last longer. Knowing the tendency to sign up and turn up only occasionally, most gyms recruit many more members than could actually fit in the facility at one time.

A company called Statistic Brain compiled data from several sources to come up with a remarkable set of figures that lay out the state of the modern fitness center. Globally, the health club industry pulls in $75 billion per year, from 131 million members. By the researchers' estimate, about two-thirds of people never use their gym memberships and the average cost is $58 per month. Based on usage rates, they estimated that $39 per month goes to waste based on underutilization.[2]

While the numbers are startling, the trend of paying and no-showing isn't. Many of us have first-hand knowledge of how much we actually use a monthly gym membership, when we have it. Especially in the era of automatically billing to credit and debit cards, it's often money we don't even see (versus writing and mailing a monthly check, which is more likely to draw our attention).

Most boutique fitness studios rely on a pay-per-visit model, whereby we cough up a fee per class (or buy classes in packs of five or 10 to get a volume discount). For a regular participant, it's almost always more expensive—three classes are enough to eclipse that national average, and five to seven would eclipse the more expensive gym memberships in big urban areas. Yet the direct relationship to a specific class may make it more likely that you'll show up.

"The gym model used to be to work hard to sign up people to a membership and hope they didn't come," says Imperial Capital's Brian Wood. "Now, operators want you there, as engagement leads to loyalty, community, and engagement that is so important to these brands like SoulCycle. If you don't show up, they will send you a reminder."

What's remarkable about the boutiques is the premiums they can command. Once fixed costs are covered, it can become wildly lucrative, simply based on the price points students are willing to pay. While the price varies by city and company, it's rare to find a class that's less than $20 a pop. Many, like Barry's, encourage—and get—students to show up several times a week.

---

[2] "Gym Membership Statistics," *Statistic Brain*, July 13, 2014, www.statisticbrain.com/gym-membership-statistics/.

The fixed costs are relatively straightforward. Barry's treadmills cost the company a predictable amount. SoulCycle and Flywheel's capital expenditures go largely to the custom bikes.

Barry and his partners figured out early on that they needed to average eight students per class to break even, and watched that number closely. Knowing that, he was comfortable teaching a class to two or three, as long as the more popular classes drew 25.

For boutiques whose techniques require less equipment, it comes down to real estate and instructors. Real estate can be a high cost, given the need to be in key locations convenient to the well-heeled clientele.

Instructors are relatively easy to come by, given the broader push toward health and fitness. There were 260,000 fitness trainers and instructors in 2012, a figure that was estimated to grow at 13 percent a year for the next decade, according to the Bureau of Labor Statistics.[3] It's not a high-paying profession; the median annual wage was $31,720 that year.[4]

Yet at a time where we're constantly told to do what we love, and the U.S. economy isn't creating lots of new jobs, getting certified as an instructor is appealing. At Barry's and other boutiques, many instructors come from the ranks of students who look up through their sweat and say, "I could do that."

As the broad data mentioned above show, it's not lucrative unless your idea really hits. Barry recalls making $250 a week in the early days—while teaching 40 classes. His business partner worked the desk. ("It was very mom and pop," he says.)

The business grew from within the classes. One student moved from working the desk to teaching to becoming an instructor and eventually chief operating officer, mirroring the career path of the founder. Joey Gonzalez, seeing the business potential for Barry's, pestered Barry for a meeting with co-founder Rachel Mumford until he got it. She gave him the desk job and he hasn't left yet. He assumed the CEO role in the wake of the North Castle transaction.

Now, he's the kind of operator Barry is not. "I have three months of college under my belt," he said. "My business is working out. Only in the last two years have I sat up and said, 'I should be more present as a businessman.'"

Even so, Barry's main job in the business is to be Barry. As one of the working faces of the company—the eponymous founder who's not just

---

[3] Bureau of Labor Statistics, U.S. Department of Labor, *Occupational Outlook Handbook, 2014–15 Edition, Fitness Trainers and Instructors*, www.bls.gov/ooh/personal-care-and-service/fitness-trainers-and-instructors.htm.

[4] Ibid.

ceremonially leading a class now and then, but really teaching a slate of classes—he's amplifying the importance of having a person representing the underlying mission, staying involved but ultimately realizing it's bigger than he is. It underscores a modern desire for authenticity that's pushing us more broadly toward experiences, products, and services we perceive to be real.

Fitness has long thrived on personalities of various stripes, be it Jack LaLanne, Jane Fonda, or Richard Simmons. Fitness DVDs continue to sell robustly—fitness DVDs in the United States were a $297 million business in 2014, growing 7.7 percent a year since 2009[5]—and apps and YouTube videos are proliferating to deliver workouts to your mobile device. Still, the desire to be in the room with an instructor you can connect with is strong, especially for Millennials. While reliant on devices and screens for many aspects of their work and social lives, they have a strong desire to form relationships, with each other and with their instructors.

The effect of the personality on the business can't be underestimated. While the per-class rate was higher than joining a gym, it was less expensive than a personal trainer, but carried some of the benefits (e.g., the personal phone calls from Barry if you missed class). "That grew the business," Barry says. "They paid and they were showing up."

Part of growing the business for Barry, oddly, was allowing the personality of the business to grow beyond just him. His visage isn't part of the logo. The chain also rotates pictures of its instructors lest any of them, including Barry, become too heavily branded.

Personalities come in several forms and fashions. There are iconic inventors who bank on their own blend of skill and charm. They either are larger than life already (Fonda) or become so through the force of their idea (Simmons). Some gain a following within the confines of a single studio. We'll see what happens when those personalities outgrow their starting bases in the next chapter. In the meantime, spinning's an interesting way to explore the phenomenon of personalities writ large and small.

Indoor cycling—hard-charging cardio workouts that use stationary bikes—was invented conceptually in the 1980s, took hold in the 1990s (*Rolling Stone* named it the hot exercise craze of 1993), and became a boutique-fitness destination in its own right during the second decade of the 2000s with the popularity of SoulCycle and Flywheel. Those companies augmented indoor cycling classes that already existed in gyms all the way down to the local YMCA.

---

[5] "Fitness DVD Production in the US: Market Research Report," *IBIS World*, December 2014, www.ibisworld.com/industry/fitness-dvd-production.html.

Spinning is actually a trademarked name, though it's taken on a Kleenex-like stature in the exercise world whereby any class that involves a high-octane instructor barking instructions to students on stationary bikes is called spinning. Its origins date back to a South African cyclist named Johnny Goldberg (also known as Johnny G) who was looking for a way to train indoors for his long-distance rides. He and a business partner, John Baudhuin, created the first Spinner bike in 1992.

While a subset of serious cyclists prefer to spin at home—or buy so-called trainers that allow them to mount their road bikes on rollers—indoor cycling is largely a group sport, and still growing.

On a steamy southern summer morning in Atlanta, two dozen young professionals and stay-at-home moms park their late-model luxury SUVs outside a Flywheel location in the tony Buckhead section of town. The vibe is friendly, owing to the fact that many in the class are regulars. Flywheel, like many boutiques, relies heavily on technology to dispense with the administrative elements, like reserving shoes and bikes. That leaves more time for easy chitchat among the staff and riders.

The soon-to-be-sweaty mingle with a just-released class, which lingered for more visiting because it's their instructor's birthday. Cake and coffee are served and pictures are taken, destined for Instagram feeds and Facebook pages. The next class dutifully files into the darkened studio, where the instructor—a wiry, hyperkinetic triathlete named Cathy O takes charge.

The Flywheel workout is intense and designed as a more aggressive counterpoint to SoulCycle, which preceded it. It's a 45-minute ride, pegged to a thumping, 10-song soundtrack, with Cathy O shouting exhortations through her headset all along. The trademark Flywheel twist is keeping score.

The Flywheel workout relies on two main metrics—torque and speed. A knob on the bike adjusts your torque (basically the resistance) and your revolutions per minute depend on how fast you're pedaling. Both figures are displayed on a small readout attached to the bike, in your eye line when you're bent over in exertion. Those results, assuming you opt in (which most do) feed the TorqBoard. It's a dynamic scorecard that measures power exerted; personal results are displayed on screens at the front of the room.

The board stands as one more collision of humanity and technology—our most basic competitive instincts, measured and displayed, in real time. It's easy to see how people get addicted in our current, measure-it-all society.

As often happens, the big established companies sought to learn the lessons from the start-ups. In the case of fitness, large-scale gyms that once relied mostly on rows of treadmills and elliptical machines by 2013 began to see how classes could be a differentiating factor in chasing the membership dollar. The *Wall Street Journal* noted in mid-2014: "People who attend classes make more trips to the gym and are much likelier to renew their memberships, data shows. Group exercise also builds loyalty by offering a spirited and social escape from days of solo commutes and time spent staring at digital screens."[6]

The story describes the delicate process of introducing a new class concept amid a growing roster of choices for a fickle audience. At the time, the Crunch gym was experimenting with an exercise class concept called Disq that was designed by former Dutch speed skaters. It involves attaching resistance cords to one's waist and ankles, with a disc on the hip to control resistance.

At gyms across the country, owners and managers perform the delicate dance of anticipating and reacting to clients' wants and needs. Oftentimes, it's a matter of simple economics; other times customers prove themselves to be irrational actors, in the words of economists.

Michael Olander Jr. is an entrepreneur in Raleigh who didn't set out to be in the fitness business, despite his long-standing affinity for being fit. Now in his early thirties, he came of age in the 1990s, as the fitness boom was beginning. An overweight teenager, he joined a local health club. "Fitness changed my life," he says. "It changed the way I felt about myself, and the way other people felt about me. Not that I was a health freak. That's an important time to be fit and popular."

At the College of Charleston, going to the gym remained part of his regular routine, a way to recover from a big night out, or to meet girls. As he went through school, it evolved from avocation to something that could turn into a job. For his independent study project, he opened a small boutique club, in the basement of a grocery store in Raleigh, where he grew up.

He saw a hole in a market of a fast-growing Southern city, where there was "a highly educated population, good restaurants and social scene, really strong employment and professional base," he says. "It was a wealthy, growing town."

The boutique was a fun project he initially considered a lark, a stepping stone along the way to a career in investment banking after he went back to school for an advanced degree, probably a combination JD/MBA. Two years into running the club, "I realized I really loved the business, and I was tired of school."

---

[6] Rachel Bachman, "A Gym's Search for the Next Zumba," *Wall Street Journal,* July 29, 2014, http://online.wsj.com/articles/a-gyms-search-for-the-next-zumba-1406589092.

Today he's the owner and operator of O2 Fitness, with locations in North and South Carolina. He's so far eschewed outside money, choosing instead to grow the business mostly organically. He's acquisitive by picking up smaller rivals who overextend and fail, leaving a facility behind. He also acquired a slate of clubs in Charleston, South Carolina, that now operate under the O2 brand. All told, O2 has two dozen locations.

While bigger rivals need certain specs for their spaces, Olander says he can be flexible. Part of his sell is that each location leverages some economies of scale from his ownership (vendor relationships, technical infrastructure), but aims to make a unique experience for its local, regular members.

He's trying, so far successfully, to make his way in what constitutes the middle market of fitness. "We'll never compete on price, or offering," he says. "We have to constantly ask, 'What's our value?' and it goes back to experience," he says. "It's about whether you feel comfortable in a place."

These outlets offer a high-touch, personalized experience that emphasizes building relationships, between client and instructor, as well as among the clients themselves.

And there lies a surprising lesson for Michael Olander. Part of his strategy is to offer a broad array—a full-service gym with all the treadmills and ellipticals, a pool, basketball courts, as well as studios for yoga, Pilates, indoor cycling, and barre.

One discovery was that charging extra for studio classes wasn't a detraction—it was the opposite. His members were willing to pay his $49 per month membership for the gym, then turn around and pay another local studio for indoor cycling or barre classes. When the same classes were offered at O2, few people showed up. Once he made members pay an extra $15 to take a class, they became even more popular. The perception of the class's quality changed once members were required to pay for it, a fascinating study in how we as consumers perceive the value of services.

"Consumer behavior is not rational," he says. "When we charge extra for those things, there's higher value placed on them. We build this club within the club."

Olander is quick to point out that he designed his locations to be malleable—with studios that can easily be converted to cater to a clientele that's eager to try the next popular thing, and by extension dump something else. It's here that he—and the big gym chains—have the advantage.

While the overarching trend toward healthier living is steady, winning customers, and customer loyalty, is tricky. The owners of chains like Olander's, as well as the boutique operators like Barry, have to be trend spotters and tastemakers, aiming to capture or, in some rare cases, create a moment of zeitgeist. Investors demand more than a fleeting moment of popularity.

"There's still a market for the health club," Olander says. "You can't just do one thing all the time." He aims to leverage the interest niche stand-alone studios draw to fitness overall, as well as the new and interesting formats they offer. "Boutiques make us better."

Barry's, for one, won a key endorsement in July 2015, when North Castle—the firm that backed Equinox to great success—took a controlling stake. The firm ultimately bet on experiences like that one, and its collective knowledge of what works best for both the body and the business of the body.

In addition to customer loyalty and science that bears out the method of combining strength training and cardio work, Barry's also has a strong brand with a concentration in growing, affluent urban markets where more of those younger, loyal customers, present and future, are opting to live and work.

Aarti Kapoor represented Barry's in the transaction, a coup for her burgeoning business advising fitness companies and the investors looking to give them money. Part of the appeal of Barry's, she says, is the strength of the company's brand, in key markets and beyond. The company opted to sign up franchisees in not-obvious markets, such as Nashville and Oslo; those locations give Barry's backers confidence that it's a concept that can play beyond Manhattan and Los Angeles.

Part of doing that is maintaining a level of consistency while catering to the locals. It's a delicate balance to be both exclusive and not. "It's a very sexy, edgy type of brand that doesn't seem accessible to everyone," Kapoor says. "And yet they've done a great job of maintaining that elevated brand while also taking a tailored approach."

That means a 9 a.m. class in Sherman Oaks, California, feels different from a 9 a.m. class in the hip Manhattan neighborhood of Chelsea, even if the general thrust of the workout is the same. Like its rivals, Barry's has to find ways, be it specialization or innovation, to stay a step ahead of the always-fickle consumer.

The smartest operators anticipate what's going to be hot next, or have the flexibility to pivot quickly to the next big thing. Sometimes that means embracing the disruptors before they disrupt you out of business. Like so many entrepreneurs before them, Barry and his ilk have to outthink younger versions of themselves, some of whom are likely on their payrolls right now. After all, Barry himself started in a traditional health club.

The overlapping elements of personality and community come into play in a meaningful way here. The boutiques have upended the traditional health club and gym industries mostly through a specialized approach that uses a different business model—paying as you go versus monthly membership. At its core, it's mostly the same business: buying or leasing some real estate and hiring people to instruct groups of people at an appointed time in a specific exercise discipline.

While investors flock to back the next Barry, there's a subcategory of the boutique world that's taking its cues from the so-called sharing economy—the catch-all business model that encompasses Airbnb and Uber—to disrupt both the traditional gyms and their boutique brethren.

CHAPTER 4

Mob Rules

Lillian So is in a San Francisco nightclub, sweating. It's 8 a.m.

It's not the end of a long night, but likely the beginning of a long day for So, a fitness entrepreneur of the most intense nature, whose approach involves mixing a whole lot of types of workouts together and presenting them in new and different places. She has a series of workouts in San Francisco, all tied to her conveniently pithy and descriptive last name—SoFree, SoFierce, and SoDefined.

For a version of SoFierce—where the music is advertised as: "Mostly hip-hop, trap, bass, booty bass, club bangers, juke, dub, dope [stuff]. NO pop music unless it's remixed beyond recognition"—she's working very much in the spirit of the locale. Behind her, banquettes normally housing hipsters ordering bottle service sit empty. So is taking her cues from the club life, as well, leading a session she's making up as she goes along. The title carries an asterisk: "*Never rehearsed or planned. This is an IRL (in real life) experience."

Says So: "You're dancing like no one's watching, but you're working out."

Workouts with So are not of the show up, do what you're told, and move on variety. This isn't a trip to the gym where you can zone out, maybe work through a mental to-do list. She wants everyone to be all in. You might be expected to share your feelings with the group. "In San Francisco, there's a studio on every corner and there's a million ways you can work out," she says. "If you want to just sweat and spaz out, there are other places. If you're in my class, you want to work on some [stuff]. You're down for that reflection piece. You have to be up for it."

So created a moveable feast of sorts for her devotees, lining up interesting venues—in addition to nightclubs, classes are held in parks, warehouses, and the public spaces of local companies. She offers one-on-one fitness training that's a level more intense and intimate even than her classes.

She assiduously cultivates her online presence, advertising her latest offerings via a constantly updated Facebook page, investing in a robust website with embedded videos, special offers, and testimonials. She speaks in the patois of a hip-hop artist or DJ (and uses the latter for some of her workouts), dropping phrases like "blow it up" into conversation repeatedly.

She's of a new breed of relentless fitness gurus aiming to separate herself from the noise of so many like her—many of whom are former instructors from studios and gyms. Most of them, like So, still pick up gigs at those places, cobbling together a nice living in some cases.

So started out in the fitness world, working in Chicago at a medical-based center called Galter Life Center. Like Barry Jay, she started at the desk, then moved to fitness specialist. She pursued a degree in exercise physiology at the University of Illinois, Urbana Champaign, then moved to a studio called Refinery before eventually opening a small studio of her own in Champaign.

"I started nerding out on it, wanting to become really more and more an expert," she says. "I wanted to be a magician who had all the tricks."

She began with a blitz of certifications, all of which she advertises on her website, from yoga to Pilates to indoor cycling. What she kept coming back to was a workout that was heavily music-driven. She entertained pursuing a career as a presenter of fitness videos, a post-modern cross between Jane Fonda and Tony Horton of P90x.

Instead, upon moving to San Francisco in 2007, she began studying yoga, at a breakneck pace ("I don't half-ass things," she says during an enthusiastic, wide-ranging conversation). She blazed through 50-hour, 100-hour, and finally 500-hour certifications, plus yoga therapy. "I just ate it up," she says. "Everything started making sense. It was the missing glue for all the dots I hadn't connected."

She identified yoga as a way to, she says, "therapize people," using fitness and movement to deliver a yogic philosophy. "Yoga is the salsa, and the workout is the chip that gets it into your system," she says. "We're always looking for that thing that will help us. We've all got our stuff, our vices."

By virtue of her clientele—wealthy San Franciscans stocked with ideas and connections, and eager to help—she got worksheets designed for start-up companies and offers to write business plans. The self-described hippie girl got serious about her brand.

The first step was putting names, with her name embedded, to her workouts. "People want to compare it to something, but that's hard," So says. "I want people to think about not just what they're doing but what they're trying to become. That's why the naming makes sense. SoFluid, you feel fluid. SoFierce, you feel . . . fierce. The workout part, the getting fit, getting thin, happens as a side effect."

What her cosmic chips and salsa needed was some sort of actual venue. She scoured the city, mostly for dance clubs in their off hours because they fit the tone she was going for. Then she made it a different sort of experience, inviting a local juice shop or soap maker to show up with samples. For her birthday, she blasted her Facebook followers with invitations for a post-workout party (she provided the cupcakes). The message, she says: "I want you to be a part of this family."

Even as her brand was taking hold, and she built a following, the geography remained challenging. Then Raj Kapoor called. Kapoor is a co-founder of Fitmob, a well-funded San Francisco start-up that was looking to upend the traditional gym model and explored several iterations along the way, ultimately combining with a competitor in 2015.

Fitmob was created in early 2013 by a gold-plated slate of Silicon Valley entrepreneurs and investors aiming to capitalize on the surge toward working out, together. The story is a high-tech meet cute of sorts, with CEO-turned-venture capitalist Kapoor and Tony Horton, who'd already found his way into millions of homes through his famously grueling P90x DVD workout set.

Kapoor discovered Horton as many did, by buying his super-popular home workout, which grinds and cajoles those who stick with it into shape over 90 days in the comfort, or confines, of their own home. If you're not one of the people who has tried Horton's workout, you almost certainly know someone who has spent a few, or many, early mornings listening to his exhortations from their living room or basement television.

Intrigued by the effectiveness of Horton's workout, and as he was getting in shape, Kapoor began synthesizing his day job with his fitness. One of Silicon Valley's elite class of so-called serial entrepreneurs, Kapoor created Snapfish, among the first online consumer photo sites, which was eventually sold to Hewlett-Packard for $300 million. He ended up as a managing director at Mayfield Fund, a top-tier venture capital firm in Silicon Valley. He served on the boards of Rubicon Project, Qunar, and was involved in 14 other investments in the Internet-slash-mobile space.

The so-called sharing economy is embodied most visibly by car-sharing services like Uber and Lyft, the latter of which counts Kapoor as an investor and board member. The sharing economy, in short, exploits excess capacity. For the car services, it's allowing drivers to either ditch their arrangements with existing livery companies or grab extra hours when they're not busy. The other best-known example is Airbnb, where the sharing economy has invaded the home rental and hotel businesses. Homeowners are able to rent out rooms, entire apartments, or houses, taking advantage of—or creating—excess capacity that brings in revenue. In the cases of Airbnb, Uber, and Lyft, all of which have grown into massively valued companies by virtue of hundreds of millions in venture capital and private equity, they are disrupting existing markets with deeply entrenched incumbents.

Here, Kapoor thought, was another industry begging to be disrupted, and he was drawn to the $75 billion consumers were spending on gym memberships each year, memberships the majority of them didn't actually use. That meant there was both money and capacity. The capacity came in the form of both physical space and with the instructors, many of whom were willing to take on more classes than they could book at traditional gyms.

Fitmob's theory echoes one employed by the boutique operators: Part of the reason people didn't show up was because the treadmill or elliptical didn't ultimately care if you were absent—and the gym owner was actually glad when you didn't turn up since he already had your money.

Fitmob devised a clever pay-as-you-go model that actually rewards you for showing up more. Here's how it initially worked: Attend one class in a week and it's 15 bucks. Two workouts and it drops to $10. Three or more, it drops to $5 per. Fitmob, which took registrations via website or mobile app, tallied it up every Sunday and charged your account. This didn't take off, as users wanted the simplicity and incentive to work out on a monthly fixed membership.

Fitmob set out to disrupt both the business model and the fitness experience and appealed to the quirky side of the exercise aficionado. Classes were held in novel locations, such as parks, and rooms rented from non-gyms with session names like "Weapons of Ass Destruction" and "Guru Gone Wild." Workouts were highly social and involved a lot of partnering up, encouraging participants to get to know one another. That's in part building camaraderie, and it's also building loyalty to the product, akin to the boutique studios that built loyal communities of regulars: You're more likely to show up if you know your friends are there.

A big difference was the presence of carefully selected professional instructors, who were hired and trained by Fitmob. For its first market, San Francisco, Kapoor told one interviewer the company screened and met with the 500 best personal trainers in the area and hired five to ensure high quality.

They later expanded to over 50 trainers and more than 100 weekly classes throughout San Francisco.

The new model didn't work, as it proved difficult to scale for both trainers and venues, as well as for consumers. The number of venues was limited and the new pricing model didn't catch on. By the fall of 2014, Fitmob shifted to offer excess inventory through an industry standard model created in New York City by a company called ClassPass. Armed with $12 million in venture capital, Fitmob aimed to expand to the Northeast, hiring a former Googler with a fitness background to roll out the service in that part of the country.

At least, that was the plan. But in early 2015, the company was finalizing another round of funding when Kapoor decided a merger with its similar New York-based rival might work better. He set up a meeting with ClassPass founder Payal Kadakia and they hit it off. The main negotiation—between Kapoor and noted angel investor and former Microsoft corporate development executive Fritz Lanman, a ClassPass investor—took two days. The deal, announced in April 2015, closed within two months.

"When you look at quality fitness inventory in each city, there aren't thousands of studios," Kapoor says. "You're talking in the hundreds range, so the supply is limited. It's difficult for more than one marketplace to win aggregating this type of supply. We asked ourselves, 'Do we want to go head to head like Uber and Lyft? Maybe it makes sense to come together. It doesn't seem like it's going to help the industry for us to spend time and resources fighting each other versus focusing on our partners and consumers.'"

ClassPass had quickly cemented itself as the go-to option for the fickle, budget-conscious urban exercise addict. Its evolution explains a lot about the mindset of its core customer. Founder Kadakia created the company, initially called Classtivity, as a one-time (one-month) sampler; the service was called the Passport, and it allowed the user to try out various workouts with the assumption that she'd settle on a favorite and join up. The Passport holder was entitled to skip around, depending on mood and availability of classes, and pick what to do that day. One *New York* magazine writer dubbed it "How to have an open relationship with exercise." It was such a good idea that people wanted to do it for more than a month.

For the suburban bulk shoppers among us, it was sort of like going to Costco: Instead of grabbing a sample of a few things and then buying, say, the frozen pizza that you tasted, Passport users decided they'd rather just make a monthly fitness meal of sampling. ClassPass became a staple for the restless Millennial who could mix and match throughout a week or month (or even the same day), especially as ClassPass expanded its offerings.

You're paying $125 (the original cost was $99, but jumped in 2015) regardless of how many classes you actually go to. But the overall economics are attractive, especially in a city where a cheap class is $25 a pop and many run upwards of $35 or $40. Show up to two classes per week and you've easily made the math work in your favor.

Both opportunities and challenges remain, says Kapoor, who stayed on for six months after the deal to get the companies integrated (Fitmob's headquarters became Classpass's office in San Francisco). He launched an international effort, managing and expanding into countries including the United Kingdom, Australia, and Canada.

While there are similarities with other sharing economy darlings like Uber and Lyft, Kapoor makes a distinction. "With Uber and Lyft, the user experience with existing inventory (e.g., taxis) was poor and the value was not just convenience but also creating a new experience," he says. "That's not the case with fitness. Consumers liked the classes; the experience was not the problem. It's primarily about reducing friction, bringing more value and variety to existing fitness experiences."

But the marketplace is difficult. "The consumer wants all you can eat and the providers want to be paid per use, so pricing and expected usage are tricky," Kapoor says. "What's the right pricing? Are you delivering enough value on both sides? There are a lot of interesting questions."

ClassPass's appeal is the ability to mix it up, to avoid getting into a virtual rut by gorging yourself on a single form of exercise. The variety also has other byproducts.

One thing ClassPass lacks is a community. Sure, there are lots of Class-Passers running around, and users may collude by text and e-mail to grab a couple of free spots in the same cycling or barre class. But ClassPass removes a key element of what makes so many of its client boutiques so attractive in the first place—the ability to show up, on a regular basis, with *your* people.

That's what Fitmob saw in Lillian So, who continues to create her signature workouts, expanding into retreats and different kinds of workouts, like a roving boutique, trying to anticipate what her followers might want next. She's making a living doing it. Others are convening like-minded fitness folks, for free.

Part of the mission is to speak to Millennials, the massive generation that's at the heart of the new fitness economy, often exercising, and often together, and applying an implicit peer pressure around wellness.

"You want to be with your friends," says Nadira Hira, a Millennial expert (and Millennial herself) who wrote about her generation for *Fortune* and authored the book *Misled: How a Generation of Leaders Lost the Faith (And*

Just What You'll Need to Get it Back). "Having someone in your close circle getting excited about a fitness activity makes it more likely you'll do it, too."

Sometimes said with admiration, other times with a sneer, the word "millennial" is meant to describe a generation of people born between 1982 and 2000. Demographer Neil Howe is credited with coining the term back in 1990, as he looked ahead to the generation coming of age at the turn of the millennium.

Their coming-of-age years were especially notable. For fans of the Billy Joel song "We Didn't Start the Fire," the Millennials' verse would have to reference: the dot-com bust, Bush v. Gore, 9/11, Iraq, Afghanistan, Great Recession, Obama, Ukraine, ISIS, immigration, Affordable Care, Occupy Wall Street, student debt, Facebook, Twitter, iPhone.

More simply, Millennials represent the single biggest generation ever—the echo is in fact bigger than the original. Millennials comprise about 86 million people in the United States alone, 7 percent more than the Boomers, with immigration potentially pushing the number even higher.[1]

Seeing Millennials in their native fitness habitats is important. On a chilly Halloween morning in New York City, roughly 75, mostly Millennial, runners are buzzing around the iconic Lincoln Center complex, on Manhattan's West Side, a several block walk from Central Park. It's a group that gets together, in some form or another, twice a week. The bustle on this particular morning is slightly higher octane—the founders of their group, known as the November Project, are showing up today.

It's already a big running weekend. Forty-eight hours later, dozens in this group will gather at mile 14 of the TCS New York City Marathon for an unofficial official water and cheer station, with an emphasis on boosting the morale of any November Project runners (probably about a dozen) set to run the 26.2 mile course through New York City's five boroughs.

Officially unofficial pretty much sums up the November Project.

The product of a shared lament about training through the Boston winter—the bar conversation that started it all happened in November 2011—the November Project spans 16 U.S. cities, pulling in anywhere from a couple dozen to several hundred eager participants each week. It's a running club mixed with a touch of Occupy Wall Street, including the occasional run-in with the cops.

The most notable, and startling, aspect: the hugging. November Project participants old and new don't shake hands. They hug. Anyone. A lot.

---

[1] Jacqueline Doherty, "On the Rise," *Barron's*, April 29, 2013, http://online.barrons.com/news/articles/SB50001424052748703889404578440972842742076.

Having read and heard about November Project—the group was on the cover of *Runner's World* in early 2014—this was my first in-person experience of what read like a genial cult. It didn't disappoint.

After the initial greeting/hugging, we assemble around a clock on a small triangle of a cement park. It is 6:38 a.m., the designated time for the workout to begin (the timing is precise—6:38 has been the official time from the beginning, one of November Project's seemingly endless mild eccentricities).

The leaders of the New York group bring us to order. Owing to the marathon, there are participants (called members) from at least eight other cities' November Project groups (called tribes). With that in mind, we're instructed to introduce ourselves to at least two visitors. More hugging ensues. We cram in closer to listen to instructions for the workout, a blend of running and plyometrics (moves that can look like hyperactive line-dancing) that the leaders seem to be mostly making up on the spot.

We jog across the street to the central square of Lincoln Center, a plaza that's been featured in movies and television shows. Avery Fisher Hall, home to the New York Philharmonic stands on the north side. The New York City Ballet lives on the southern piece of the plaza.

The workout itself is unusual—boot camp with a dash of whimsy, as if you discovered that the drill sergeant was wearing electric pink socks. We start in planks (a static push-up) and are called by birth month to the various stations. The first activity is dips using the stone benches. After 10 of those, we jog three-quarters of the way around the plaza, to another set of benches, where we do step-ups. Then it's on to a game of leapfrog—groups of six people, most of us strangers to each other, crouch butt-to-head while each of us hops over the other. Then we repeat the circuit.

By the time I get back around to the leapfrog station, the police officers who to that point looked on with amusement, finally decide that dozens of weirdly dressed people climbing and hopping and running around Lincoln Center probably isn't a great idea. We reassemble back at the park across the street.

The balance of the workout consists of running around the tiny park, stopping every loop for a set of hoisties. Those involve partnering up, joining hands and then crouching and jumping (preferably shouting "Hoisty!" each time). This goes on for about eight minutes. At one point I realize I'm doing a hoisty with the editor of *Runner's World*. I play it cool and try not to fall down.

The final piece of the workout is a series of push-ups—in pairs, again— that the leaders describe as [Expletive deleted] yeah push-ups. We face our partners and each time we push up, slap opposite hands and shout/grunt/

wheeze "[Expletive] yeah!" There are 50 of them to do. I have the pleasure/horror of doing this with a woman a decade younger than me who I don't know—fortunate, given that I collapse after the fiftieth.

November Project is intensely social, from start to finish. Despite a near-constant stream of encouragement and high fives, clusters peel off from the workout to gab and catch up. Most in the group, it appears, know one another and I'm told later that at least one engagement and another serious relationship were born out of this weekly workout.

After the push-ups that shall not be named, we gather for the traditional group photo, which will show up on the group's Facebook page later that day. There's a series of announcements, mostly related to the logistics of handing out water and cheering at Mile 14 of the marathon.

The leaders then turn to the business of the next workout (after a special Marathon Monday run). The following Wednesday will be a PR Day, one of a recurring series of chances for participants to post their personal best on the regular course adjacent to Gracie Mansion (the home of New York City's mayor, located in the upper part of Manhattan).

As a bonus of sorts, the group also will take yearbook photos, individual shots that have become a popular feature of the November Project (the New York group's Facebook page is a collage of the yearbook photos taken the previous summer). The photos are tangible, shareable evidence of one's November Project participation; many use them as profile pictures on social media.

This owes in part to November Project's target demo. Aside from a guy visiting from Boston for the marathon and a couple others, I am, at 40, dramatically pulling up the median age. (This fact makes me that much more reluctant to fully embrace the hugging ritual. The wider the age gap, the more I'm aware of the thin line between cool middle-aged guy who's up for anything and creepy.)

Hoping that most people take me for the former, I tag along with the friend who convinced me to visit November Project and join a small gang for breakfast, after several in the group, naturally, consult apps on their smartphones for the closest bagel shop, with good Yelp ratings. On the walk and over bagels loaded with cream cheese, I learn a little about some of the regulars: one's a designer at Ralph Lauren, another works in the enforcement office of the National Hockey League (the guy who helps decide which players get suspended, and for how long), yet another is a schoolteacher. All are accomplished young professionals.

This is the November Project target market and broadly describes many disciples of Bojan Mandaric and Brogan Graham, the two founders who I note during the workout are never formally introduced, or even mentioned.

(At the same time, they are easy to spot—both are towering, cut figures, each wearing intentionally gaudy plastic medallions and chains that look like they're lifted from a Mr. T costume).

They're big dudes with bold ambitions around fitness, albeit with humble beginnings. Former crew teammates at Northeastern University, the pair was lamenting over beers their tendency to hit the snooze button rather than work out through the nasty Northeastern winter. They made a pact, in November 2011, to keep each other honest. After making it through that cold spell together, tracking their progress with a Google Doc, they invited a few others to join. What began as their bro vow spawned a grassroots movement.

Their marketing prowess is at once subtle and ubiquitous. While the group doesn't collect email addresses (much to the likely chagrin of race directors, shoemakers, and apparel manufacturers), its social media reach—centered on a Facebook page for each of its markets—is deep. As of early 2016, the Facebook page for the New York group had almost 5,000 "Likes" (the Boston page had more than 27,000).

Traditional media, though, helped fuel it. The *Runner's World* cover story that helped November pivot from a cult-like, unwieldy organism that encouraged embracing sweaty strangers into a full-fledged national network closes with a scene from a somewhat typical Boston morning workout that ended with hundreds of sweaty runners serenading one of their fellows on her birthday, while body-surfing her up the crowd. "Suddenly, we are no longer individuals with work pressures and insecurities and demanding touchscreens, but a glistening, 500-armed creature of joy," Caleb Daniloff wrote.[2]

It's a largely Millennial movement, and a strong signal of the power that generation (loosely defined as born between 1982 and 2000) has over this new fitness economy. While November Project is free, the shoes, apparel, and race numbers its tribe members snap up aren't.

The group fitness movement extends beyond the November Project and firmly into the for-profit world.

Rick Stollmeyer, whose company MindBody provides boutique fitness studios, spas, and salons with their backend scheduling and payment systems, says he puts people into two general categories when it comes to exercising.

He describes the people who have their thing—usually running, maybe hot yoga—and that's pretty much it, "their *one* thing," he says. Stollmeyer puts himself in the other category. He has a personal trainer, does some yoga,

---

[2] Caleb Daniloff, "Hugs, Sweat and Cheers," *Runner's World*, November 8, 2013, www .runnersworld.com/runners-stories/hugs-sweat-cheers.

indoor cycling, runs, walks. He said that makes him, in practice at least, more like Millennials, who tend toward the varied approach.

It's beyond cliché these days for successful people, on stage, in television, or in print, to preach passion as one's North Star, in life and in business. "Follow your passion," we're told, and the rest will work out. Don't get into something for the money, we hear—from people who already have a lot of it.

And yet, this fitness economy is driven by people who are intensely, well, passionate about what they do. They appear to genuinely love their work in a way that not everyone does. This is not a thank-God-it's-Friday crowd; they thank God—or the Buddha, or some other spiritual being—that it's Monday (or any day, since most of these businesses draw customers seven days a week, many on weekends).

One thing that makes this story easier to tell is that passion—this topic of mind and body—is something that almost everyone involved simply loves to talk about, at length.

Stollmeyer is a prime example. He bubbles with enthusiasm over the mission of his company and the industry he supports—more than 40,000 fitness and wellness businesses, with more than 1.1 million customers of their own. To him, being fit has turned the corner into the mainstream consciousness— that for a growing segment of the population, exercising regularly is the equivalent of not smoking.

That comparison is notable, given the recent history of cigarette smoking, or not, as the case may be. As recently as 30 years ago, smoking was, if not encouraged, only mildly discouraged. It's only in the past 15 years that smoking bans have taken hold in major cities like New York and Los Angeles; those bans were once thought to be unthinkable. Now it's hard for many people, especially young people, to remember or consider what a smoking section in a restaurant (or an airplane!) would even look, feel, and smell like.

So it's no surprise that Steve Feinberg is telling me his story over a green juice and avocado on toast in a café on the Upper East Side of Manhattan.

A day or two of stubble give his 39-year-old face an even more boyish look and he's wearing a fleece advertising an endurance race over a bright blue compression shirt with his Speedball logo on it. He's got 250 instructors strewn in seven countries around the world, preaching and teaching his brand of fitness.

Feinberg had a Barry Jay-esque road to Damascus moment when he ditched a very different life in favor of fitness.

Feinberg's epiphany came while he was outside a martial arts studio on Long Island, spent from a day detailing cars, on his way to meet a buddy who was working at a local McDonald's so the two of them could go out for the night.

Feinberg was 19 years old and a recent college dropout, the latest in a string of academic failures that had brought him home to live with his mom, and scrape by on the $7-an-hour, under-the-table job of cleaning cars.

He took karate as a kid, but quit one summer because the local school where instruction took place didn't have air conditioning. He never thought about taking it up again, his youthful athleticism having generally disappeared in a haze of booze and cigarette smoke ("among other more interesting recreational pursuits that altered reality," he says), through high school and into college (where he'd talked his way in, before he stopped going to class altogether).

But here he was, on Merrick Avenue, entranced by a pair of guys performing an ancient ritual involving a sword and shield. They finished and looked up at him through the window. Startled, he walked away, but one of the fighters rushed out to catch him and convinced him to come back the next day for the first in a series of martial arts classes. He charged the fee for the lessons to a credit card he shouldn't have been using, walked over to his buddy at McDonald's and told him he wasn't going out: "I'm starting kung fu training tomorrow," he said to his utterly baffled friend.

Feinberg's mother, a retired teacher who'd reluctantly let him leave college to come home, was disappointed and angry that he'd spend money he didn't have. She felt he'd been turning something of a corner. After work three days a week, he was taking psychology classes at Nassau Community College, sometimes dozing off owing to the 10 hours spent earlier in the heat, cleaning cars. But it was better than skipping class to hang out at the fraternity and do…nothing.

And then came kung fu.

Feinberg's laughing as he tells parts of the story, noting that he still kids his mom about the hard time she gave him when he started the classes, now that his company is global. "I tell her, 'Do you still think this is playtime?'" he says.

Speedball is a group fitness workout that combines music (and in classes Feinberg leads, his own singing and rhyming) and movement, all while holding, or swinging, a specially made, patent-pending medicine ball. Feinberg teaches the class himself about 14 times a week in New York, at six Equinox locations, giving him access to a high-end, affluent, influential crowd that loves to talk among themselves about their latest and greatest workout. He supplements that with personal training work, as well as training, and working out with boxers. ("The guys you see on NBC on Saturday nights," he says.)

At the boxing gym, he's also a coach, working with professionals and amateurs on strength and conditioning.

Like Lillian So, Feinberg is a new breed of fitness entrepreneur who's taking a concept and trying to build a business around it. Spurred often by satisfied, deep-pocketed, well-connected clients, Feinberg, So, and others have built brands around themselves, their services, and even products (like the ball), and pursued deals with fitness chains, created videos, and ultimately drawn followings of both instructors and students.

Like Barry Jay, Feinberg learned by starting at the front door of a studio, though for Feinberg it was a step even further removed. He worked his way through the martial arts school world for several years, not giving much thought to fitness. The head teacher at the school was a party DJ on the side who was well-known in that corner of Long Island, and he encouraged his fellow instructors to use music at the beginning of instruction, when students were warming up and stretching. That innovation anticipated the creation of Tae Bo, created by Billy Blanks, which blends boxing with a lot of lower-body movement, fueled by music.

Feinberg's studio took notice, and began offering a cardio-driven, martial arts–based workout. What began as a couple of classes became a dozen a week and, importantly, the students were an entirely new category for the school. Feinberg wasn't just teaching kids and teens anymore—he was teaching their moms, as well as local gym-goers who liked the notion of actual martial arts experts creating a music-driven exercise (versus fitness instructors simply co-opting martial arts moves).

Feinberg and his boss started talking about expansion, with Feinberg pushing to open a new studio in a nearby town that he would run and be part owner of. Those plans fell apart, leading Feinberg to leave the school for good.

Along the way, he had picked up instruction certifications, so he took a job at Reebok Sports Club NY. It took him deeper into the now-booming world of group fitness. Part of his workout regime was boxing and he became a regular at a gym favored by some of the top New York–based fighters. He competed as a boxer, and trained other fighters. He began to understand what he calls "the demands of functional movement." The medicine ball, a staple of boxing gyms, was a part of many workouts.

He realized he could marry his worlds, and moved the medicine ball into the fitness center. Speedball was born.

As fitness clubs, especially on the high end, have sought to keep up with demand for group fitness, they've entered an arms race of sorts to offer the latest potential breakout class, led by popular instructors. Usually offered as part of the membership, classes can lend a—to use an especially appropriate business term—stickiness for members. Loyalty to an instructor, assuming he or she stays with that studio or chain, translates to loyal clients.

There's something in it for the instructors, too, beyond the money (often a set amount from the gym, sometimes augmented based on how many members attend a given class). They get the seal of approval from a known fitness brand. That often leads to exposure beyond the studio. Feinberg says an overseas deal in Europe, where he trained instructors in his method and therefore gets a cut of their profits, came after fitness-interested investors came across Speedball during a regular review of Equinox's schedule, posted on its website.

The beauty for Feinberg as a businessman is that Speedball is his, to own and expand and defend. Even while he's teaching Speedball at Equinox in New York, Feinberg licenses the method by training instructors, selling them the gear—the ball (branded as the SpeedBALL) and optional, branded apparel—as well as a soundtrack that he curates himself.

He's trained upwards of 220 instructors in Speedball, using technology for initial training, but relying heavily on his personal enthusiasm to truly indoctrinate. "Before I show up, they learn the method, the biomechanics," he says. "They learn how to use the music, they get information that makes them better instructors."

That's in part out of enlightened self-interest. Very few instructors limit themselves to one type of class—most, like Feinberg did, have a range of certifications to give them flexibility across studios and potential clientele. Feinberg knows what the gyms and studios are looking for. "A huge part of the business model is empowering them to be better professionals across whatever they teach," he says. "That makes them more attractive to the operators."

Those operators, in turn, are more likely to throw a Speedball class on the schedule if they have a trusted instructor on the books already. To further woo operators, Feinberg's a presence on the fitness conference circuit and flies around the country making the case in Chicago, Texas, and other non-New York and non-L.A. markets.

His plan for world domination is largely digital. As he was proving the concept at Equinox, he went looking for ways to push video content that would enhance the brand. After a couple of false starts, he connected with Peter Heumiller, a founding partner of a firm called All Screens Media, created to back companies at the nexus of media and fitness. Heumiller is something of a pioneer in pushing exercise beyond just DVDs, as well as understanding how to give what Feinberg calls "a fair share" to the instructors-cum-entrepreneurs.

Feinberg formed a joint venture with All Screens, called Speedball Media and Merchandise, that aims to create a generation of Steve Feinbergs and Lillian Sos. Using a template based on Feinberg and Heumiller's own experiences, he sells would-be fitness gurus a package whereby they can create a brand, design and find a manufacturer for their own equipment, even seek additional funding. "We can help people make anything they want," he says. "We're creating a brand factory."

Feinberg and So learned the fitness side, but needed the media expertise and found it in various ways through ever-evolving partnerships. Other gurus-as-brands come with a deep knowledge of the media side, including one particular guy who had it quite literally beaten into him.

Diamond Dallas Page was an entertainer before he became a guy selling yoga to dudes.

I arranged with his publicist to meet the wrestler-turned-yoga guru at a midtown Manhattan hotel one spring evening. He was in town making the media rounds. (Two months later, he was the centerpiece in a long *New York Times Magazine* story under the headline "The Rise of Beefcake Yoga.")

His publicist gave me very precise instructions on where they'd be in the hotel, instructions that were completely unnecessary. A heavily muscled, 6-foot-5-inch dude in a tight black shirt holding court in a gravelly, cigarette smoke-cured voice stands out.

Sometimes the athlete is the one selling his own product, where the personality is effectively the product. DDP, as he was and is known to both wrestling fans and his newer yoga disciples, is a relentless tweeter, retweeting and replying to users of his DVD-based program. He stands as an example of a personal brand and company anchored in personality and fueled by technology. Twitter is only a part of it.

Page was a household name for those who followed professional wrestling in the late 1980s and early 1990s. He came to wrestling in his mid-30s and went on to become world champion, and at a time when wrestling was selling out arenas and minting money via pay-per-view events. While pro wrestling takes its knocks for being more entertainment than sports, there is a lot of it that is quite real. In other words, while outcomes may be scripted, there's an immense amount of physicality to it, a lot of actual collisions, body slams, kicks, and punches.

In 1998, he found himself laid up, the result of one too many hits. His back was basically broken, or enough that he couldn't do anything close to the hard-core, weight room–oriented workouts that had turned him into a world champion wrestler.

His then-wife and still–business partner was the one who suggested he try yoga. His response wasn't suitable for polite company; the sanitized version is "Hell no." But he succumbed and the seed for DDP Yoga was planted.

He is affable, profane, and demonstrative. Slightly too big for the hotel lounge chair where he sits, he pops up often during our conversation to demonstrate a specific move. He extends one leg and holds it at a 45-degree angle to his body. A neighboring bar patron, looking for a quiet drink with his date, opts to move to the opposite corner of the bar. Clearly not a wrestling or yoga fan.

DDP says he'd just as soon have no one call what he does yoga, but at this point, he's stuck with the name. He's not so interested in the roughly 20 million people already practicing. "I want the people who wouldn't be caught dead doing it," he says.

As he used yoga to rehab from his broken back, he began to zero in on the notion of a high-octane yoga-based cardio workout for the everyday person. The original name of his company and product was YRG—Yoga for Regular Guys.

Now he's 59, and building a company worth about $10 million, with visions of taking it to 10 times that, a multimedia empire that he describes as "the Netflix of fitness."

That nod to the popular video rental and streaming service is notable, as DDP's popularity would be a sliver of where it is now without his relentless use of media, social and otherwise. Beyond his Twitter followers, he's on Facebook and has leveraged YouTube videos to great effect. He knows his personality is at the center of this slightly off-kilter endeavor.

To augment the retweeting and "liking," he spends time almost every day calling 5 or 10 people who recently bought his DVD series. Few people buy a DDP Yoga program without knowing who he is, so they're pretty excited to get that phone call. He asks how they found out about it, and given the high referral rate, it's usually a friend or family member. So DDP asks for their number, and calls to thank *them*.

His time in the world of professional wrestling made him appreciate the power of a curated and carefully managed public persona. The wrestling swagger comes through in person, and on screen. He's leveraged his own brand and network, in wrestling and beyond, to amplify his efforts. He ran into the musician Rob Zombie, an acquaintance, a few years ago when they were both buying Christmas trees in Los Angeles. Zombie noted how good DDP looked; DDP sent him the DVD program and Zombie became a devoted user. When DDP wrote his 2013 book, *Yoga For Regular Guys: The Best Damn Workout on the Planet!*, Zombie contributed the foreword. His first draft started, "Yoga. Give me a . . . break" with some additional obscene language fit for the wrestling ring. Another chance encounter, at an airport, introduced Page to a fan named Steve Yu, who went on to become the president of DDP Yoga.

Page has gone on to convert other former pro wrestlers to his method. The *Times* piece revolved around his work with Jake "The Snake" Roberts, arguably one of the best-known wrestlers of his generation (his signature move, the DDT, involved slamming an opponent's head into the mat or concrete outside the ring, followed by Roberts placing his snake on his prone prey).

At his induction into the Wrestling Hall of Fame in 2014, held at the Smoothie King Center in New Orleans, Roberts made reference to his post-wrestling descent into drugs and alcohol, which rendered him a virtual shut-in.

"All you have in your heart is shame and pain," he told the crowd, according to the *Times*. "And you can't do what you love anymore, so what do you have left? Not much. Not much at all. And if you are alone, like I was, you make some bad choices. But for some reason, one person sticks a hand out. And that person for me was Diamond Dallas Page."[3]

Page's outstretched hand pulled Roberts all the way into Page's spare bedroom, where Page oversaw a complete overhaul of Roberts' life and body. He kicked a crack cocaine habit and finally booze, after a series of relapses. Page, ever the media promoter, turned Roberts' story into a movie—*The Resurrection of Jake the Snake*—that was screened throughout the United States in 2015.

Having a growing roster of devotees who are certified tough guys helped spread the word, and counter any concerns about yoga appealing only to lithe, New Age women. Within the ranks of the World Wrestling Entertainment (WWE), at least 40 wrestlers have used the program, according to the *Times.*

Page is also heavily reliant on the regular guys, and that's where social media, and especially YouTube, have made a huge difference. With DVD sales as the main revenue source, Page's most effective marketing channel is YouTube, where he posts get-pumped-up videos and testimonials. The most popular and effective has been one starring a guy named Arthur Boorman.

A wounded Gulf War veteran, Boorman used video to document what is by any description a remarkable transformation.

A five-minute video of his workouts, filmed by his son and edited by Page's team, is at times slightly uncomfortable to watch, as Boorman struggles

---

[3] Alex French, "The Rise of Beefcake Yoga," *New York Times Magazine,* August 17, 2014, www.nytimes.com/2014/08/17/magazine/the-rise-of-beefcake-yoga.html.

to find his balance, repeatedly falling over. The video has been viewed in excess of 12 million times. His devotion to Page helped propel the DDP Yoga program; within a month of posting the Arthur video, Page sold $800,000 worth of DDP Yoga DVDs. The video also inspired others, with Page's help, to create their own testimonial videos.

Video is the cornerstone of Page's empire-building. For several years, he held sessions at his suburban Atlanta home, which he dubbed "the Accountability Crib." Now, all classes are at his DDP Yoga Performance Center, located in the Atlanta suburb of Smyrna. There, he leads live weekly classes and shoots content for his new DDP Yoga Now app. He envisions more documentaries like the Jake the Snake film and more heavily produced versions of the Arthur video.

At the heart of the whole endeavor is building a DDP community through traditional media like video, with social media as a powerful accelerant. For every person Page could draw to the Accountability Crib, there were hundreds more, maybe thousands, maybe tens of thousands, he could reach through Twitter. By early 2016, he had in excess of 380,000 Twitter followers, many of whom he exhorted through barrages of retweets and replies.

For all the of-the-moment feel (the videos, the tweeting), Page has a lot of the traditional hallmarks of an evangelist who's seen the error of his previous ways, complete with the fervor and enthusiasm only converts can pull off.

And what he ultimately professes to his growing flock is that his program isn't something you do, it's meant to be part of who you are, and that means thinking not just about that half an hour or hour a day you're blending *vinyasas* and body slams, but thinking about what you're putting on, and in, your body.

CHAPTER 5

Dress the Part

Chip Wilson was practically late for his own wedding because he was too busy selling yoga pants.

The founder of Lululemon marks his 2002 wedding day as a turning point in his company's life. What was then a one-location retailer in Vancouver, British Columbia, mushroomed into a $7 billion juggernaut. That made Wilson famous (and, at times, notorious). It made him a billionaire several times over, and helped launch a fashion category that did not exist before.

The yoga pant, as popularized by Wilson's company, is the iconic apparel item of the fitness economy. In its utility and ubiquity, the sleek, expensive, casual piece of clothing epitomizes how fitness has shifted for many people from something we do to who we are. Giving people, especially women, something that doubled as activewear and streetwear reflected a broader move, Wilson says. "There was a mindset shift, toward longevity and health, and away from drinking and smoking and working."

Today, Lululemon apparel, with its tiny, stylized *a* logo, is ever-present on the sidelines of soccer games, in carpool lines, at coffee shops, and on airplanes. The pants and tops spawned a raft of imitators, including some of the biggest names in athletic apparel, as well as a new term—athleisure—for the style of clothing that seems fit for the gym, but is worn many places besides. Such casualwear doesn't come cheap, and the product's popularity and price point (upwards of $100 for a pair of Lulu pants) points toward the affluence associated with this type of fitness fashion.

The Lululemon story is one of innovation and anticipation, peppered with missteps and misstatements, course corrections and rapid growth. It starts as a classic entrepreneurial tale, where a big thinker boldly moves in a way few of us have the guts to, and helps create a new market in the process.

Chip Wilson saw a chance, and he took it, and he knew it the day of his wedding: "I said, 'I've got something here,'" he says. "Either I've got to make it big or I'm going to get run over."

Lululemon was born in 1998 when Wilson, who'd been in the business of surfing, skating, and snowboarding apparel and equipment, opened a store in Vancouver, British Columbia. The Lululemon name was the product of a 100-person survey, selected from 20 names. Wilson identified that the company needed to be more than a store, highlighting the community aspect of the endeavor. He wanted it to be a place where the staff was smart and able to engage customers not just on what they were wearing, but also about how they were living. "It was a people development company as much as an apparel company, because I only wanted to work with people I loved and respected," Wilson says.

Vancouver was, and remains, the perfect laboratory for companies like Lululemon and entrepreneurs like Wilson. Gregor Robertson, the city's mayor, is a tall, athletic guy whose preferred mode of transport is a bicycle.

Robertson says Vancouver, by design and climate, encourages the sort of culture embodied at companies like Wilson's. "It's a dominant way of life, to be outdoors," Robertson says. "The combination of contemplative and active is part of the city's DNA."

Part of it, he says, owes to the way the city is laid out, with many buildings looking out toward the sea, rather than in, on each other. "We're an outward-facing city," he says.

Wilson says all of it changes the people who live and work there, down to how they define success. "An alpha male or an alpha female, they're completely different," he says, especially versus hard-charging financial hubs like New York. Where Manhattanites measure success on money or position, a Vancouverite's more likely to brag about his or her run, ride, or hike. Wilson himself can barely have a conversation without a mention of, or invitation to, the Grouse Grind, an insanely vertical hike in Vancouver he takes on daily, if not more. He counsels that everyone benefits from sweating for an hour a day.

His timing was impeccable, and Lululemon became one of those companies that both benefits from and helps define a trend. Big money came calling. Representatives of Advent International, a well-known global private equity firm that backed companies like Party City and The Coffee Bean, first encountered the company at an outdoor sports equipment convention in 2004, having identified the broader wellness trend several years earlier. Six months after the first encounter, and a series of cold calls to the company by junior investors at Advent, the apparel maker said it was seeking funding.

Advent invested in Lululemon in 2005 with the idea of expanding the management team, product lines, and geographic reach. The next two years were frenzied, as Lululemon tapped executives from across the retail and consumer world and built a company that could scale its operations globally. From its base in Canada and a handful of other stores in the United States, Lululemon opened outlets in Los Angeles and San Francisco, among other American cities, and also went far afield, to Tokyo and Sydney.

By the end of 2007, the year of its initial public offering, Lululemon had 80 stores. Advent said, citing Thomson Reuters data, that out of 177 offerings that year, Lululemon was the third-best performing IPO. The company continued to consistently grow fast. Up until 2013, sales rose 30 percent or more for 14 straight quarters. The company posted its first $1 billion revenue year in 2012.[1]

Lululemon became a poster child for the industry, and for how private equity firms might exploit the trend toward fitness and wellness. This was a situation where an investor saw an opportunity not in the activity, but in the adjacent elements. Advent also saw what Wilson had identified: this wasn't just about the clothes, it was about a way of life.

Advent created a case study it posted on its website as an advertisement of sorts for would-be future investments, and its own investors. Advent sold some of its stake in the IPO, and then sold down its ownership into 2009. When the last of those shares were sold, Advent delivered an eye-popping return to its investors, making eight times its original investment.

Wilson remained and stood as the company's biggest investor, as well as an irascible spokesman for the business and the broader trend. Plainspoken, he was a journalist and TV producer's dream, a popular conference speaker who kept audiences engaged. Which is of course what ultimately got him in trouble.

The first problem was product related. A popular version of Lululemon's tight-fitting yoga pants were, it turned out, too sheer. In the course of a yoga class or any other activity that stretched the fabric, anyone in back of the wearer got a full view of whatever was underneath the pants. A well-read *Bloomberg News* story explaining the flaw after the fact ran under the headline "Lululemon Sheer Yoga Pants Undetected Until Bend-Over Test." The company pulled the product amid a social media storm and offered refunds. The mistake cost the company 27 cents per share in earnings that year.

---

[1] Sapna Maheshwari, "Lululemon Sheer Yoga Pants Undetected Until Bend-Over Test," *Bloomberg News,* March 21, 2013, www.bloomberg.com/news/2013-03-21/lululemon-forecast-trails-estimates-on-pulled-transparent-pants.html.

What should have been an unfortunate but straightforward product recall took a turn when Wilson appeared on Bloomberg Television. Pressed about why the product didn't work right, he said women's size and shape played a role. "Frankly, some women's bodies just don't actually work for it," Wilson said, referring to the yoga pants. "It's more really about the rubbing through the thighs, how much pressure is there over a period of time, how much they use it."

The backlash was immediate, and fierce. Twitter and Facebook feeds lit up denouncing his comments, forcing him to apologize, which he did via a video posted on the company's Facebook page.

The stock dropped 4 percent in the wake of his comments, showing how wide his misstatements spread, how much it worried investors counting on the continuing popularity of the brand, as well as the insane power of social media in shaping public perception of a brand. Wilson's much-heralded successor as CEO, Christine Day, had already announced her departure within months of the recall. She took a job as the CEO of Luvo, a company that makes healthy fast food.

Her replacement was Laurent Potdevin, who joined Lululemon from TOMS, the do-well-by-doing-good shoe company that donates a pair of shoes to a needy child for every pair it sells. Potdevin set out to put the company on better footing, assuring both shareholders and consumers that the company had learned its lesson and was focused on all the right things.

Wilson, still a board member and substantial minority shareholder, stayed vocal, for a time. He said publicly he was looking for a backer to finance a takeover of the company, through which he'd take the company private again. His preferred option was to change the board in order to change management. Words flew, and the stock languished amid the feud, as investors fretted about whether the company could recover amid an increasingly competitive market for its apparel.

In late July 2014, after weeks of negotiation, Advent stepped back in. No other investor was more familiar with the company and its potential. Advent saw a chance to get back in by buying half of Wilson's remaining stake, roughly 14 percent of the company's shares, for $845 million. In addition to diminishing the founder's voice, Advent regained two board seats, filling them with two Advent partners instrumental in the original deal.

On the day of the announcement of Advent's return, and Wilson's implicit concession, the stock rose almost 4 percent. (Representatives of Advent and Lululemon declined repeated requests for interviews for this book.)

The next quarter made clear that something of a revival had already been underway. In September 2014, the company announced quarterly results that beat analysts' estimates and raised its forecast for the full year. The stock jumped to its best price in three years.

The trigger, in addition to Wilson's dilution by Advent, was the successful rollout of a line called & Go that was designed to be worn outside of the studio or gym and still fit the athletically casual mindset. Lululemon also saw a boost from its men's line, both for workout clothes and for & Go apparel. In the intervening period, Lululemon stock bounced around. The stock dropped 6 percent in 2015, the third straight annual decline. The company found itself dealing with the decidedly unsexy and, at times, difficult parts of running a growing global business, including distribution costs and inventory management.

For his part, Wilson was largely onto the next adventure. He put some of his Lululemon riches into a new family business, conceived and run by his wife, Shannon, and son, JJ, called Kit + Ace. That company is meant to pick up to some extent where Lululemon leaves off, with a higher-end line of clothes designed to be worn at work and throughout a nonsporting social life.

Fashion has played an interesting role in the evolution of fitness, informing how we look and even our goals in doing all this crazy stuff in the first place.

Today's fashion, especially for men, raises a chicken-and-egg question when it comes to the modern body. That is, did we get skinnier to fit into tighter clothes, or did wardrobes slim down to cater to the fitter man?

What's not in doubt is the bias in current fashion to a slighter build. Lost to history and Arsenio Hall's closet are the double-breasted suits of the 1980s and 1990s (to wit, when I first typed double-breasted while jotting down notes on my iPhone, it autocorrected to double-breastfed; the term didn't even exist, according to Apple's vocabulary sensibility). Many pants don't have pleats, as men favor flat-front suits and chinos that make it much more difficult to hide a few extra pounds.

The slim trend appears to be born, at least in part, out of the men's metrosexual fashion of the late 1990s and early 2000s, when straight men began leaning toward looks previously associated with gay men. Television shows like *Queer Eye for the Straight Guy* begat lines at retailers including Banana Republic that incorporated looks and color palettes previously thought of as feminine. Advertising, too, took on a different tone, with models for apparel makers such as Abercrombie & Fitch appearing shirtless and lacking any body hair.

The rigors of the modern workout regimes served to push those trends further. For men, it became (mostly) acceptable to wear skin-tight shorts and fitted tops for cycling and triathlons—and to click through the aisles of Whole Foods in their cycling shoes afterward to pick up a smoothie. The more serious competitors (or those who want to appear serious) shaved their legs, chests, and arms to increase their personal aerodynamics on the bike and in the water.

Men also moved to tighter-fitting shirts, ditching the looser look that peaked in the 1990s. The trimmer fit is a throwback to the 1960s, spurred by a variety of cultural factors, including the popularity of the show *Mad Men*, set in a New York agency during the Sixties and Seventies. Celebrities, too, adopted the cleaner, slimmer look. Women noticed, and pushed their boyfriends and husbands toward that look. Once again, the Internet played a role, putting fashion in front of men's faces.

Retailers reported flipping percentages of regular and slim fits. In 2014, 60 percent of Nordstrom's men's dress shirt sales were trim or extra trim, with the balance regular cut. Five years earlier, regular fit accounted for 60 percent.[2] The same *Bloomberg News* story reported an increase in the extra-slim category, whereby designers were cutting several inches from a shirt's width.

For both men and women, spending more time in workout clothes that doubled as carpool and coffee-run wear was the product of athletic clothes that were better designed and more stylish, a far cry from the mesh shorts and ratty T-shirts once acceptable for a jog around the neighborhood or trip to the gym. (We'll completely skip over the era of the tracksuit as evening wear.)

Sport-specific clothing is a massive industry in its own right. For the triathlete, there's Tyr, a family owned, Long Island-based company that started in the goggle-and-swimsuit business back in the mid-1980s and seized more recently on the triathlon frenzy.

Tyr's story tracks the explosion in interest in endurance sports, and their move from fringe to mainstream. The company started in Huntington Beach, California, the brainchild of a former Olympic swimmer named Steve Furniss, who captained the 1976 U.S. swim team in Montreal, and Joe DiLorenzo.

Tyr takes its name—pronounced tier—from the Norse god of warriors, and stands as an example of an endurance company whose employees live its mission, and its products. The current CEO is Joe's son, Matt, who took over running the company shortly after graduating from Villanova in 2008.

---

[2] Cotten Timberlake, "Slim Shirts Get Slimmer as Nordstrom Courts Fitter Guys," *Bloomberg News,* June 4, 2014, www.bloomberg.com/news/2014-06-04/slim-shirts-get-slimmer-as-nordstrom-courts-fitter-guys.html.

"In 1985, fitness was coming of age, and they wanted to make swimsuits that were fashionable and appealing," the younger DiLorenzo says. "That was where we started. The tri was not nearly as developed as it is now. . . . We've grown along with the endurance fitness business."

While Matt DiLorenzo grew up around the business, he wasn't raised as a swimmer or triathlete, favoring more traditional youth team sports like hockey, basketball, and baseball. When he rejoined the company full-time after a few years on Wall Street, he signed up for a triathlon. "I thought, 'I need to do this to understand what our customers go through,'" he says. "I got pretty into it."

The Tyr staff tend to be the same way—"healthy and somewhat fitness conscious," DiLorenzo says, noting that "not everyone is doing a 10-mile run at lunch." But there's a high level of interest in the continuum of yoga, spinning, and running, or the obvious—swimming. "You can just grab a suit and goggles," he says. "It's all around you. It just kind of absorbs you, especially when you see other people doing it."

That social aspect is a critical component of the broader movement, specifically as it relates to the business of fitness apparel. "America loves gear," DiLorenzo says. "That's what we like to do. You get to research it. It's part of the experience and it's fun."

The gear is where technology plays an important role, in a couple of ways. There's the technology behind the equipment and apparel itself, and then there's the role social media plays in feeding the aforementioned obsession.

To that point, "shopping and research is part of the experiential component—that's part of the social aspect," DiLorenzo says. "You can talk and talk about this stuff. It may not make a difference, but the athletes are talking about it all the time. The forums and blogs are littered with 'Have you tried this?' It really builds that community."

Among the most popular online communities is SlowTwitch.com, a sort of message board on steroids (which is also a topic, especially in the post-Lance Armstrong doping admission world) that's grown to have its own newswire of sorts. The site is crammed with news and information—and opinions—with lots of partners and sponsors presumably clamoring to be heard by the visitors to the site.

Athletes of varying skills pile onto the site, providing advice, commentary, and straight-up bragging. On that site, as well as the *Runner's World* message boards, it's not uncommon for the bottom of a poster's message to feature his or her personal bests.

Then there's the technology that's actually in the gear and apparel, technology that's advertised relentlessly and promises to give weekend warriors an edge, any edge. As it is in the virtual world, real-world running and cycling groups feature almost nonstop discussions on shoes, clothes, and everything else a runner or cyclist might need, or think they might need.

Here, traditional media still plays a powerful role, with magazines like *Runner's World* filling its pages with editorial and advertising that blends our enthusiasm for fitness and consumerism. Rodale, the publisher of *Runner's World,* also owned the now-defunct *Running Times,* whose reader tended toward the more serious amateur athlete. Races buy full-page ads through the magazines, and smaller ads toward the back, alongside various products meant to solve problems from plantar fasciitis to chafing. Every other sport or activity has its own publication (or more) to keep competitors up to date. *Yoga Journal* is the go-to for that crowd. Cycling has *Bicycling* and triathlons have a number of titles, as well (there's both *Triathlon* and *Triathlete*).

Buying what's advertised got increasingly easier with the dawn of the Internet—much to the dismay of local independent retailers, who increasingly found their customers showrooming their stores (showing up, trying on shoes or other apparel, and then finding a lower price somewhere online).

The local running and cycling stores—like their counterparts in the bookselling industry—pressed their value around community, arguing that personal attention and expertise can't be found on the web. While true to an extent, the amount of information and advice available from global sources a click or two away grew exponentially.

The Independent Running Retailer Association introduced a campaign to encourage people to shop at places near to them, rather than online or at a big box retailer. Called "Lace Up Local," the effort noted that $100 spent at an independent store put $68 into the local economy, versus $43 at a national chain. Appealing to the notion that many races have charitable components, the group also reminded visitors to its site that local stores donate to local charities at twice the rate of the national chains.

The market Lululemon helped create continued to grow around it, as more-established retailers saw the market expand rapidly. Gap Inc., whose brands include its namesake chain, as well as the high/low pair of Banana Republic and Old Navy stores, bought Athleta, then a catalog business, in 2008 and made it part of its brick-and-mortar empire.

Athleta sought to exploit Lululemon's fitness halo, while pressing advantages that came with being part of Gap. Athleta offered consistently lower prices than Lululemon—usually 30 percent less by one estimate—at stores often located in close proximity. While Lululemon had an intentionally small selection and rarely discounted merchandise, Athleta more frequently rolled out new lines and quickly put out-of-date merchandise on the sale rack.[3]

Wall Street analysts noted that Athleta stood to gain during Lululemon's recall woes, as well as the broader growth of the category. The brand used Gap's ample resources, especially in e-commerce, where cost-conscious shoppers often scoured for bargains. Gap also was growing its physical footprint aggressively; the company opened 65 Athleta stores in its fiscal 2014, and said it would open 30 more the following year.[4] Athleta is aimed squarely at women—its slogan is "Power to the She."

Other retailers joined in, designing lines of clothes that could double as workout and hangout clothes. Urban Outfitters embraced the concept, adding an in-store element called Without Walls in a handful of outlets, which it planned to expand. The company created a big online presence for Without Walls, playing to its target market of young shoppers. The site featured products from brands such as Vans and Patagonia and the name is meant to evoke and encourage a lifestyle lived actively and outdoors.

In September 2014, Sports Authority introduced a new clothing line called Bloom. Calling it one of the company's biggest launches in the past several years, a Sports Authority executive noted that it was aimed at the 25 to 40-year-old, and for wider use. "This is not just for the yoga studio, this is a lifestyle collection. Our objective is to cast a wider net within the yoga market."[5]

Sports Authority described a plan to create small stores within a store dedicated to yoga, presumably to make affluent women shoppers more comfortable within a traditional sporting goods store where they're more likely used to shopping for youth soccer cleats.

The athleisure trend was measured in a number of ways and like many fashions, the leading edge was with teenagers. A study in early 2014 found that leggings were the top fashion trend; activewear accounted for almost 30 percent of clothing purchases, up from 6 percent in 2008.[6]

---

[3] Shas Dey, "Athleta Versus Lululemon," *The Motley Fool,* May 12, 2013, http://beta.fool.com/edliston/2013/05/12/athleta-versus-lululemon/34193/.

[4] Sarah Mahoney, "On Softer Sales, Gap Expanding Athleta," *MediaPost,* February 28, 2014, www.mediapost.com/publications/article/220516/on-softer-sales-gap-expanding-athleta.html.

[5] Sharon Edelson, "Sports Authority Launches Yoga Collection," WWD.com, September 2, 2014, www.wwd.com/fashion-news/fashion-scoops/sports-authority-launches-yoga-collection-7856041.

[6] Nicole Goodkind, "Teens Abandon Denim for this New 'It' Pant," *Yahoo! Finance,* April 15, 2014, http://finance.yahoo.com/blogs/daily-ticker/burn-your-jeans--teens-are-abandoning-denim-for-a-new--it--pant-143502837.html.

Weekly lifestyle magazine *InStyle* wrote, "athleisure represents a bigger, and likely permanent, sea change in fashion. . . . The reasons are many, but the most obvious cause stems from people who are embracing healthier lifestyles, while also demanding more functionality from their wardrobes."[7]

Under Armour made its way to the trend from another angle, starting with the hard-core male athlete initially—its name alone sounds like the polar opposite of Lululemon. Yet the Baltimore-based apparel maker moved swiftly into the athleisure market during the past several years, embracing it as a new way to appeal to its existing male customers as well as move deeper into women's wardrobes.

As part of that effort, Under Armour pursued its previously successful strategy of signing up celebrities and athletes (or sometimes celebrity athletes). The company did a deal with supermodel Gisele Bundchen, as well as with ballerina Misty Copeland and pro surfer Brianna Cope.

The method illustrates the sharp contrast in the Lululemon and Under Armour business models. Lululemon sells only through its stores, relying on a high-touch, personalized approach dating back to the community built around the first Vancouver location. There are no paid celebrity endorsers, though Lululemon certainly benefits from famous people showing up Lulu-clad in public—or better yet, in the pages of celebrity magazines.

Under Armour, meanwhile, is practically ubiquitous in both advertising and retail, from its own outlet stores to department stores in every corner of the United States (again in contrast to Lululemon, which has resisted even going to suburbs of major metropolitan areas in favor of hip urban locales).

As with the sports themselves, the acceptance and proliferation of the apparel into mainstream retailers was a meaningful step forward, and was critical in establishing fitness as a lifestyle and not just a series of activities.

That's what the Wilsons have in mind with Kit + Ace. The company's name comes from a fictional man and woman whose lifestyle the apparel maker is meant to support. Its foundation is a trademarked concept, Technical Cashmere, which Shannon Wilson conceived to match her active lifestyle, and that of the affluent, on-the-go consumers like her. She and JJ Wilson, Chip's son and her stepson, run the company.

Chip Wilson for the moment is an investor and consultant to the company, but in late 2015 made noises indicating he might engage on a more serious level with Kit + Ace. The company has already lured some former Lululemon executives into the Kit + Ace mix, where there's also the same lifestyle/spiritual-oriented culture the Wilsons imbued at Lululemon.

---

[7] Eric Wilson, "Now You Know: Just How Far Should You Take the Athleisure Trend?" InStyle. com, July 16, 2014, http://news.instyle.com/2014/07/16/what-is-athleisure/.

At Kit + Ace, the mission is to lean further into the megatrend—athleisure and the active lifestyle—that made Lululemon successful and made Chip Wilson a billionaire. Wilson says his goal is to launch five companies, Kit + Ace being the first, that are adjacent to, but don't compete with Lulu. After all, he's still that company's largest shareholder. Clothes may make the woman and man, but many in the fitness economy are spending as much time, and money, thinking—sometimes obsessively—not just about what they wear, but what they eat.

The food and fashion element of the fitness economy breaks down into two roughly defined parts—what we wear and eat that's directly tied to the activities themselves, plus the derivative fashion and food choices coming from a lifestyle that favors a certain type of body and routine.

The first is relatively easy to define—that's the market for all the equipment we buy to run, bike, and swim, go to a class at a boutique, or practice yoga. Sporting goods stores are bumping up the amount of space devoted to these sports, noting the demand and high prices the apparel commands.

The second is harder to capture because it reflects a broader societal change that extends beyond getting fit. Then there's the causality question—that is, does exercising more beget healthier food habits, or does eating healthier make us more willing and able to exercise?

Anecdotal evidence abounds. Take almond milk, a niche product if ever there was one. (Count me among those who didn't even know it existed until a couple of years ago.) Many others have learned, apparently. By mid-2014, almond milk was generating $700 million in annual sales. One producer, WhiteWave, boasted six straight quarters of at least 45 percent sales growth.[8] Part of what drove the uptake was athletes, as almond milk became a familiar topic on websites and blogs devoted to the best food for training. Like other fitness-related crazes, almond milk has its detractors, especially amid a historic drought in California. Creating almond milk involves adding a lot of water, a precious resource in a state that grows 80 percent of the world's almonds.

The modern everyday athlete has fueled a segment of the food industry devoted to healthier choices. With professional athletes like Novak Djokovic touting the benefits of a gluten-free diet, what once was considered fringe is mainstream when it comes to eating, too.

Organic food moved from the purview of aging hippies and earth mothers to the mass market, especially the affluent segments, with the arrival and

---

[8] Vanessa Wong, "America's Almond Milk Boom Tops $700 Million in Sales," *Bloomberg Businessweek,* August 8, 2014, www.businessweek.com/articles/2014-08-08/the-almond-milk-boom-silks-huge-sales-lead-the-way-trounce-soy.

popularity of Whole Foods (jokingly called "Whole Paycheck" for its frequent sticker shock), as well as everyday grocery chains like Stop & Shop devoting significant shelf space to organic brands. Sales of organic products rose 11.5 percent in 2013 to $35.1 billion, according to the Organic Trade Association. Organic food growth averaged more than 10 percent growth a year (versus overall growth of roughly 3 percent) and accounted for about 4 percent of U.S. food sales.[9]

Part of this stems from a generally better-educated consumer. Books like *Fast Food Nation* and *The Omnivore's Dilemma* are hard to forget for their insights into where our food comes from. More recently, Katie Couric and Laurie David's documentary *Fed Up* provided a startling view of the obesity crisis and its causes, which brings up a major and troubling paradox: How, in an age of record obesity, is one segment so focused on health and wellness?

Academic research shows that healthy eating and affluence are linked and specific healthy foods are associated with higher income. A 2008 American Journal of Clinical Nutrition noted that "grains, lean meats, fish, low-fat dairy products, and fresh vegetables and fruit are more likely to be consumed by groups of higher SES (socioeconomic status). In contrast, the consumption of refined grains and added fats has been associated with lower SES."[10]

This trend isn't necessarily new. The researchers cite a study from the mid-1980s where a survey of British adults found non-manual workers consumed four times more whole grains than manual workers.[11]

The connection between a healthy diet and a regular exercise regime is not hard to make, though social mores play a role as well. The ability to eat rich foods in plentiful portions once was a sign of success and affluence. That's a concept that dates back centuries, and held true well into the twentieth century. Think of the term fat cats. It was only in the latter half of the last century and the first part of the new one where phrases like "You can't be too thin or too rich" came into vogue.

Owing to the complexity of how economics, nutrition, and exercise play off each other, arguments around affluence and exercise tend to feel circular—the rich have more information, easier access to higher quality foods, and the leisure time to devote to exercise. The poor have none of those things. What's cause and what's effect?

---

[9] Organic Trade Association, "America Appetite for Organic Products Breaks Through $35 Billion Mark," May 15, 2014, www.organicnewsroom.com/2014/05/american_appetite_for_ organic.html.

[10] Nicole Darmon and Adam Drewnowski, "Does Social Class Predict Diet Quality?" *American Journal of Clinical Nutrition* 87, no. 5 (May 2008): 1107–1117.

[11] Ibid.

It's clear that higher quality education includes more information about healthy eating and exercise. First Lady Michelle Obama's Let's Move campaign is aimed at creating healthy habits for kids, including those who might not otherwise get the necessary encouragement around physical activity.

What's not in dispute is the move toward healthier eating exploded. The term *superfood* gained traction, as doctors and nutritionists pushed kale, blueberries, and quinoa on a public eager for advice on how to eat better. Vegetarianism and the more extreme veganism took hold among a broader population. Mark Bittman, a *New York Times* writer (and himself a longtime runner), wrote a book called *VB6: Eat Vegan Before 6:00 to Lose Weight and Restore Your Health . . . For Good* that laid out a philosophy of eating to appeal to the modern, busy citizen.

The 6 in question was 6 p.m. and Bittman's program, which he followed himself, called for a plant-based diet until the evening, at which point he gave over to his desires to eat meat and other foods that would fall out of a full-on vegan's purview. It was radical in a way, in part because Bittman's plan conceded our shared imperfection and many people's unwillingness to give up the simple pleasures of good food (after all, many people took up a heavy exercise routine to be able to eat whatever they wanted, with little consequence, given their weekly calorie burn). He admitted to cheating on a regular basis—eating a piece of bacon for breakfast, for instance—but argued that following the general outlines allowed him to drop weight and boost his energy levels.

My own super-food discovery of sorts was steel cut oatmeal, made with almond milk instead of dairy milk, and topped with some brown sugar and blueberries. I swore by it in training and folded it into my routine, preaching its attributes to just about anyone who would listen. I was one voice among many, apparently. McCann's, an Irish oatmeal maker whose history dates back to 1800, in 2005 sold 1 million tins in a year for the first time.

Activity-specific food and drink—the stuff we consume right before, during, and after running, biking, and working out—grew into a huge business in its own right. By 2009, sports nutrition, not including sports drinks, was a $4.6 billion market worldwide, according to researcher Euromonitor.[12]

The subsector devoted to energy drinks was massive in its own right. Gatorade and Powerade, as well as niche drink brands, broadened their marketing from team sports to individuals, promising hydration for the high-octane weekend warrior.

---

[12] International Markets Bureau, *Overview of the Global Sports Nutrition Market*, Agriculture and Agri-Food Canada Market Analysis Report, August 2010, www5.agr.gc.ca/resources/prod/Internet-Internet/MISB-DGSIM/ATS-SEA/PDF/5569-eng.pdf.

The sports drink category—pegged at $6.9 billion by one researcher in 2012, was predicted to grow to $9.3 billion by 2017—on the strength of the powerful existing brands as well as new companies.[13] In addition to products like Muscle Milk, which caught on with endurance athletes, there were other well-funded entrants. Basketball star Kobe Bryant said in early 2014 that he invested in a sports drink called BodyArmor, which was founded in 2011. Bryant struck a deal to invest $4 million to $6 million, for roughly 10 percent of the company, *Forbes* wrote at the time.[14]

Among the most surprisingly popular markets is the one for gels—energy, protein, and caffeine delivered usually through single-serving foil packets that fit in a shorts pocket (there's an entire line of shorts under the brand Race Ready, that has specially designed pockets for gel packets). They're attractive to runners and cyclists because they're easy to consume on a run or ride. Among the most popular brands were GU (pronounced goo) and PowerGel, a line of gels from the maker of PowerBar, a popular protein bar.

While relatively small compared to the market for sports drinks, there were still 18 distinct gel manufacturers in the United States in 2014, according to a website called *Energy Gel Central.* (The fact that such a site exists is both impressive and scary.)

In each case, the makers and marketers were looking for, and promising, an edge to the average athlete looking to be above average relative to his or her peers. In any regular running or cycling group, and in the pages of the magazines and websites devoted to each sport, there's constant talk about hydration and nutrition. It's the source of pre-race sleepless nights, and fodder for post-race post-mortems. Too few fluids (or too many), the wrong food (or the wrong amount) all are valid reasons for not reaching one's race-day goals. Constant experimentation is the norm.

As 2015 drew to a close, Moelis' Kapoor was spending more time looking at the food section of the health and wellness ecosystem. She knows investors are looking for big markets and a huge part of the shift to a healthier lifestyle involves more awareness of what we're putting in our bodies; in meetings with companies she frequently hears words like fresh, clean, transparent. "It's an active space, and a massive category," she says.

---

[13] Brian Warmoth, "Sports Drinks: A $6.9B Market—and It's Only Getting Bigger," *Food Dive,* October 10, 2013, www.fooddive.com/news/sports-drinks-a-69b-marketand-its-only-getting-bigger/180655/.

[14] Kurt Badenhausen, "Kobe Bryant Invests Millions in Sports Drink BodyArmor," March 24, 2014, www.forbes.com/sites/kurtbadenhausen/2014/03/24/kobe-bryant-invests-millions-in-sports-drink-bodyarmor/.

While still focused on the body, Chip Wilson is also intrigued by the mind. Wilson is an investor in whil.com, a website meant to bring meditation to the masses, in bite-sized chunks. Its tagline: everything's gonna be alright. A subscription-based service, the website and associated app deliver tailored, brief meditations meant to relieve stress, help you sleep better, improve your relationships, and boost creativity.

Wilson is especially interested in mindfulness in the workplace, keying off his experience building distinct employee cultures that not only acknowledge, but celebrate, the everyday blurring of lines between our lives and our work. It's also an acknowledgement that while we focus so much on our bodies, it's our minds that may need even more attention.

Having spent years encouraging his teams to be active, Wilson is now using the Kit + Ace staff as a test case for whil in the workplace. Most meetings start with a meditation grabbed from the site, lasting from one minute to 10. For Wilson, it's a reflection of his own evolution. "I used to be able to satisfy myself with a 10-K in the morning," he says. "Now that's not enough to keep me focused throughout the day." The ability to drop meditative sessions into the workday sets him, and he says his colleagues, to be more successful.

The focus on physical fitness leads, it seems, to a deeper search for meaning. And that helps explain why the ancient practice of yoga moved from the fringe to the mainstream and into a starring role in the new economy of mind and body.

CHAPTER 6

Looking for Meaning

Sunday morning means different things to different people. For generations of Americans and others, Sunday was a religiously prescribed day of rest, or at least the day your parents made you wash your face, put on something nice, and go to church.

If you play a word association game with many modern weekend athletes, Sunday would prompt the response: long run or long ride. The road is the new church.

I like to think I manage to experience both sides of this. I'm a regular, Catholic churchgoer. To get to Mass on Sundays, I actually drive past the high school where my weekend running group congregates. It has struck me many times that the purposes, and the results, aren't so different. (Hopefully the liberal Jesuits who taught me in college would be mildly amused by this comparison.) To that end, I point out a piece about a religious scholar named Stephen Bullivant, who made good on a promise to complete a marathon while reciting the rosary the entire way.

In the piece, he explained: "As readers of *The Canterbury Tales* will be well aware, the motivations for such 'spiritual exercises' are often decidedly mixed. Mine are no exception. A large part of it is simply the desire to have done a marathon. . . . This was one last try to satisfy that ambition and I called— frivolously and selfishly, perhaps—on the patronage of Mary, Our Mother of Perpetual Help, to keep me injury-free."[1]

---

[1] Stephen Bullivant, "My Marython," *America*, December 5, 2013, http://americamagazine .org/my-marython.

This mind–body connection, with the spiritual acting as the connective tissue, comes up time and again in interviews and writings about why we hit the road. There's no doubt that, as Bullivant alludes to, some of it is rather narcissistic. But it's socially acceptable—as illustrated above, a priest can get away with it, for goodness sake.

Connecting the body with the mind and soul is a strong driver of the current fitness obsession and the similarities between what's happening in that high school parking lot and my church up the street abound. Spirituality is at once both intensely personal and naturally communal. In a place of worship, we are alone and together simultaneously. While a group run or ride is somewhat more boisterous, any runner will attest to quiet moments of introspection even amid the chatter of the group. The community aspects of running and cycling clubs are in some cases replacing the shared purpose once found in the pews of a church.

There's a documented modern tendency to eschew formal religion and religious institutions while maintaining some sort of informal spiritual life. Research from the Pew Research Center in 2012 pointed out that roughly a fifth of all U.S. adults are "religiously unaffiliated," the highest figure ever in its polling.[2]

The research found "that many of the country's 46 million unaffiliated adults are religious or spiritual in some way. . . . More than half say they feel a deep connection with nature and the earth (58%), while more than a third classify themselves as "spiritual" but not "religious" (37%).[3]

"Young people are looking for anchors," says author and Millennial expert Nadira Hira. "A lot of this is about connecting with people who are at your stage and phase of life. Millennials are looking for sources of stability and support and are generally skittish about the old model of doing that, particularly religion. This is a generation that resists restriction, and religion feels restrictive."

Organizations and institutions, some religious in nature, have laid claim to the spiritual benefits of running, and as an antidote to the craziness of everyday life. In his book, *Running with the Mind of Meditation*, Sakyong Mipham writes:

In the modern culture of speed, we seem to not do anything fully. We are half watching television and half using the computer; we are

---

[2] Pew Research Center, "'Nones' on the Rise," October 9, 2012, www.pewforum.org/2012/10/09/nones-on-the-rise/.
[3] Ibid.

driving while talking on the phone; we have a hard time having even one conversation; when we sit down to eat, we are reading a newspaper and watching television, and even when we watch television, we are flipping through channels. This quality of speed gives life a superficial feeling; we never experience anything fully. . . . When we are running . . . we are engaged in one of the most intimate and meaningful acts that might occur during the day.[4]

Ascribing such heady notions to exercise makes it feel, and seem, more important. Now it's not just about getting fit for swimsuit season or to make oneself generally more attractive. It's not even about following your doctor's orders to get your cholesterol levels down. It's about connecting with your very being.

Robin Harvie, in his book *The Lure of Long Distances*, echoes Mipham's theory about running as an escape: "In those hours when we are cut off from telephone calls and the nagging reminders of our daily responsibilities, we enjoy an illusion of complete self-sufficiency in which we want for nothing."[5]

Inherent to both men's argument is the idea that running takes place outside; it's hard to capture that illusion of self-sufficiency on a treadmill. Harvie's view of running is heavily informed by Henry David Thoreau and Ralph Waldo Emerson, who found deep meaning in nature.

Running marketers have seized on the idea of running as an escape to a more primal feeling. Flip through the pages of *Runner's World* or more specialized magazines like *Trail Runner*, and you find runners pictured in sweeping vistas, often alone, a small figure in a vast swath of nature.

It's human counterprogramming, a physical escape from an unrelenting virtual world. I felt it one time on a trip to Northern California. I'd spent three days preparing for and hosting a high-tech conference, on a tricked out stage with video cues, wireless microphones, and producers in my ear giving direction.

The morning after the conference ended, I woke up with a few hours before my flight. After dispatching with a few emails, I broke away and soon found myself on a thin ridge high above Marin County, the fog rolling across and filling in the valley on either side. I was completely alone and went the better part of an hour without seeing another human being. Faced

---

[4] Sakyong Mipham, *Running with the Mind of Meditation* (New York: Three Rivers Press, 2012), 78–79.

[5] Robin Harvie, *The Lure of Long Distances* (New York: PublicAffairs, 2011), 17.

with a turn that would take me back to my hotel, and questions, and phone calls, and work, I kept running. I wasn't tired, but I stopped occasionally to just soak in the view. After a few miles navigating rocks and roots, and an occasional fleeting concern that I could fall to my death, I turned to go back.

I emerged from the clouds to a sweeping view of San Francisco Bay, the Golden Gate Bridge. Harvie and Mipham were ringing in my ears.

So was Fred DeVito.

I turned to him several months earlier to learn about his New York fitness studio, which had drawn a following largely based on its ability to connect mind and body.

DeVito created the exhale and the Core Fusion workout. Core Fusion has a yoga derivative and its general philosophy sits at the nexus of mind and body, an ethos reflected in DeVito's calm manner.

I first spoke with him by phone on a spring Friday, while he was sitting in his car on the way out to East Hampton, where he and his wife/business partner, Elizabeth Halfpapp, have a home, near one of their exhale studios. The location attests to the clientele, which moves en masse during the summer from the sticky concrete Manhattan jungle to the Hamptons out on Long Island.

Our conversation moved quickly from the physical to the metaphysical and back. DeVito has the ambition of an entrepreneur but the sensibilities and grounding of someone who thinks about the body and mind a lot. "I look at exercise as a moving meditation," he says. "Our entire society is trying to reach a higher level of consciousness. We're trying to see the world from a higher vibration."

DeVito and Halfpapp have been married for more than three decades. They chose not to have children, he told me, to spend time teaching. "This is my life, and my wife's," he said. "We can reach a lot of people in a transformational way."

The pair met in high school in central New Jersey, and after college, DeVito played bass in a jazz band while Halfpapp went to ballet school. She got a job at a then-new exercise studio on the Upper East Side of Manhattan run by Lotte Berk, a London-based instructor. Berk had created an eponymous method of exercise that used a ballet barre.

As the business grew, Halfpapp became a manager, and then moved to Los Angeles with DeVito, where she opened a Lotte Berk studio. A year later, they returned and DeVito became an instructor, encouraging men to practice at the studio. He taught six classes a day, and he and Halfpapp began to draw a loyal following of people who came to the studio regularly, for years. "Our student body went from single to married to married with children," he says. "We lived all that with our clients."

As the 1990s came to a close, the couple saw a chance to evolve beyond the Lotte Berk method and open their own studio. A student named Annbeth Eschbach joined them, as a co-founder and the CEO, to form the basis of what's now exhale.

DeVito points to the terrorist attacks of September 11, 2001, as a pivotal point in the evolution not only of his own business, but in the movement toward mind–body wellness overall. "Post-9/11 was when people changed," he said. People started to think about their well-being "on a day-to-day basis."

In the months after 9/11, in fact, was when exhale won its first funding, from a group of investors who saw the same thing DeVito did. In an age of increasing physical and economic uncertainty, people were turning inward and looking for something to cling to, at least for a time.

That shift meant wellness became an all-in lifestyle instead of an existence where exercise is ghettoized on the schedule—a morning jog or a dreaded trip to the gym. "It's a lifestyle," DeVito says. "People want to live longer and start thinking a lot about what they need to do. They start to find restaurants that serve healthy food. They go on active vacations instead of going on a cruise and overindulging."

Wanting to embrace the lifestyle fully offers opportunities for expansion geographically (locations in summer vacation spots so clients don't have to leave their routine back home) and technologically. Two decades into teaching, DeVito and Halfpapp created their first DVD, and now they have produced a dozen. The pair has also written a book (*Barre Fitness: Barre Exercises You Can Do Anywhere for Flexibility, Core Strength, and a Lean Body*) and has explored whether to offer streaming video of its classes.

DeVito isn't alone in appealing to the soul, body, and mind simultaneously, aiming to scratch a deep existential itch.

Other forms of exercise are pointed about their spiritual component. SoulCycle—the New York-based spinning juggernaut—promotes the idea right in its name and in its classes, right down to the candles in the room. Its marketing materials are filled with notions of using exercise to connect with ourselves on a deeper level.

Part of this pivots back to the generational elements mentioned earlier. Author Daniel H. Pink, who writes often about how our minds work, discussed this in his book *A Whole New Mind*. He noted that "[p]ursuits devoted to meaning and transcendence, for instance, are now as mainstream as a double tall latte." Pinning it squarely on Baby Boomers, he goes on: "[A] s individuals age, they place greater emphasis in their own lives on qualities they might have neglected in the rush to build careers and raise families: purpose, intrinsic motivation, and meaning."[6]

The sway that the Baby Boomers hold is notable here. The sheer size of the generation makes them a powerful commercial force that has a deep impact on the rest of the marketplace. Generation X picked up the mind–body thread with gusto and forty-somethings have flooded yoga studios during the last decade. This cohort, as young adults, lived through the late 1990s tech boom as well as the subsequent bust, then watched the cycle repeat itself to some extent with the economic fervor of 2004 to 2007 and its requisite crash. All that macroeconomic and personal drama has sent us toward new solutions to calm our crazed minds.

Millennials have largely grown up in a world where whatever tensions Generation X held onto—between being a good corporate soldier and seeking work/life balance—don't exist. Millennials are straightforward about their priorities, placing less emphasis on making money, and more on Pink's "purpose, intrinsic motivation, and meaning."

All three groups, for those different yet overlapping reasons, are flocking to a centuries-old practice that more obviously than just about anything else, seeks to connect mind and body: yoga. The activity holds a place in the modern affluent world as antidote to modern life.

Yoga, despite some of its trappings—perfectly designed studios stocked with bricks and designer water—is a stripped-down exercise, one that comes with not just permission to, but an insistence on, cutting off. There is no technology that can make you a more accomplished yogi. You can't be better than the person three feet away by shelling out more for a mat or a towel (though my modern, consumer self did wonder a few times about the fancy, yoga-specific towels that fit *just so* on a yoga mat, versus my bath towel grabbed from the linen closet).

There's also the elimination of outside influence. No studio I know of allows anyone to check email or take a call during a class, which is exactly how we want it. In fact, most of us in that studio would gladly pay $25, or a lot more, for 90 minutes to ourselves, silent and undistracted.

Yoga sits, quietly, at an intersection of postmodern angst, narcissism, and spiritual longing. Its appeal derives largely from the fact that it's generally good for you, and because participating is a way to say something about you to the rest of the world. It imparts a worldliness and perceived serenity on the practitioner. It feels like a vestige from yoga's roots on the

---

[6] Daniel H. Pink, *A Whole New Mind: Why Right-Brainers Will Rule the Future* (New York: Riverhead Books, 2005), 60.

fringe, and an inherent mysticism that pervades both historical and current practice.

Yoga instructors and practitioners speak in words and phrases that, inside and outside the studio, likely would sound ridiculous in any other context (and probably do in this context, to some): "I feel centered," "I'm listening to my body." The social scientists would note the singular personal pronoun in both of those sentences—while a group activity, yoga is not a team sport, and plays hard to our individualist streak. The perception of worldliness and serenity helps explain why so many who practice yoga, especially only occasionally, manage to drop it into cocktail conversation. It also helps explain the popularity of yoga pants—a socially acceptable piece of apparel that gives the impression you are a yogi.

Roughly 20 million Americans regularly practiced yoga as of 2012, a 29 percent jump in four years, according to *Yoga Journal*. It's a population that's overwhelmingly female (upwards of 80 percent, according to the survey). Like the other sports, practicing yoga (and to be clear, you practice yoga, you don't just do yoga) has come to mean more than going to a room and bending yourself into weird positions once or twice a week. Like the other exercises and activities described earlier, doing it on a regular basis begins to define who you are, even when you're not contorted.

But for many, it's intimidating to start, for a variety of reasons. The writer Claire Dederer, in a memoir called *Poser* that used yoga as a way to tell her life story, writes it this way: "I thought yoga was done by self-indulgent middle-aged ladies with a lot of time on their hands, or by skinny fanatical 22-year-old vegetarian former gymnasts. I was also unsettled by the notion of white people seeking transformation through the customs of brown-skinned people—basically, to my mind, a suspect dynamic."[7] Spoiler alert: Yoga changes Dederer's life and allows her to survive and contextualize a whole series of dramatic life changes.

Later in the book, she's still mulling the appeal to people like her: "I still wondered what yoga was, exactly. In America, was it just a gentle way for dorks like me to get in shape? These poses, honed and refined over thousands of years, were like a safe harbor."[8]

Trying to explain yoga's popularity requires an exploration of what yoga actually does, and what it's become. Science writer William J. Broad wrote an excellent book, *The Science of Yoga: The Risks and the Rewards,* that sought to find the answers.

---

[7] Claire Dederer, *Poser: My Life in Twenty-Three Yoga Poses* (New York: Picador, 2011), 7.
[8] Ibid., 91–92.

Part of its increased appeal is the increasing number of variations, especially those that focus on the physical benefits akin to other more obvious workouts like running, cycling, and weight lifting. Broad writes: "[M]odern yoga, by accident or design, has lost much of its contemplative nature and adopted some of the sweatiness of contemporary exercise."[9]

Culturally, yoga pivoted around the turn of the twenty-first century into something normal people felt comfortable doing and talking about. Once limited to hippies huddled in not-well-advertised studios, it's a breakout sport of the past decade. Most every gym offers it. Cruise ships and resorts feature classes at several levels. Women (and men) who you think would not even entertain the idea of showing up for yoga roll out a mat.

While men haven't flocked to yoga the same way women have swarmed running, the phenomena are similar. Getting men interested in yoga unlocks the other half of the population, and helps spread some more macho variations like Bikram—a type of yoga practice in a very hot room—and even DDP Yoga, which was discussed earlier. Broad and others noted that this was in fact taking yoga back, way back, to its own roots. For centuries, yoga was a practice for warriors, who were exclusively male. Women were, in fact, forbidden to participate. Now that women are dominant, classes meant to attract men spring up now and again. A neighborhood buddy of mine told me about a class he and some pals were going to, branded unofficially as Bro-ga.

Once the numbers started growing, misconceptions faded, which begat bigger numbers. "It's become demystified," says Colleen Saidman, who with her husband Rodney Yee is one of the most influential and popular yoga instructors and personalities. "It's always been incredible for mind, body, and spirit. But it was perceived as a cult or a religion."

Yee said that for many, yoga is a replacement for organized religion, at a time when many are asking the Big Questions, and very publicly. "Even though it's a material world, we all have a deeper impulse," he says.

Celebrity has played a major role, and just as she did with marathons in the mid-1990s, Oprah played a role in shaping public opinion around yoga. Yee and Saidman both appeared on her show, and Oprah was an early strong voice about recognizing the importance of one's spiritual side.

In 2011, celebrity yoga collided on one of Oprah's television shows, when Jennifer Aniston—while telling Oprah that yoga had changed her life—presented Oprah with a personalized yoga mat.[10] At that point, Oprah had been

---

[9] William J. Broad, *The Science of Yoga: The Risks and the Rewards* (New York: Simon & Schuster, 2012), 49.

[10] *Oprah*, www.youtube.com/watch?v=x-5azf8jHBo.

talking yoga for more than a decade, and like she did for books and many of her so-called favorite things, her attention and support moved product. Yee appeared on Oprah's show in 2001. That year, one of his DVDs became Amazon.com's second-best selling video for the year.[11]

A growing number of celebrities, some obnoxiously, have boasted of their yoga prowess. Sting was among the first and most vocal about it, to the point that *Buzzfeed* wrote a story in 2014 titled "43 Celebrities Who Swear By Yoga. Besides Sting." Their list included Julia Roberts, Madonna, and Woody Harrelson, as well as younger stars like Russell Brand and Reese Witherspoon.[12] "The celebrity world has had an incredible effect," Yee says.

Saidman and Yee both note that many of the celebrities chose to attend classes, underscoring the community component of the practice and echoing much of the sentiment around the boutique fitness classes (some of which also benefited from implicit celebrity endorsement). Many or all of the stars could afford private yoga instruction, safely within the walls of their Holly-wood Hills compounds or sprawling Tribeca lofts. "We have desires to huddle together," Yee says. "It's just like milk and cookies in your kindergarten class."

Says Saidman: "As animals, we're drawn to that setting. It's very natural to our beings."

The balance between the personal and the communal has informed Yee and Saidman's practices and businesses from the beginning. Their ability to marry the two has formed a growing and profitable empire. While yoga has thrived in the social setting of the studio, it's also found a thriving business through books and DVDs that allow would-be yogis to work out in their homes.

Yee and Saideman were among the key architects of moving it from fringe to mainstream. The ubiquity of Yee's DVDs, along with a rugged travel schedule that puts both of them in a place to personally interact with students has spread both their brand and yoga. My first conversation with them took place over the phone during a brief summer lull. I called their Long Island home and talked to them together. They each picked up a receiver, almost like I was calling home from college and talking to my parents.

After talking through the why, we started talking about the what. In particular, about Yee's videos, which arguably are the most visible of all yoga

---

[11] Deirdre Donahue, "Look at This Man's Body: This Is What Yoga Can Do," *USA Today*, April 24, 2002, http://usatoday30.usatoday.com/life/books/2002/2002-04-24-rodney-yee.htm.

[12] Emily Hennen, "43 Celebrities Who Swear By Yoga," *Buzzfeed*, February 18, 2014, www.buzzfeed.com/emilyhennen/43-celebrities-who-practice-yoga#ar7xls.

videos. Through a partnership with Gaiam, his ponytailed, trim (and often shirtless) form sits on sporting goods and bookstore shelves around the world.

The videos, Yee says, are something of a gateway to practicing yoga. Even with its growing popularity and the natural comfort of being around other people, picking up yoga is intimidating. As it's become more popular, more and more people have gotten really good at it, which in a way makes it even more intimidating to be a beginner. "There is a great social aspect to class, but there [are] a lot of people who are shy," Yee says.

"Especially men," Saidman says.

The first video was produced in 1989, followed by three more in 1992. That kicked off the series, which now numbers around 30 videos, some of which now feature or include Saidman. The videos are relatively simple in their form—calming and straightforward, with Yee leading a session in his soothing voice, often with a lovely background.

A former student who became Yee's wife, Saidman started Yoga Shanti in 1999 and, even though she started her studio more than a decade after Yee, the technology and business acumen was basically the same. She and the other instructors constituted the whole staff and the initial investment for the studio was $1,500. "We'd run to the bank to make change," she says. "We wrote everyone's name down on a piece of paper and used index cards."

Yee's experience was similar: "We had a basket that people dumped money in."

In both of their cases, it was in part because they didn't set out to build big businesses. Yee says early on, people who didn't practice yoga weren't even sure what he did. "People thought we were talking about 'yogurt,'" he says. "You did it because you wanted to share knowledge. It wasn't going to be a livelihood."

As a business, Yee says yoga is in its infancy. "I feel like it's just getting its feet wet," he says.

The growing modern popularity is largely tied to physical benefits that put yoga alongside more obvious cardio activities, Broad wrote. While some of the research about the physiological benefits were dicey, he says, it was enough to kick-start a wave that's only gaining momentum. "From a business angle, the claim was pure gold. It could turn a simple form of exercise requiring no costly equipment or investment into a dazzling profit center.[13]"

Those profits are what attracted investors to back yoga studios, yoga apparel makers, and other companies selling goods and services to yogis and

---

[13] Ibid., 66.

would-be yogis. CorePower Yoga, a Denver-based operator of studios, had $60 million of revenue and 74 studios in nine states when it sought private equity money in 2013.

CorePower won an investment from Catterton Partners, a private-equity firm focused on consumer and retail products. Catterton had backed the likes of Bloomin' Brands (operator of restaurants including Outback Steakhouse) and Baccarat, a home luxury brand. Catterton had identified the fitness trend and also invested in Flywheel, the indoor cycling studio, as well as Pure Barre, the Spartanburg, South Carolina–based company backed by WJ Partners. The firm also backed Protein Bar, a restaurant chain offering healthy food options like quinoa bowls and protein drinks, and Sweaty Betty, an active-wear company. In early 2016, Catterton combined with the private equity arm of fashion giant LVMH to form L Catterton.

Yoga has also become popular with athletes, an increasing number of whom—female and male—tout its ability to help them recover from, or avoid, injury.

That's how it was pitched to me, and how I ended up at my local yoga studio on a frigid January morning.

My previous yoga adventures had made me feel somewhat geriatric—lots of gentle stretching and soft voices. Here, the voices were soft, but it was in service of kicking my butt. I dropped two pounds in class that day, sweating profusely, wiping my mat so I didn't slip in a puddle of my own making. And yet the music was soothing, the room mostly dark, and the tone encouraging.

One thing that struck me was that despite a friendly teacher who made sure she knew each of our names, there was essentially zero chitchat among the students in class. I wasn't complaining, but I was surprised, having guessed that a midmorning yoga class might be a bit more like a coffee klatch. This was about the business of ourselves, individually. We could chitchat another time.

Throughout most of the class, my heart rate was up and my breath was short. My sweat was prolific. The instructor that day was in a relatively kind mode, encouraging us to make a silent intention at the beginning of class, to use the time away from the world to really disconnect from it. The intensity of the workout makes that easier than I thought. I couldn't spend a lot of time ruminating on a missed deadline given how much I was struggling to keep my balance. Our instructor used the word yummy several times to describe certain postures, a questionable word choice, at least to me. Very little beyond the couple of minutes devoted to corpse pose—lying still in the dark, finished with the workout and actually just breathing—fit that description.

And yet, the sum of the parts was simultaneously exhilarating and, in the end, relaxing. My muscles felt loose and tested. I found myself in the subsequent days striking an occasional pose (out of sight of anyone else, mind you) in order to clear my mind, or deal with an especially stressful moment at work.

A few weeks later, I went back with a different instructor who was more rigid, even a bit snappy. She chided one of the students for taking a sip of water, noting that we would come to a break soon. Instead of a gentle instruction to shift positions, she clapped to signal a change in the pose. It felt more mission than meditation, a little bit of Navy SEAL mixed in with our *namaste*. I started to understand why this style of yoga—hot, fast-paced—was the one drawing more and more Type-A athletes to studios.

The athlete/yoga connection led me, via a mutual friend, to a former Nike account executive named Ellen Bain. She left the comforts of the corporate world to start Train with Yoga. It's geared toward the high-octane athlete—professional and otherwise—who wants to integrate yoga into their routine and lifestyle.

She started as a yoga skeptic, a successful executive-cum-athlete who couldn't shake injuries. Tired of going to the chiropractor, she was constantly looking for solutions. "I read an article that said Kareem Abdul-Jabbar partially attributed his longevity in the NBA to yoga," Bain told me. "I initially thought it was incense and chanting. He played in the NBA until he was 42. That got my attention. It was the beginning of my love affair with yoga."

As she dug in, she read *Power Yoga* by Beryl Burch, and later got to know her personally. Power Yoga as a concept helped Bain relate to ashtanga yoga, then relatively obscure. Bain was interested in a system that built strength, flexibility, and concentration, while also helping heal injuries. Here was an activity that both challenged the body and calmed the mind, and brought her into a welcoming and tight group that only seemed to grow.

"For me, it was initially just from the physical realm, but I learned it was so much more," Bain says. "It became a way of life to train my mind and body. I moved a lot in my business career and it was a great source of community in the various places I had the opportunity to live. It slowly became my main social conduit. It was spiritual but not religious. Some of the best friends of my life post high school and college I've met on the mat."

Emboldened, she turned yoga into her full-time work, creating Train with Yoga to serve athletes who also took a cue, most unwittingly, from Abdul-Jabbar. She worked in New York, Los Angeles, and Santa Barbara, California, at Equinox and a California company called P3, helping enhance the performance of athletes through yoga.

Her job was in part to spread the message to the pro athletes, many of whom weren't immediately into yoga. But it was working. And history was on her side. "Yoga's been around for 2,000 years and this train isn't turning around any time soon," Bain says. "It will only get bigger as we make it more acceptable."

It's getting there, if the business world is any indication.

According to author and journalist Laura Schadler, "Today health insurance companies cover yoga as a therapy for heart disease, schools teach meditation, nonprofits use yoga as a means to serve disadvantaged youth, and soldiers use it to manage combat stress."[14] Her conclusion: "Yoga, despite how dramatically different it might look [now versus centuries ago], is still about that truth. And therein lies its appeal."[15]

But what is it that makes the truth so much more appealing today than, say, 20 years ago, when people were practicing yoga in far fewer numbers? Society right now has a growing obsession with authenticity—a fancier way of talking about truth. Social science provides some additional answers. Jennifer Smith Maguire, a lecturer in mass communications at the University of Leicester, tells me that yoga underwent a transformation as it got more popular and moved into the mainstream. Newer instructors "stripped out the selfless notion and turned it into an individualized exercise."

This observation is fleshed out in her fascinating book, *Fit for Consumption: Sociology and the Business of Fitness* that was first published in 2008. The book was the ultimate byproduct of a research project that began almost by accident. Several years earlier, pressed for a graduate course topic at the turn of the new year, Maguire noted the tendency of herself and friends to join health clubs in a flurry of good New Year's intentions. She saw a prime opportunity to explore modern consumption in a new way.

What she discovered goes to the heart of this new economy of fitness: we are not just allowed, but encouraged and expected to work on our body and our *self*. To thread it into the larger economy, where the majority of the middle, and certainly upper, classes are engaged in a white-collar service economy, our relationship to our bodies and leisure changes.

Maguire writes: "[R]ising living standards and the mass production of consumers transformed self-improvement into a mass, middle-class project." She quotes none other than the author Tom Wolfe, who saw this coming in 1982: "The new alchemical dream is: changing one's personality—remaking,

---

[14] Laura Schadler, "How Did We Become So Obsessed with Yoga?" KQED, March 10, 2014, http://blogs.kqed.org.

[15] Ibid.

remodeling, elevating and polishing one's very *self*. . . and observing, studying and doing on it. (Me!)"[16]

Another social scientist named Lisa Wade, a prolific researcher and blog-
ger, puts it this way in a conversation: "This idea of us being individuals and
having identities that we need to explore and discover, let alone is difficult to
discover, is a foreign idea before the 60s and 70s," she says. "The idea of working on one's self is a completely new idea."

Many of the latest and greatest exercises skew expensive, especially the
studio-based activities that require either special equipment, high-level
instruction, or both. Yoga is an activity where some feel it's gone far enough
beyond its roots to require a correction.

Because of its long history, yoga poses an interesting conundrum as it
expands. While its jump to the mainstream was driven largely by an affluent
segment of the population—clad in Lululemon and able to afford both the
time and money required for steady, serious practice—there have emerged
backlashes that seek to take it back to its roots. Take, for instance, Yoga to the
People, meant to appeal and attract a set that's turned off by the commercialization of practicing yoga.

With locations in Millennial progressive hotbeds like Seattle and Berkeley,
California, the Yoga to the People mantra, posted on its website, captures it
well. Its spirit and practice—no set fees—call to mind the November Project.
Here's the mantra:

> There will be no correct clothes
> There will be no proper payment
> There will be no right answers
> No glorified teachers
> No ego no script no pedestals
> No you're not good enough or rich enough
> This yoga is for everyone
> This sweating and breathing and becoming
> This knowing glowing feeling
> Is for the big small weak and strong
> Able and crazy
> Brothers sisters grandmothers
> The mighty and meek
> Bones that creak

---

[16] Jennifer Smith Maguire, *Fit for Consumption: Sociology and the Business of Fitness* (New York:
Routledge, 2008), 19.

Those who seek
This power is for everyone[17]

The mantra recalls a sort of religious creed, and one that's meant not to separate, but embrace. And that ethos seems increasingly important at a time when exercise is used as a way to set apart the more successful.

Access to health and fitness shouldn't be limited to those with the resources of both money and time, though Wade paints a disturbing social portrait of healthy bodies developing as a show of power. "People seek to distinguish themselves from the less powerful groups," she says, and historically physical presentation has been the easiest way. "When everyone worked outside, it was considered beautiful to be pale. When food is scarce, it's beautiful to be fat… The more obesity is a signal of being lower class, the more aggressively people will try to be thin."

Wade points to her own experience as a successful academic who's unable to afford what many in affluent urban centers commit to their fitness regimes. "I'm a college professor and this is out of my reach," she says. "Doing cardio plus yoga can easily get you to $100 a week and it's not unreasonable for some to spend $200 a week. Who is doing this? This isn't just 'not poor' Millennials. It's people on the other side of a shrinking middle class."

With that in mind, there's room for efforts like the November Project and Yoga to the People to thrive. There's also hope in the trend that fitness becomes more integrated into a lifestyle that manages to blend individualism with a sense of broader social good. Here, technology is again providing assistance, by making it easier to use one's fitness prowess to raise money for charity.

---

[17] Yoga to the People, http://yogatothepeople.com/about-us/mantra/.

CHAPTER 7

Charity Case

Edward Norton was a movie star looking for some money.

Robert Wolfe and his brother Jeffrey had an idea how to get it. Shauna Robertson, a movie producer, put them all together. Like many before and after him, Norton was running the 2009 New York City Marathon for charity. Unlike those who joined a group like Team in Training or Fred's Team, Norton had identified his own specific cause; a little-known environmental group in Africa called The Maasai Wilderness Conservation Trust.

Norton has long been known for being at least slightly off the beaten Hollywood path, in terms of what he does for his work, and outside of it. His film choices are at times aggressively counterintuitive and seem meant to invite controversy—*American History X*, where he played a former neo-Nazi, and *Fight Club*, the hyperviolent adaptation of the Chuck Palahniuk novel. More recently he was featured in two films nominated for the Best Picture Academy Award in 2015, *The Grand Budapest Hotel* and *Birdman*.

Norton could go what had become the traditional route—an email blast to a bunch of family and friends. But he figured there might be a better way.

Halfway across the country, in Detroit, the Wolfes had sold their stakes in an outdoor retailer called Moosejaw. Not even 40 years old, they'd decided the next company would be built around the idea that raising money for causes you're passionate about should be fun. They thought a platform should exist for giving, the exact same way that LinkedIn is a platform for your professional life.

"Our goal was to change the world and have an impact," Wolfe says. "How the hell do we figure out how to make giving back fun? We want to flip the model entirely so that charity is no longer boring, burdensome, or guilt-ridden."

In the quest for a test case, Robert Wolfe called his long-time friend Robertson, then a movie producer at the peak of her game—her credits include *The 40-Year-Old Virgin*, *Superbad*, and *Knocked Up*.

Like the Wolfes, she was at something of a crossroads, asking big questions about what she wanted to do for a living. Wolfe described what he and his brother were working on. Robertson, who at the time was dating Norton (they've since gotten married), suggested he might use this new fund-raising platform for his New York/Maasai project.

Norton set a modest-for-a-movie-star goal of $75,000 and along with the Wolfes and Robertson, built a website. From the first moment, it looked and felt different. The site cajoled and good-naturedly bribed would-be donors with Norton-related prizes, including a signed *American History X* poster.

The final tally: $1.2 million. More than validated, the foursome created a company called CrowdRise to bring the platform to the famous and nonfamous alike. The basic idea is Kickstarter for charity, an easy way for anyone to raise money. The Kickstarter analogy is underscored by CrowdRise's financial backers, led by Fred Wilson of Union Square Ventures. Wilson, the highest-profile New York-based venture capitalist, also invested in Kickstarter.

In 2014, CrowdRise raised $23 million for its own purposes, in an investment round led by Wilson, who said when the round was announced that he estimates the online charity market is worth at least $30 billion annually, with the potential to reach as much as $70 billion.[1]

CrowdRise already had won the financial backing of Twitter founder Jack Dorsey and venture investor Chris Sacca for his seed round. Wilson assembled a powerful roster for the more recent infusion; Spark Capital, CAA Ventures, and Bezos Expeditions were among the new investors.

Here's how it works: CrowdRise touts that a user can set up a fundraising page in exactly 21 seconds, for a race, or even to encourage people to donate to your favorite charity in honor of your birthday. There's no time limit to what you're doing and few other restrictions. CrowdRise, in the quest to capture and define a community of people, has what it says is the only loyalty program in giving. Users earn CrowdRise Impact Points, which lead to prominent placement for your cause on the website and can also be used to earn CrowdRise apparel, which isn't for sale in any other way.

---

[1] Alexia Tsotsis, "Fred Wilson Leads $23M Funding for CrowdRise, a 'Charity Water' for Everyone," *Techcrunch*, April 21, 2014, http://techcrunch.com/2014/04/21/fred-wilson-leads-23m-funding-for-crowdrise-a-charity-water-for-everyone/.

CrowdRise is a for-profit company. The business model is straightforward: CrowdRise charges a small processing fee, which donors can opt to cover themselves. They choose to do so at a high enough rate that the charity or beneficiary ultimately receives more than $98 out of every $100 raised, Wolfe says. It's the official fundraising platform for the Boston Marathon, New York City Marathon, Ironman, and Tough Mudder.

While CrowdRise started with something of a top–down approach, and worked with the aforementioned partners to gather customers. By 2015, the company was shifting to marketing directly to gather new users. Wolfe directed a team to build an app designed to keep users connected with each other, encouraging more consistent engagement. CrowdRise leaned into the notion of being a club its members wanted to be a part of.

By virtue of its roots as a cool, word-of-mouth start-up (Wolfe told me during a February 2015 phone conversation that their first outbound salesperson started that day), CrowdRise users skew toward the young professional, Wolfe says, an image the company clearly cultivates.

As Barry's Bootcamp grew on the strength of its celebrity clients, CrowdRise has gained a following from its own roster of famous people; Will Ferrell, Olivia Wilde, Judd Apatow, Paul Rudd, and dozens of other A-listers have used CrowdRise to raise money for select causes.

And CrowdRise hasn't been shy about leveraging those connections, drawing new, noncelebrity fund-raisers in, as well as rewarding donors with personalized swag from the famous like Norton's personalized posters.

Perhaps owing to its celebrity-powered roots—and the particular famous people who've embraced it, the most distinct element of CrowdRise is its tone. The website is littered with winking asides, good-natured snark, and comments, questions, or movie quotes that slide right into the absurd. Wolfe says a staffer said a line from the movie *Stepbrothers* was "totally out of place."

"I said, 'That's exactly the point,'" he says.

Wolfe says the off-kilter culture is imported directly from Moosejaw, the retailer he started at age 21, with no retail experience. By his description, the store sounds like something that exists only in a Shauna Robertson-produced script. "People would come into the store and I'd ask them if they wanted to play Home Run Derby in the parking lot," Wolfe says. "I wasn't trying to market to them. I just genuinely wanted to play Home Run Derby." Customers who came in during March Madness would find themselves ignored because the staff was too busy watching the games on TV, Wolfe says.

Moosejaw, which sells outdoor apparel from brands like North Face and Patagonia, set the tone for what CrowdRise would become. (Even today, on the part of the Moosejaw site that sells its branded T-shirts, it says, "I'd buy these for my friend if he weren't so imaginary." It's a short philosophical hop from there to CrowdRise's tagline: "If you don't give back, no one will like you.")

Wolfe, in his provocatively friendly way, says it's probably not the best way to run a company. Asked about his management and strategic vision, he demurs about the overarching grand plans for CrowdRise, noting that he prefers to be very much in the proverbial weeds. "Micromanaging is underrated, particularly when technology makes it so easy to stay really well-connected," he says. "'Flat' organizations are cool and fun, and looking at what's five feet in front of you, in addition to a year or two out, is often underrated."

What's in front of him is a massive segment of the new fitness economy, where technology, physicality, and meaning intersect. Charities are a gateway to the big live participatory athletic events, a fun way to get fit with your friends, a dose of altruism added for good measure. Tens of billions of dollars flow in and around all of these events, and ultimately into the hands of (hopefully) worthy causes.

Paul Schaye grew up in Boston, in a house that was steps from the Boston Marathon course. His life changed when he got a bicycle. "It was like getting the keys to the car," he says. "On a bike you could go anywhere."

He covered most of his native city by pedaling and soon anywhere became close to a reality. By high school, he was taking bike trips through Canada and Europe through the American Youth Hostel program, eventually leading his own ride in Nova Scotia. The nine cyclists carried everything on their bikes, camping every night along the way.

After college at University of Massachusetts–Amherst, Schaye moved to New York to start what began as a successful, if somewhat typical, career in consulting and finance. After working at PepsiCo and Booz Allen, he founded his own firm. Named for his Boston neighborhood, Chestnut Hill Partners works with private equity firms to find deals and recruit management teams.

We met in that context. While we talked frequently about private equity, we talked almost as much, if not more, about running, cycling, and triathlons. Every conversation or email included the question: "How's your training?"

While cycling was and remains his main sport, he evolved into a triathlete after befriending Joe DiLorenzo, a founder of Tyr, a company that started in the swimwear business and went on to become a major outfitter for the modern triathlete. DiLorenzo in 2003 convinced Schaye to do the bike leg of a triathlon relay out in the Hamptons. The following year, Schaye opted to do the whole thing himself instead of relaying. He completed the Olympic distance triathlon and "was hooked," he says.

What I didn't know when I first met Paul in 2007 was that he was battling stage IV cancer. His particular strain was a rare gastrointestinal tumor that had spread to his liver.

We became friends as he staged a remarkable recovery. After multiple surgeries and complications, he returned to form, riding his bike or spinning, pausing only when he had to have a follow-up operation. Occasionally he'd ask for my advice about a fundraising note to send out to friends and contacts for endurance charities he supported.

Cycling was his gateway into charity, long before he got sick. He participated in the early Boston to New York AIDS Ride, a three-day trek that raised in excess of $7 million, as well as its predecessor, a seven-day ride from San Francisco to Los Angeles known originally as the California AIDS ride.[2]

Schaye also signed up for the Pan-Mass Challenge (PMC), a ride across Massachusetts that began in 1980 and bills itself raising more than any other athletic fundraising event in the United States. In 35 years, riders have raised $455 million for cancer research.

For Schaye, the PMC is the thing. He organized a group to ride with him—and when he was sick, without him—dubbed Paul's Posse. The group includes his doctor, who specializes in the so-called orphan cancers that Schaye fought, and which struggle to win funding because of their rarity. In the past decade, the Posse has raised in excess of $2 million on its own.

Schaye, who carries himself with a calm confidence of a guy who stared down death and won, puts riding in context. "Let's be honest, this is playtime," he says. "But it's not so egocentric—you're running or riding for a greater purpose."

Beyond the PMC, Schaye also supports Cycle for Survival, an indoor, spinning-based fundraising event that's quickly become a juggernaut. Started in 2007 to raise money for rare cancer research at New York's Memorial Sloan Kettering, the one-day event by 2014 was held in 13 cities, with additional small satellite locations.

Cycle for Survival capitalizes on the fever around spinning. Equinox became a founding sponsor in 2009, and hosts the events each year. Through 2014, the charity had raised $51 million, making it one of the fastest-growing athletic fundraising events in the United States.

In the summer of 2014, Schaye committed to ride for part of the first day of the PMC, held in early August of that year. A couple days after the event, I got a brief, exuberant email with the subject line, "Mission FULLY Accomplished." The body said simply, "We did it . . . All 112/90," a reference to the miles logged each of the two days.

---

[2] AIDS Ride, www.markrobinson.net/AIDSRIDE/aidsride.htm.

Schaye is a spiritual descendent of a movement that began almost 30 years ago, when Georgia Cleland had a 45 percent chance of making it to three years old. It was 1988, and she'd been diagnosed with a rare form of leukemia. Her suburban New York parents were understandably distraught. Largely tapped out, they looked for new and different ways to pay for her treatment.

Her father, Bruce, was an avid runner. He decided to ask his friends for money in return for running that year's New York City Marathon. He organized 38 runners who raised $322,000 and ended up creating the largest athletic fundraising organization in the process.

Today, Team in Training raises about $70 million annually. Bruce Cleland has handed off the day-to-day running to Georgia, now in her thirties, who ran her first half marathon in 2011. The chances of survival for Georgia's same cancer today stand at 95 percent, according to the Leukemia & Lymphoma Society, the main beneficiary of Team in Training.

It's a juggernaut, pulling in $1.2 billion in donations since Bruce Cleland's first ask in the late 1980s. Team in Training (TNT) meets both the criteria of its name, gathering dozens of like-minded people for a specific event. In return for raising money, TNT provides training programs, organized work-outs, coaching, and mentoring. On race day, TNT team members wear distinctive purple gear; full-throated, dedicated cheering sections propel them through the racecourse.

Team in Training's defining moment in the modern marathon era was the inaugural Rock 'n' Roll Marathon in 1998, where TNT became the exclusive national charity. The race, the largest-ever, first-time marathon, drew more than 19,000 people. Elite Racing CEO Tim Murphy, the Rock 'n' Roll creator, pushed TNT to bring more racers than it originally intended.

Charities typically guarantee a certain number of runners from its ranks by buying the bibs and then giving them to participants in return for raising a certain amount of money. Team in Training initially agreed to guarantee about 1,500 runners for the first Rock 'n' Roll. Knowing his ambitions for the race, Murphy pushed for more, said Tracy Sundlun, another Elite Racing executive and long-time running coach and race promoter.

Murphy also wanted to exploit Team in Training's national reach and asked the charity to promote the race in each of its chapters. Given the high profile of the training teams, Murphy was counting on a word-of-mouth effect for his race. It worked all around.

With about 5,500 runners toeing the line (roughly 25 percent of the total field), Team in Training raised $15.6 million that year. In the first 10 years of the ongoing partnership, TNT runners in the San Diego race alone raised

$125 million.[3] "Team in Training changed the face of fundraising," Sundlun says.

Training with a group like Team in Training provides a social architecture of encouragement and support, and racing for a cause sits at the center of the new fitness economy. It's an athletic gateway drug, the means by which folks who never seriously considered themselves cut out for endurance sports manage to run a marathon, or complete a triathlon. Often a charity race introduces a participant into a world they want to continue to be a part of, even if they don't raise money again.

Being on a team is appealing, satisfying a primal human need for belonging and encouragement. For an activity as daunting as running a marathon, standing alongside other newbies and supported by kind veterans provides a deep level of comfort.

Then there's the cause itself, which provides a motivation for many, especially people like Bruce Cleland, who have someone very specific in mind.

I'd add a third, slightly more cynical, motivation. For some more experienced athletes, charity provides cover for what's ultimately a selfish endeavor. A number of runners conceded this to me, asking not to be identified. One says, "It helps defray the being-away-from-the-family guilt." Another puts it more bluntly: "When you're riding your bike for five hours on a Saturday, it's harder for anyone to argue with you when you say you're helping cure cancer."

Wolfe, for one, has little time for this theory, or at least a more optimistic twist. An avid runner—he ran, and raised money for the Maasai with Norton back in 2009—he says he's never thought of charity as validating a selfish impulse, nor do any of his running buddies.

What he does see, in himself and in other CrowdRisers, is a desire to use charity as an excuse, and megaphone for touting your own fitness.

"When I ran 10 miles in the rain on a Tuesday night, I wanted to tell everyone about it," Wolfe says. "The best excuse to tell your friends about your miserable training is to tie that into the fact that you're raising money for charity."

This is where the tagline—"If you don't give back, no one will like you"— is both funny and true. "Everyone at the heart of it wants to be well-liked," Wolfe says. "If raising money for charity can be something awesome that you tell the world about and your network praises you for it, and you feel great about it and that turns into a kick-ass cycle of people raising money over and over again for their causes...maybe we can change the world." Wolfe's

---

[3] Press Release, *Track and Field News*, http://trackandfieldnews.com/index.php/display-article?arId=14311.

team also amplifies the in-crowd cool through the merchandise that can only be earned by successful fund-raisers. It's another manifestation of the get-the-joke tone of the company. The names of the merchandise on the site make sly reference to obscure movie characters, like Ari and Uzi in *The Royal Tenenbaums.*

With gear you can't just buy, but have to earn, CrowdRise is playing an angle familiar to amateur weekend athletes everywhere, folks who can generally afford to buy any T-shirt or jacket that strikes their fancy. Having something that effectively can't be bought has that extra, incalculable value that only comes from feeling cool.

CrowdRise stands as both an amplifier and disruptor of a booming industry of raising money through races. For a decade or more, it's taken the form of a gentle, good-natured spam of sorts—the emails that land in most of our email boxes every week, asking for a contribution tied to completing a run, bike ride, or triathlon. The list of charities attached to endurance events is ever-growing: Leukemia & Lymphoma Society, American Heart Association, Susan G. Komen, Fred's Team, Livestrong.

The numbers are big. The American Cancer Society's Relay for Life series raised $335 million in 2014, giving it the top spot in the annual Peer-to-Peer Fundraising Top 30, which tracks events geared toward raising money.[4] For context, the thirtieth-biggest event—American Foundation for Suicide Prevention's Out of the Darkness Community Walks series—pulled in $12.5 million.

The list is a fascinating look into what's appealing to both participants and givers and the moves within the rankings point toward what's waxing and waning. To wit—and this signals a different kind of endurance that has nothing to do with running, walking, or riding—a new entry to the 2013 list was Movember. That's the increasingly popular gimmick of growing a mustache during the month of November in exchange for charitable contributions. The 2014 take for those confident enough to sport a hairy lip for a few weeks: a robust $23 million, placing it twenty-second on the Peer-to-Peer list.

To understand the mechanics of the list—and the role of giving in the world of endurance sports—I went to the source. The annual ranking is the brainchild of David Hessekiel, an erstwhile journalist who in the late 1990s pivoted from publishing to the world of advising people on how to most efficiently do good.

---

[4] Peer-to-Peer Fundraising, www.peertopeerforum.com/wp-content/uploads/Infographic-2013-Peer-to-Peer-Fundraising-Thirty-Results.pdf.

He started the Cause Marketing Forum, a firm that advises and convenes companies around how to structure their charitable work, in 2002. More recently, in 2007, he created what was originally known as the Run Walk Ride Fundraising Council. In 2014, the group officially changed its name to the Peer-to-Peer Forum, a nod to the changing nature of giving (including events like obstacle racing and moustache growing).

Hessekiel met me one morning near his home office in Rye, New York. He was nursing a recently operated-on knee, promising a friend who sat down nearby that he'd be back on the tennis court soon. He carries the confident air of a convener: a centerpiece for both Cause Marketing and Peer-to-Peer is an annual conference where practitioners gather to dig into the latest and greatest approaches.

From our table in the tony Westchester suburb, he notes that a number of notable nonprofits in the middle of the event space are headquartered in the northern New York suburbs and southeast Connecticut, presumably owing in part to New York City's place in the broader financial landscape and the money generated a few miles away in Manhattan. Team in Training's office in White Plains is next door to the March of Dimes.

Hessekiel obviously has thought a lot about what motivates people to give through these sorts of charities, and he himself ran his first marathon back in 1997 for charity. His late father died of pancreatic cancer then and Hessekiel ran with Team in Training, which by that time was the go-to run-a-marathon-for-charity organization.

His own work shows how different the landscape is. Team in Training remains a dominant endurance charity, with $58.5 million raised through its participants in 2014, putting it eleventh on the Peer-to-Peer list. But that number pales with what Team in Training once garnered. As recently as 2010, Team in Training pulled in more than $97 million, putting it fourth on the list. At its height, Hessekiel told me, it raised $120 million in a year.

What happened? It appears that the pie isn't keeping up with the number of organizations clamoring for our charitable dollars. "It's getting diffuse," Hessekiel says. Were he to participate to honor his father's memory now, there'd likely be a way to direct the money he raised directly to pancreatic cancer research, rather than leukemia and lymphoma, which Team in Training supports.

It's also easier to raise money, he says. The infrastructure and personnel necessary for a group like Team in Training even a decade ago simply aren't necessary to support would-be individual fund-raisers. Technology has made it absurdly simple either for more local or specific charities to engage an audience. "Some things that used to seem like insurmountable tasks just aren't," Hessekiel says, evoking a variation of Wolfe's brag-about-my-run email. "Now it's 3 a.m. and I can set up a fund-raising page for a race, because I miss my dad. It doesn't involve writing letters to everyone you know, or walking around the neighborhood, asking for money door-to-door."

While endurance sport charities like Team in Training stress the team part of it, if it's just about raising money for a race, there are other, more individual ways to accomplish the same goal. CrowdRise and its ilk have in many cases eliminated or diminished the need for a middleman, or at least changed what that middleman looks like.

As Norton's experience in New York shows, the big races are still where much of the charity work takes place, even if the money is raised on an individual basis. Charities large and small feed off the energy inherent in the crowds of participants and spectators. Racers raising money for charity flout their associations, turning themselves into moving billboards for good causes.

Some of the world's largest races caught onto charity early and used the notion of giving to swell their ranks. The connection between raising money at the largest marathons in a methodical, organized way is generally attributed to the London Marathon.

The London Marathon bills itself as the largest fundraising event on the planet (in 2007, its haul of 46.5 million pounds put it in the *Guinness Book of World Records*). The race has facilitated in excess of 600 million pounds ($1 billion) of giving since the first charity was included in 1984 (the race itself started three years earlier). The charity component started modestly, with the Sports Aid Foundation granting some entries as a way to help raise money. By 2014, roughly three-quarters of the more than 35,000 runners agreed to raise money for a cause and the race—now known as the Virgin Money London Marathon—has roughly 750 charities that benefit.[5]

Much of that happens through a two-decade-old program called the Golden Bond, whereby charities buy five places in the race every year for 300 pounds each, and then give them to runners who agree to raise a four-figure sum. According to the marathon's website, there's a waiting list for the Golden Bond. There's a related program, called the Silver Bond, which guarantees a place every five years. About 15,000 spots are set aside for charity runners.

---

[5] "History of the London Marathon: Charity History," www.virginmoneylondonmarathon.com/en-gb/news-media/media-resources/history-london-marathon/charity-history/.

While it came later to the United States, the American races, too, became major annual fundraising anchors. In the six years ending in 2013, the New York City Marathon saw its number of charities jump to 324 and the number of runners tied to charities double.[6]

Part of the charity appeal is the experience. Like London, New York and Boston—the two most prestigious races of that distance in the United States—use charity as a way to get in, and one that comes with perks in addition to the whole helping other people thing.

Both races are difficult to get into, for different reasons. New York has for more than 15 years resorted to a lottery to admit the vast majority of its field. (A handful of elite runners are invited, others receive a guaranteed entry by posting a fast qualifying time or a combination of completing nine other New York Road Runners races and volunteering at another.) In the 2014 lottery, 77,087 people entered and 9,170 received numbers, about a 12 percent success rate.[7]

For the charity runners, race day is filled with VIP perks. Dedicated private buses whoosh past the official race transport for the rest of the field, depositing the charity runners at dedicated tents (usually with the far more important dedicated Porta Potties cordoned off for their exclusive use). After the race, another members-only tent awaits, this one for a post-race party where runners can greet their family and friends for a more civilized round of congratulations and refreshments.

Runners for charity teams also wear special, team-provided tops that make them easier to pick out by the dedicated fans in the dedicated cheer zones. Anyone who's run a distance race knows that someone—anyone—shouting your name or affiliation can provide an enormous boost, especially in the later miles.

This social and support element—on race day and through training—is a critical component to charity's appeal within the endurance sports equation. For almost everyone, completing a marathon or triathlon is difficult and the infrastructure is impressive and attractive. As Team in Training says on its website: "It's like having a personal trainer plus the companionship and support of a team."[8]

---

[6] Mary Pilon, "Hitting the Wall: For Marathon Charities, Numbers Are Slowing," *New York Times*, October 25, 2013, A1.

[7] Alison Wade, "New York City Marathon Registration Opens Thursday," *Runner's World*, January 14, 2015, www.runnersworld.com/newswire/new-york-city-marathon-registration-opens-Thursday.

[8] Team in Training, www.teamintraining.org/il/firsttimehere/FAQ.

While people get hooked on the activities by raising money the first time, there's evidence that they don't keep shaking the virtual cup, opting in subsequent races to pay their own way rather than securing a spot through donations. Ahead of the 2013 New York Marathon, New York Road Runners conceded that its charity numbers were down significantly, even as the race took people in through the lottery system.[9]

Charity runners aren't created equal, consultant David Hessekiel says. In his estimation, they fall into two distinct buckets. The first group is passion-driven. They're people like Bruce Cleland who are racing and raising money for very personal reasons, like a sick child, spouse, or friend. They'll get in touch with every single person they can think of and make a strong, personal pitch. Often, they'll blow right past their goal.

The second group is driven by a different kind of personal reason. They want the experience of a certain race. For the Boston Marathon, entry requires meeting stringent qualifying standards. The average American male marathoner is 40.2 years old and the median finishing time in 2013 was 4:16, according to Running USA. The Boston qualifying time for that age cohort is 3:15 or below. For women, the average age was 36.6, and median finish was 4:41. Her qualifying time for Boston is 3:40. In short, to run Boston, you need to run a full hour faster than most people.

Beyond knowing someone who can get you in, the only other way to the starting line is to raise money, and like New York, Boston has used its iconic status to encourage people to raise money in order to run the storied route from Hopkinton to Boylston Street. Boston runners in 2014 raised a record $38.4 million, largely around the heightened awareness after the 2013 bombing. The previous year's total was $20 million.

As with the Boston tragedy, there are factors that are difficult to quantify or predict that drive giving. Celebrity is another intangible yet potent force (Edward Norton's success in raising money for the Maasai came in part because he's a famous actor).

Nowhere was celebrity more powerful than the case of Livestrong, the uber-charity created around the cult of Lance Armstrong, the once-worshipped and subsequently disgraced cyclist who used his triumph over testicular cancer to create one of the most powerful athletic-oriented charities in history.

---

[9] "Numbers Down for NYC Marathon Charities," Competitor.com, October 28, 2013 http:// running.competitor.com/2013/10/news/numbers-down-for-nyc-marathon-charities_87497.

Setting aside for a moment the drama around Armstrong's ultimate admission that he created a dizzyingly complex scheme to use banned substances to compete in and win a record number of Tour de France competitions, his contribution to the charity landscape is hard to dismiss.

First, Armstrong's willingness to talk openly and fiercely about his own struggles helped remove long-standing stigmas around cancer, probably permanently. Coupled with other charity efforts like the Susan G. Komen breast cancer initiatives, cancer treatments—and cancer victims and survivors—were more comfortable talking publicly about their own experiences.

It was also an effective way—intentionally or unintentionally—to elevate the Armstrong brand. As detailed in Juliet Macur's book, *Cycle of Lies: The Fall of Lance Armstrong*, by surviving cancer and talking about it, Armstrong "could very well transcend the provincial roots of the sport."[10] His personal narrative elevated cycling into a different realm, especially in the United States, where the sport lacked the visibility and fan base it had in Europe.

A huge part of that visibility came from the cancer narrative, which Armstrong and his team leveraged into a hugely powerful organization to raise money for cancer research and provide support for cancer patients for whom Armstrong regularly took a personal interest.

And then there was the yellow wristband, which was brilliant in its simplicity as an outward symbol of survival and/or support, as well for its sales and marketing. For a measly dollar, you became a visible supporter of a good cause.

Nike began producing the bracelet in 2004, as Armstrong prepared to pursue his sixth Tour de France victory. The rubber bracelet concept originally was designed for basketball players, who could wear them on the court without them interfering with their game, noted Chris Brewer, of the Livestrong Foundation, in a taped interview for a website called Facing Cancer Together. The color was yellow, to evoke the leader's jersey in the Tour. Nike produced 5 million bracelets, which felt like a big number, Brewer said. "We thought we could maybe sell 500,000 of them," he said. "We were trying to figure out where we were going to store 4.5 million wristbands."[11]

More than 80 million ultimately were sold, until Nike discontinued them in 2013, along with the rest of the Livestrong line, which included a range of apparel.

---

[10] Juliet Macur, *Cycle of Lies: The Fall of Lance Armstrong* (New York: Harper, 2014), 18 percent on Kindle edition.

[11] Facing Cancer Together, http://facingcancertogether.witf.org/living-with-cancer/the-story-behind-the-yellow-livestrong-wristband-81312.

Anecdotally, for those of us who have participated in a number of races, charity seems like a major force, a dramatic accelerant for participation in endurance sports. At least one expert knocked that theory down a peg.

Jeff Shuck is an affable Indianan whose job is to help other people raise money. His firm, called Plenty, works with nonprofits and for-profits looking for a sophisticated approach to convincing people to give. He's organized or been a part of hundreds, probably thousands, of events. After we speak on the phone, he sends me a white paper his firm produced on why people give money.

The athletic piece sits in the middle of the list and he notes that endurance events are effective to a point. But he pushed back on the notion that charity was a huge feeder.

Charity acts a gateway for some, and something of an excuse to others. As already mentioned on the positive side, it effectively cajoles some people who might otherwise never run a half marathon or marathon or complete a triathlon, to get out and do it. It can jumpstart a latent desire to be healthier and fitter, triggering all the mental and physiological benefits discussed in previous chapters.

"The idea of a walkathon has been around for generations," Shuck says. He traces it back to 1938, when President Franklin D. Roosevelt oversaw the creation of the March of Dimes as a new way to raise money for the newly formed National Foundation for Infantile Paralysis.

As with many charity founders who came before and after, Roosevelt's own history informed his charitable interest. His personal struggles with polio prompted him to form an organization that would help fund research. That work led to a vaccine that effectively eradicated the disease.

The notion of actually marching wasn't the original intent. The phrase was coined in 1938 by an entertainer of the time named Eddie Cantor and was a pun meant to reference a popular newsreel—*The March of Time*. Cantor's innovation was to make the appeal wide using the most popular medium of the time: radio. He saw a radio-based appeal work to raise money for flood relief, and convinced radio producers to run 30-second spots for his March of Dimes campaign.

In another move that would be replicated for decades to come, he enlisted the help of other entertainers, like Jack Benny, Bing Crosby, and Kate Smith. The radio spots asked adults and children alike to send a dime, or whatever they could spare, directly to the White House. There was a time peg, as well. By 1934, annual Birthday Ball fund-raisers were held on FDR's birthday, January 30th, to raise money for polio research. The march in 1938 was to lead up to that year's balls.

By January 29 of that year, $268,000 in donations (mostly in dimes) arrived at the White House, many in envelopes from kids wanting to help other children with polio. That's roughly $4.3 million in today's dollars. The president took to the radio to thank the American public for its generosity, out of a sense of efficiency: "Literally, by the countless thousands, they are pouring in, and I have figured that if the White House staff and I were to work on nothing else for two or three months to come we could not possibly thank the donors," he said.[12]

More than four decades later, and after polio had been effectively cured, the March of Dimes took on a more literal meaning. In 1970, the first walkathon took place in San Antonio to benefit the March of Dimes. First called Walk-America and now known as the March for Babies, the program has blossomed into more than 900 annual events and has raised in excess of $2 billion.[13]

The more recent progenitors were walks that started in the 1980s and 1990s to support causes like AIDS and cancer research. Walks were appealing because almost anyone could do it. Research of late shows that those very simple events, far less demanding than a triathlon or marathon, are increasingly appealing. "It's not a test of wills, it's a walk," Shuck says.

From a business perspective, the future of charities fueling endurance participation seems robust, if diversified. The ever-growing number of specialized events indicates that the days of a dominant charity like March of Dimes or Team in Training is likely over.

Sports-driven charities find themselves competing not just with one another, but with for-profit companies infringing on an area once dominated by nonprofits. One interesting negative force on charity is big Wall Street money. With more and more private equity flowing to events, it becomes more difficult—and expensive—to make your race distinct, Shuck says. That's because private companies can and usually do spend more to make more. As long as they can increase the bottom line, or justify increased cost with higher revenue at a related event, they'll spend it.

That's not the case with a charity event, which has to be cautious about every dollar, always mindful about how much of each dollar goes to overhead and production versus the charitable cause. While some will still gravitate to events for their pure motives, many more people will head for the sexier, more fun events—the ones with awesome goodie bags and cool post-race parties

[12] March of Dimes, "Eddie Cantor and the Origin of the March of Dimes," www. marchofdimes.com/mission/eddie-cantor-and-the-origin-of-the-march-of-dimes.aspx.
[13] CBS Pittsburgh, "March of Dimes—Celebrating 75 Years," April 16, 2013, http://pittsburgh.cbslocal.com/2013/04/16/march-of-dimes-celebrating-75-years/.

and bands along the course. Raising money by doing something physical to earn it is far from a radically new concept, Shuck says.

With the process of raising money being as simple as ever, thanks to the Internet and platforms like CrowdRise, and people like Paul Schaye able to marshal millions of dollars from friends, family, and contacts, and Millennials increasingly focused on doing well by doing good, we may be seeing our physical and charitable worlds begin to collide.

Robert Wolfe says his company, and the underlying notion of charity as something fun worth sharing, got a boost from an unlikely source in mid-2014: The Ice Bucket Challenge. As the notion of standing and getting a bucket of ice dumped on your head caromed around the social media universe, it not only raised record amounts of money for the ALS Association (more than $100 million in 30 days), it also helped change—Wolfe says permanently—the perception of charity as a bleak chore.

"There is no cause more serious than ALS," he says. "My guess is that if someone went to ALS, or any cause for that matter, and said 'We're going to drive awareness and raise money by dumping ice on our head' the reply would have been that it's the dumbest idea ever. But, people want to have fun. And, if you can make it fun then it can resonate. My guess is that millions of people know a lot more about ALS than they did two years ago, and that's pretty great."

The Ice Bucket Challenge's success further validates the notion that the best and most effective charities blend the virtual and the live, by leveraging the absurd speed and reach of the Internet into a very real experience. What's more physical than getting ice dumped on your head?

As the physical amplifies the virtual, and vice versa, the result is activities that form a bigger portion of one's daily existence—something to talk and tweet about, and something you actually do. Wolfe's CrowdRise is another manifestation of what Chip Wilson managed to make of Lululemon, which became not just something to wear, but a reflection of who you are.

"It's a part of your life, not an addition to your life. I like baseball and oranges and I raised a thousand dollars for Stand up for Cancer," Wolfe says.

CHAPTER 8

Work and Working Out

Most people opt to relax the day before they start their new job as president of a company. Others choose to compete in an Ironman.

Mike Zafirovski, then the president of Motorola's handset division, was driving with his family to O'Hare Airport in Chicago in the spring of 2002. It was a Thursday and they were bound for Lake Placid, New York, excited for Zafirovski's long-planned Ironman debut. He was participating under the auspices of CEO Challenges, a race-within-a-race concept Ironman was launching at the event. As a top executive, Zafirovski was getting white-glove treatment for him and his family—intimate dinners with top athletes as speakers, training advice, special viewing areas along the course for his wife and kids.

They were almost to O'Hare when Zafirovski's boss, Christopher Galvin, the CEO of Motorola, called. "I need you to come see me," Galvin said. Zafirovski reminded him that he was on the way to Lake Placid. Galvin himself had been among those who'd donated thousands of dollars to the charity Zafirovski was racing for. He asked if they could just talk on the phone. Galvin was undeterred. Zafirovski took him off speakerphone and picked up the handset; this wasn't typical Galvin, with whom Zafirovski had a friendly relationship. "Please come to the office," he said. Zafirovski turned around, dropped his family off and headed for Motorola's suburban Chicago headquarters.

He arrived and headed through the executive suite, passing his friend and Motorola president Ed Breen along the way. The two men briefly greeted each other. Zafirovski had taken himself out of contention for the president's job less than a year earlier, which Breen eventually got. He wanted to keep working on Motorola's flagship handset business, which was struggling against larger rival Nokia.

Inside Galvin's office, the CEO (and grandson of Motorola's co-founder) told Zafirovski that Tyco, the giant conglomerate, would announce that afternoon that Breen was its new CEO. Zafirovski was now taking the president's job—and was scheduled to be at a press conference for the following day. Instead of relaxing with his family and prepping his mind and body for the looming Ironman, Zafirovski stayed in Chicago to address reporters, then flew to Lake Placid Friday night.

The timing was more challenging owing to Motorola's scheduled analyst meeting the following week. On Tuesday, several hundred analysts and investors would meet at Motorola headquarters for presentations from senior management. Zafirovski had already prepared his group's remarks—a joint effort involving a half dozen other executives to lay out the latest in handsets. Now Galvin asked if he'd be comfortable giving Breen's portion, an overarching kick-off speech to set the tone for the conference. Zafirovski knew it was important for his own credibility in his new job, and for investors' confidence in Motorola's future, that he deliver a compelling speech.

Saturday, the day before the Ironman, Zafirovski holed up in his hotel room going over notes and writing his presentation. He made it to the CEO Challenges team dinner with his family and then went to bed. Two major milestone events—ascending to the presidency of a global corporation, and completing an Ironman—were happening more or less simultaneously.

Skipping the Ironman wasn't an option for him. "If you get that close and don't do it, you'll probably never do it," he says, more than a decade removed from that weekend. He finished in 13:38 and hung around for a Chicago-based friend who came in after him. The pair took off from Lake Placid at 1 a.m. and got home at 3 a.m., giving Zafirovski little sleep before his 8 a.m. rehearsal. He pushed through the day, greeting the company's analysts at a cocktail party that evening. "I felt great," he says. "But walking up and down stairs was challenging."

Zafirovski embodies a broad and deepening trend, where the business world—from the executive ranks to the rank and file—fuels the business of mind and body. Fitness junkie CEOs, along with corporate programs designed to create healthier, more productive, and happier employees have pushed fitness deep into our workaday lives, as a perk, a status symbol, or a way to get ahead with the boss.

Zafirovski was at the starting line in part because a guy who worked for him effectively dared him to. At Motorola's analyst meeting in 2001, he led a group run in the baking Chicago summer heat. Even those desperately trying to impress the boss dropped out, while Zafirovski finished seven miles. He took pride, and still does, in his athleticism, which dates back to his childhood in Macedonia, where he was as standout soccer player and accomplished swimmer. He ran his first marathon with little training, vowing to do at least one each decade; he's completed more than 10.

An email from an engineer who worked for him proposed that Zafirovski train for an Ironman, an idea Zafirovski dismissed almost immediately. "But he was persistent," Zafirovski says, and continued to invite him out for training runs, making the case over the course of months. Zafirovski finally relented, and found out that there was a new program for top executives at the Lake Placid Ironman.

CEO Challenges was the brainchild of Ted Kennedy, then an executive at World Triathlon Corp. (WTC), which owns and produces the Ironman series. He came up with the idea after learning that almost 1 in 10 (8 percent) of the participants in the 2001 Lake Placid event were CEOs or equivalent (i.e., running major divisions at large companies or senior partners in professional firms).[1]

Kennedy's notion was that Ironman could recruit even more high-level executives through a white-glove program that mirrored a CEO's life in his or her day job—personalized training programs, special transportation, intimate dinners with famous athletes, and networking with their peers, among other perks.

With Ironman's blessing, Kennedy sent out paper invitations—this was 2001 after all—to the qualifying participants, offering the added perks, for an added cost.

(Kennedy says he mispriced it the first year, charging $3,500 to the CEOs; that wasn't a meaningful premium given the package included the $750 entry fee, several nights at a five-star hotel adjacent to the start and finish line, transportation, and meals. In later years, participants paid $5,500.)

Kennedy figured he might get half a dozen CEOs to sign up, a good beta test. He got 15, including Zafirovski.

Kennedy's CEO Challenges caters directly to those executives, notably through an annual competition that determines who is the World's Fittest CEO. The company is now a division of Life Time Fitness, a publicly traded company based in Minnesota that runs a chain of fitness centers, as well as races. Part of its portfolio is the Leadville 100, a famously grueling endurance race held in Colorado and memorialized in the book *Born to Run*.

Membership in the CEO Challenges network is limited to those who head companies with at least $1 million in annual revenue, giving Kennedy a

---

[1] Shirley Won, "Some CEOs Measure Their Success Mile by (Painful) Mile," August 14, 2007, www.ceochallenges.com/news/2007/08/14/some-ceos-measure-their-success-mile-%28painful%29-mile.

broad target market. The mean size of companies represented is $20 million in sales. The other stats indicate at least a few massive companies are in the mix: the total annual revenue represented by competitors is $1.9 trillion, and the average sized company is $3.2 billion.

CEO Challenges aims to blend the trappings of the CEO life with the rigors of competition that are a natural extension of many chief executives' personalities. While competing in an Ironman or similar endurance race already is something of an exclusive experience, CEO Challenges creates an even more VIP experience, setting up meet-and-greets with athletes and rolling everything into a single price. Portions of that fee go to charity, primarily the Challenged Athletes Foundation.

For Ironman, it was an idea steeped in enlightened self-interest from a sponsorship perspective: CEOs who were into the idea of endurance sports were more likely to instruct their marketing division to sign up as sponsors. "If a CEO is passionate about a sport, that's typically the sport the company invests in," Kennedy says.

After the surprising turnout the first year, the numbers rose, for a time. The following years drew 25 and 35, respectively. He opted at that point to cap it at 30 in order to ensure a high level of service for those who participated.

The program appealed to CEOs on a number of levels, he says. First, it was a way for a naturally hypercompetitive set to differentiate themselves, especially as endurance sports hit the mainstream in a major way. "By 2000, Betty in accounting had done a marathon," Kennedy says. "So CEOs say, 'You think a marathon is tough, try an Ironman.'"

And CEOs, like all of us, like to be around their peers. CEO Challenges, by definition, was exclusive and the competitors found themselves sweating, and networking, with people with similar day-to-day lives. "It's a race against people who had to travel all over the place, attend board meetings, and take care of their families," Kennedy says.

The group went to great lengths to keep those often-ignored families happy, too. Already away from home a lot, the sell for a CEO at home got easier when they told their families they too would get high-end treatment, with fancy meals and amenities. Staff would whisk them to the best viewing points. Triathlete widows and widowers, and restless kids, liked that treatment.

The key for Kennedy was putting himself in his customers' mindset, where money is not an obstacle. He recruited star endurance athletes like Paul Newby-Fraser for kick off dinners and brought in exercise psychologists to give advice.

In 2005, Kennedy spun CEO Challenges out of Ironman as a separate company. The Ironman events remained the core offering, with Kennedy's new outfit running the program as an outside contractor. He says WTC surprised him in 2008 by not renewing that contract, opting to run its own program for CEOs, in house.

The timing couldn't have been worse for someone in the business of CEOs, a fact underlined at one of Kennedy's first races as an independent producer. He managed to recruit AIG, the global insurance and financial services firm, as his title sponsor and one of the company's senior executives was competing in a half Ironman-distance race outside of Toronto. It was September, 14, 2008.

He showed up for the race distracted, and Kennedy, assuming it was pre-race anxiety, assured him that he was well-trained and prepared for the event. He handed Kennedy two mobile devices to hold during the race, noting that he'd like to get them back as soon as he crossed the finish line.

The race itself was miserable, raining throughout, Kennedy recalls. The executive endured three flat tires during the bike portion, but finally crossed the finish line. Kennedy delivered the devices. Glancing at them, he told Kennedy he needed get back to New York immediately. Kennedy reminded him of the dinner that night, with then-Ironman world champion Craig Alexander.

"I can't stay," he said, according to Kennedy. "You'll read about why in the papers tomorrow."

On September 16, AIG agreed to what eventually totaled a record $182 billion bailout, one move in a series of devastating actions involving Wall Street and the U.S. government that sent the country and world into crisis.

In the teeth of the worst recession since the Great Depression, top executives shunned extracurricular activities. Not only were CEOs focused on running their businesses, anything that brought attention to a chief executive—especially a seemingly selfish, seemingly indulgent activity like an endurance race—was highly unpopular.

"It was probably the worst time in modern history to be in the 'Hey look at me, I'm a CEO' business," Kennedy says. While Ironman races dipped slightly in participation, Kennedy's company was on the verge of extinction.

What saved him was a pair of events for the Young Presidents Organization, which asked Kennedy to organize mini-endurance events for its retreats. Through the recession, he hunted for new races to drop the CEO Challenges concept into, like Escape from Alcatraz and a cycling event with well-known cyclist George Hincapie.

He keyed in on the Leadville 100, which brought him to Life Time in 2010 for a discussion. Two years of on-again, off-again conversations with the company ensued. Early on, Kennedy says, there wasn't much to sell. Without Ironman, he was rebuilding, and endurance races were recovering from the broader economic hit, with CEOs slowly emerging from hiding.

Now he has access to 10 Life Time salespeople, and a marketing group. Life Time has a portfolio of more than 60 races that Kennedy can consider adding his concept to. There are also non–Life Time events like Spartan Race, where Kennedy created a partnership for his clients who are looking for something new and different. The inclusion within the Life Time family gives Kennedy access to an even broader population of top executives looking to better themselves and find kindred spirits who are keen on demonstrating high performance across all aspects of their lives.

Kennedy's original theory is more than intact—anecdotally, the top jobs at companies across industries are held by men and women who take their bodies and minds seriously, favoring a look that's more slim suits with a green juice over double-pleats with a cigar and Scotch. Corporate America has largely left behind the steakhouse and the golf course as bastions of its top executives.

Participating in races and other public events—even just working out regularly at the company gym—allows chieftains to satisfy their own needs to relieve stress and maintain a holistically healthy lifestyle while also modeling that behavior for the workforce. The boss sets the tone, in the office and beyond. Employees take their cues on everything from dress code (see Steve Jobs and Mark Zuckerberg for their influence on what to wear to work) to management styles (aggressive screamers tend to set a certain tone). So the notion of the CEO as a serious athlete has implications for how employees see a particular boss, as well as how those employees see fitness in their own day-to-day lives.

Part of it is simply humanizing. Evidence that a big boss has ground out a marathon or triathlon puts them on something of a level playing field with an underling who has similar interests. Maybe more importantly, there's a sense of implicit permission to indulge, as it were, in such activities outside of work. That is, if a CEO is making the time to fit in a run or a swim before or after work, I might feel better about doing the same.

With apologies to supply-side economists, we might refer to it as trickle-down fitness, whereby the wealthiest and most successful choose to pursue such activities, setting health and wellness as a kind of status symbol. Now, it becomes cool to spend your nonworking time riding a bike or hitting the gym rather than indulging in less healthy activities.

At more and more companies, the leader is blurring the lines between work and workout into nonexistence. The implications are vast, as they both join and influence the rank and file, broadening the fitness economy audience.

Strauss Zelnick is a scion of the family that ran Twentieth Century Fox, where he once served as chief operating officer. He's the chairman of the video game company Take-Two Interactive and runs an eponymous media-focused private equity firm, Zelnick Media Capital. The best way to get to Zelnick is to meet him for a workout. He tells his staff, "You can have an hour with me anytime you want," provided you're willing to spend that hour on an adjacent workout machine or in some sort of state of exercise.

Zelnick stops short of requiring his staff to work out, but it's hard to see how someone could walk around his office with a doughnut in each hand. "It's a powerful message when the boss and others look pretty good," he says. Encouraged to do so—"there are no demerits for leaving the office for exercise"—people tend to take advantage of it, and end up transforming themselves.

Like many educated adults looking to stay in shape, Zelnick started as a runner. Around 2000, his regular running partner, complaining about his knees, convinced him to buy a bike. A skeptical Zelnick plunked down $3,000, an amount that made him to decide to put it to use. He took immediately to cycling, mainly because he was able to actually have a conversation with his buddy.

A few years later, Zelnick's wife suggested, to his surprise, that he go see her trainer. "She told me, 'For a guy who spends a lot of time in the gym, you don't look so good.'" That caught his attention. Like many in finance and other highly competitive, measurement-happy industries, he threw himself into the data, making his body his project.

He describes a typical week, which spans eight to eleven workouts, including weights, cardio, hot yoga, running, cycling, and CrossFit. In season, he skis. (He aims to take one full rest day a week, but concedes, "I don't always.")

Several days a week, he convenes what he calls #TheProgram, a group that comprises 60 people and some portion gathers 4 times a week at 6 a.m. He foots the bill for everyone, roughly $2,000 a month for various classes at Equinox. The group even has its own Instagram account (@theprogram_nyc).

For him, it's an investment that drives his competitive self, and pushes his sensibilities to a much younger mindset. "I genuinely feel 25 years old," he says. "Because I feel like that, I'm inclined to think like I'm 25. . . . It drives my investment philosophy."

Marrying what once were considered outside interests with day-to-day business life has the potential to further push fitness into our collective consciousness, especially if those practitioners—as Strauss clearly can—demonstrate how those activities accrue to their own career development, and bottom line. The linking of outside interests and work are a meaningful shift in the way we work, and reflect how both technology and our need for community have infiltrated our work lives, says Henry Albrecht.

Albrecht runs a company called Limeade, a company based near Seattle that has almost 200 employees. A former product guy at the software company Intuit, he started Limeade back in 2006. Its goals are lofty, and built around how companies can better engage their employees to make them healthier and ultimately more productive.

His professional and personal goals collide happily all the time. Ten days before we connected on the phone, he ran his first-ever mud race, with his wife and two children, then 7 and 13 years old. "We live and work in these beautiful glass towers with the Internet connected at all times," he says. "There's something really awesome looking at your wife and kids covered in mud. There's something primal."

Unlike some of his fellow CEOs, he himself isn't an endurance sports junkie; he prefers to play recreational basketball. At an annual tournament near Seattle called Hoopfest, his team was one of hundreds competing on what ultimately was a sprawl of pick-up basketball games. "It's a weird and awesome spectacle," he says.

He says Limeade has "a very disproportionate amount of marathoners, half marathoners, and ex-jocks. Those are people you can rely on to not let you down. They're not going to give up easily." His colleagues reflect their customers, many of which are run by former athletes and want that ethos embedded in their companies.

"There's the idea of the corporate athlete," Albrecht says. "The higher up you go, you hear it more. More of those people have addressed issues of stress and mood balance in a conscious way. They have high emotional quotients."

Millennial expert Nadira Hira says her generation's tendency to blend their work and social lives, as well as what they expect work to be, means a largely different approach.

"When you're going to work, you don't want to feel this is something soul-killing," she says. "You're starting from a place where you want to be able to connect with people, yourself, and your work, meaningfully. Millennials all look at work that way, whether it's at the juice shop or in finance."

While it's easy to roll your eyes at team-building exercises, Limeade found that companies that do nonwork activities with their fellow employees perform at a higher level, and opportunities around fitness abound. "People feel an emotional connection to work," Albrecht says. "The definition of employee engagement is people who in the absence of extra pay will go the extra mile."

Sometimes literally. Albrecht has seen events like walking challenges where employees sign up to compete with one another for prizes. Such activities ultimately have external effects that help the company's public image and recruit people who are drawn to that sort of culture. "Inside the company, it builds teamwork, connections to the community," Albrecht says. "It's a talent optimization and retention strategy, but it's also a marketing strategy for the brand. Compensation and other things may be roughly similar, but only one of the employers you're looking at is super-embedded in this community."

With that in mind, it's getting rarer to see a company of any meaningful size that *doesn't* have some sort of wellness program with a fitness component. Companies, fueled by enlightened self-interest with a strong sense of the bottom line, are pushing fitness and wellness programs down through the ranks.

For two nights every June in midtown Manhattan, the end-of-day rush hour has a different feel. While suited commuters head south down Park Avenue toward Grand Central, packs of bankers from brand-name banks and investment houses move toward Central Park, for an annual event called the JPMorgan Chase Corporate Challenge.

The Corporate Challenge dates all the way back to 1977, when New York Road Runners created the run in its home city, pitting teams from local companies against one another. By 2014, it had blossomed into an event involving more than a quarter-million people representing more than 8,000 companies. The world championships, featuring top finishers from around the world, took place in London in October.

Massive events like the Corporate Challenge point toward a larger trend of company-directed or at least company-encouraged, fitness and wellness. From 2009 to 2014, the average amount of incentives offered by companies, on a per employee basis, more than doubled to $594, according to a study conducted by Fidelity Investments and the National Business Group on Health.[2]

A *Harvard Business Review* study mapped corporate wellness to profits in 2010. The piece noted that healthcare giant Johnson & Johnson saved $250 million in healthcare costs over a decade. Sliced a different way, the company got $2.71 back for every dollar spent on such programs. The authors

---

[2] Dan Cook, "Employers Budgeting More for Wellness Incentives," BenefitsPro, February 21, 2014, www.benefitspro.com/2014/02/21/employers-budgeting-more-for-wellness-incentives.

point to both higher profits due to better-managed healthcare costs—healthy employees cost you less—as well as the tendency for healthier employees to be happier in their jobs. Effective health and wellness programs led to voluntary attrition rates of 9 percent versus 15 percent with ineffective programs.[3]

That finding points to a different aspect of the equation, beyond lower healthcare bills. There's recent science indicating that healthier employees not only show up more regularly, but perform better, as well.

In his book *Spark: The Revolutionary New Science of Exercise and the Brain*, John J. Ratey cites a 2007 study around cognitive flexibility. The study, he wrote, compared participants' ability to perform a mental exercise after half of them watched a movie and the other half ran on a treadmill. The results were stark, with runners performing the task better, and the movie-watchers staying the same. He writes: "Cognitive flexibility is an important executive function that reflects our ability to shift thinking and to produce a steady flow of creative thoughts and answers as opposed to a regurgitation of the usual responses. The trait correlates with high performance levels in intellectually demanding jobs."[4]

While CEOs influence their employees, there are certain corners of the business world that set the tone for the rest of us worker bees. In that regard, Wall Street and Silicon Valley stand out as leading indicators of future fitness trends. It's no coincidence that both of these places are awash in technology, money, and ambition, making them the perfect petri dishes.

New York City plays a vital role in the American consciousness, regardless of whether folks outside of the city want to admit it. Trends in music, fashion, and food tend to incubate in Manhattan and its environs.

Fitness is no exception. Its surge in popularity fits in with New York's ethos—a collection of relentless, enthusiastic, and competitive strivers from all walks of life, many of whom come from other places with the express intent of making it here. Ratey's *Spark* research is relevant again in this context, given the popularity of endurance sports and fitness inside firms defined by their so-called intellectual capital.

Wall Street—broadly defined to include investment banks, trading desks, and various flavors of investment funds such as private equity and hedge funds—is a natural place to find the sort of competitive men and women

---

[3] Leonard L. Berry, et al., "What's the Hard Return on Employee Wellness Programs?" *Harvard Business Review,* December 2010, http://hbr.org/2010/12/whats-the-hard-return-on-employee-wellness-programs/ar/1.

[4] John J. Ratey, *Spark: The Revolutionary New Science of Exercise and the Brain* (New York: Little Brown, 2008), 54.

(mostly men) for whom endurance sports can calm their anxious minds, cater to ample egos, and help ensure an appealing appearance. And Wall Street isn't limited to New York City. Its influence and practice extends across major American cities like Chicago, Dallas, and Atlanta, as well as global capitals like London, Hong Kong, and Dubai, where brand-name firms and their offshoots have expanded.

For the hardcore, there's the Wall Street Decathlon, an annual competition that pits the best athletes from various financial institutions against one another across 10 events. It's covered by the likes of uber-blog *Business Insider* (which produced a slide show of the ripped bankers and traders under the headline "51 Wall Streeters Who Are Ridiculously Cut") to Bloomberg, which assigned a reporter from the sports desk to cover it like any other major sporting event.[5]

Those guys are the extreme of the extreme. To a man, they were either collegiate or, in several cases, professional athletes. The pictures look like they were cut-and-pasted from a report on the NFL tryouts.

The less extreme, yet still dedicated to a crazy extent, are legion among banks and funds. Lincoln Ellis, an investor and founder of Astor Janssen Holdings, splits his time between New York and his native Chicago. He worked for a handful of financial services firms during a 20-year career, including Morgan Stanley, putting him in direct contact with like-minded amateur athletes.

He came to endurance sports early and recalls watching the iconic Ironman finish of Julie Ross in 1982, when she essentially crawled across the finish line. "The desire, grit, and sheer willpower to do this was fascinating," he says. Three years later, a 15-year-old Ellis used his neighbor's driver's license to register for the Lighthouse Triathlon in Racine, Wisconsin. He placed second in the 16–19 age group.

During the next two decades, he dipped in and out of cycling and triathlons, completing his first Ironman in 2010 in Louisville, Kentucky (he's since completed three more). He has also competed in numerous long bike races, including the 2014 Triple Bypass, a two-day event in Colorado that covers three separate passes in the Rocky Mountains, with 10,000 feet of total elevation gain. (For the advanced/crazy, there's a Double Triple Bypass, where riders basically turn around and come back.)

By virtue of his Ironman training, Ellis is slender and earnest, a postmodern investor with a hint of hipster (I complimented his jeans one time

---

[5] Erik Matuszewski, "Barclays's Rubin Wins Wall Street Decathlon by One Second," *Bloomberg News*, June 23, 2014, www.bloomberg.com/news/articles/2014-06-23/barclays-trader-rubin-wins-wall-street-decathlon-by-one-second.html.

and he conceded he bought them at Uniqlo, the Japanese discount apparel maker with a Fifth Avenue outpost; their jeans, he says, seemed to be made for the triathlete's body—skinny, with pronounced quads). Over a series of (very healthy) lunches, phone calls, and emails, he lays out his insider's view of the Wall Street/athlete archetype.

By Ellis' reckoning, the wave of driven bankers, lawyers, and executives that descended on the cycling and triathlon world during the early part of the 2000s were drawn by the possibility to excel in something else they could manage. "I call them, as they are already known in other contexts, the Type As. There are a lot of these people who think they are, or want to be, 'the ones in control,'" he writes to me one evening in an email. "This is a very task-driven, box-checking world where everything can be measured. They can be less-than-pleasant as training partners."

Some of this group, he says, evolved into what Ellis called the Seekers, a category where he places himself. "They were probably Type As at one point, but really do the work for the spiritual fulfillment that comes out of accomplishing a physical feat. Make no mistake—there's competition and gamesmanship and there's an occasional geek-out around equipment and race times. But the point of all the time spent is much more a focus on the journey."

The final group in Ellis's architecture is the Groupies. He does not like them. "It's great that the sport has more fans and participants but I must admit I find this population extremely confusing. How is it that you can go run 13 miles and then eat a stack of pancakes? Why are you drinking five nights a week and then trying to 'weekend warrior' your fitness? Commitment is commitment. This group can be, or appear to be, uncommitted."

Herein lies one of the more interesting burgeoning conflicts of sorts, as these sports pivot into the mainstream. For a certain segment of the population, mass appeal signals that it's time to find something else. Like the indie band that's suddenly allowed its ad to be used in a car commercial, or the hot new restaurant that's now gotten good notices in the *Times,* some of the more hard-core athletes are surrendering traditional endurance to the hoi polloi.

"I have to say I feel the tidal wave of endurance is receding," Ellis writes. "The broadening of the base is now in place. I'm not sure where it goes from here, but it seems like a peak in the market to me." Falling into his role as investor, he concluded, "Then again, I'm always bearish."

Nowhere is the cool new thing more important than in the ecosystem of technology companies and the investors who love them. The trend is similarly, maybe even more powerfully, reflected in Silicon Valley, where many argue much of the nation's real innovation happens. There's arguably even more fertile ground for these sports coming to the fore, given the affinity high-tech companies have for recruiting and retaining employees by appealing to their whole selves, not just their brains.

Northern California also has a long history of appealing to the outdoorsy nature in all of us. It's practically impossible to spend more than half an hour in the Bay Area's natural areas and not want to take a hike, bike ride, or run.

Max Levchin, a founder and former CTO of PayPal, spoke at a Bloomberg technology conference in June 2014 about his own affinity for cycling and how it plays into his entrepreneurship and leadership. Levchin, still in his twenties, has embarked on a slew of post-PayPal projects. He's working on a new consumer finance company called Affirm and another called Glow. He also serves as the chairman of Yelp and on the board of Yahoo! (His personal website is sparse, featuring only 13 lines of text, including the gentle warning: "You are welcome to contact me via whatever channel you like, but please do not be offended if I never respond, as I tend to be very busy."[6]) Part of what keeps him busy is an intense cycling habit, where he rides with like-minded, successful entrepreneurs and investors.

For many executives, pursuing endurance sports is part innate competitiveness, with some ego and example-setting mixed in. Many profess their avocations proudly, through interviews and social media. John Legere, the CEO of T-Mobile USA, is an avid marathoner—and Tweeter. A healthy dose of his tweets are fitness-related. Other executives use the sharing features of the wearable fitness hardware like Fitbit and Jawbone to compete with one another, privately and publicly.

Beyond the formal competition is a subtler version, and in the Information Age, everyone's personal best is only a few clicks away. Boston Marathoners have become accustomed to their at-work colleagues tracking them in real time during the race, held on a Monday. Having a near-stranger parrot back your splits is simultaneously flattering and slightly creepy.

Part of that familiarity speaks to the broader popularity Ellis referenced. With endurance sports no longer living solely in the realm of fitness nutjobs, an everyday colleague has a sense of what's a respectable time, likely because they or a spouse have participated in a race, be it a 5-K, 10-K, or half marathon. Maybe they've sweated alongside other employees, at a nearby fitness boutique or on a company-sponsored team at a local race.

Companies in the business of fitness, like MindBody, are natural places to find an emphasis on pushing well-being and work together. The biggest provider of software used by studios to schedule classes, keep track of their

---

[6] www.levchin.com.

members, and get paid, MindBody has from the start made sure its employees can take advantage of the types of services its own customers provide.

CEO Rick Stollmeyer knows that the movement is following all of us from home into the workplace and his fervor manifests itself in the work of his employees. In 2014, inspired in large part by the NBC hit show *The Biggest Loser*—the show's host Alison Sweeney is an investor in MindBody— the company created a program for its employees to encourage a somewhat radical change in health. While a company like MindBody tends to draw a certain type of person—young and fit—not everyone looks and acts like they just showed up from yoga class—though, like an increasing number of companies, MindBody subsidizes health classes. Employees there get a debit card with $65 worth of use-it-or-lose it credit per month for boutique fitness sessions, or even spa treatments—given that some of the company's clients are more traditional spas and salons.

He also realizes that part of what drives a fitness lifestyle is subtle, or not so subtle, peer pressure. That is, if a coworker is chatting/bragging about her killer spin class or great run over the weekend, we're at least slightly more likely to entertain the idea of doing something active, assuming we have the ability and basic desire to do so.

For its version of *The Biggest Loser* (while a fan of the show, Stollmeyer concedes to not loving the name, especially for corporate team-building pur- poses so he called it MindBody Evolve), MindBody solicited applications for a 90-day intensive regimen of workouts and, more importantly, tracking. Each of the 65 participants in the original cohort in early 2014 were given a Fitbit or similar tracking device and submitted to regular weigh-ins and checkups. Stollmeyer's team was able to monitor and calculate progress, including hundreds of thousands of steps taken, and dozens of pounds lost.

What surprised even him, he says, was the qualitative change, pivoting back to the gentle and effective implicit peer pressure, or encouragement. "They have a glow in their face, a spring in their step," he says. "The thing that's hard to quantify is their effect on everyone else."

At the end of 2014, MindBody was monitoring its second 90-day group, with similar results. And while there was clearly a benefit to his own company's morale and culture—a culture where the core values are printed everywhere, including the website—he was also using his employees as a test kitchen of sorts for a new product. He hoped to use the experiment to hone a concept MindBody could eventually sell to other companies, who could launch their own 90-day programs for their own employees.

It's no surprise that Silicon Valley has embraced all these efforts, and hard. The workers' paradises at companies like Facebook and Google go to extreme lengths to focus on the whole employee. Free, (mostly) healthy food, nap rooms, and state-of-the-art gyms all encourage the rank-and-file to take care of their bodies in ways very few companies did in past generations. The subsidized cafeterias, once seen as a major perk, have given way to stocked cafes and free massages.

Our jobs continue to push themselves deeper into our social lives. Technology allows (or demands) constant access to email, and therefore work. For many of us, it's routine to engage in some form of work communication from the moment we wake up until the moment we fall asleep.

This is an important development, as it radically changes our relationships with each other, and even with our own minds and bodies. As professor Anne Bardoel writes, "On the football field, the boundary marks the edge of the field. Inside the boundary, the ball is in play; beyond the boundary it is out of play. The trouble with the boundary between work and personal lives is that it is very permeable . . . [W]orkplaces are greedy institutions and technology has allowed them by stealth to expand the boundary line and encroach on our personal lives."[7]

This owes largely to the popularity of smartphones, our constant companions. While the aforementioned stalking happens, we're often offering that information to the world voluntarily. Through social media—Facebook posts, tweets, Instagram posts from the finish line—we're putting a lot more of ourselves out there.

Amid this flow of personal, even intimate, information to a broad scope of people, who we choose to spend time with, and how, has also changed. A 2014 survey conducted by LinkedIn—a company with deep insights into all of our work habits, especially from a social media and networking perspective, came up with some fascinating results. Millennials especially make fewer distinctions between friends at and outside of work, and are more likely to talk about personal issues and details with colleagues than members of older generations. The survey found that Millennials placed heavy emphasis on at-work friendships (57 percent said it made them feel happy) and, importantly, three out of five cited "socializing in-person" with colleagues as contributing positively to their work environment. Only half of Baby Boomers felt the same way.[8]

---

[7] Anne Bardoel, "Tool or Time Thief? Technology and the Work-Life Balance," July 29, 2012, *The Conversation,* http://theconversation.com/tool-or-time-thief-technology-and-the-work-life-balance-8165.

[8] LinkedIn Corporate Communications Team, "Millennials More Likely to Divulge Personal Details When Speaking to Colleagues at Work Compared to Baby Boomers," LinkedIn, July 10, 2014, https://press.linkedin.com/site-resources/news-releases/2014/millennials-more-likely-to-divulge-personal-details-when-speaking-with-colleagues-at-work-compared-to-baby-boomers.

CEOs have a sense of that, and are increasingly looking for ways to engage their employees.

Skullcandy CEO Hoby Darling likes to declare Powder Days and join his employees on the slopes near the company's Park City, Utah headquarters. Like Zelnick, the best way to get a one-on-one meeting with Darling is to ask him to go to the gym, or for a run.

One of Skullcandy's advantages is its headquarters, home to former Olympic skiing venues and the annual Sundance Film Festival. The company sells headphones and speakers to the younger, hipper set. Darling, a former Nike executive, landed the top job at Skullcandy in part based on his ideas about rejuvenating the company's culture. A key part of his solution: employees and executives need to work out more, and together.

The average age of a Skullcandy employee is 27. Working and sweating together promotes a level of collegiality and intimacy that's appealing to a young demographic already comfortable with sharing—in conversation and online—pretty much everything about their lives. As Darling got to know his employees outside of the office, it led to marked changes at work, even in the physical layout. He ditched private offices in favor of an open floor plan, a move he said increased the speed of decision making because he could just turn his chair or pop up and talk across the desk. Fewer meetings also mean more time to ski, bike, or run.

While Darling and Zelnick's proto-fitness version of a CEO man feels extreme, the shift toward a more fitness-oriented lifestyle and workplace has infiltrated a business class that once socialized over Scotches and steaks, not yoga mats and elliptical machines. The speed of modern life has also made that last mostly male bastion of networking—the golf course—a lot less popular.

As golf's popularity fades, broadly and among the business set, a number of sports and activities are vying to become the new golf. On the eve of the 2014 PGA Championship, *Bloomberg News* reporters Michael Buteau and Eben Novy-Williams wrote a story with the headline "Golfers Swap Spikes for Sneakers in Endurance Sports Boom."[9]

The number of regular golfers fell every year from 2003 onward. In 2013, the sport saw a 19 percent drop, to 24.7 million players.[10] A portion of those ex-duffers were trading in clubs for bikes and running shoes.

That's in part because the bosses—like Zafirovski, Zelnick, Darling, and Albrecht—either quit the game, or never took it up to begin with. Business

---

[9] Michael Buteau and Eben Novy-Williams, "Golfers Swap Spikes for Sneakers in Endurance Sports Boom," *Bloomberg News*, August 7, 2014, www.bloomberg.com/news/2014-08-07/golfers-swap-spikes-for-sneakers-in-endurance-sports-boom.
[10] Ibid.

and networking happens where people actually spend time. Thus, more networking happens in the SoulCycles and yoga studios and on bike rides.

More than one journalist has referred to it as sweatworking. Cringe-inducing terminology aside, the practice is an antidote to the breakfast, lunch, drinks, and dinner circuit that historically defined many jobs, especially those that involve face-to-face interaction with customers. Side-by-side downward dog poses do force a level of intimacy that breaking bread doesn't. "For some reason it lets you break down barriers you wouldn't be able to if you were just sitting next to someone at a bar," Tracy Roemer, a co-owner of a Chicago boutique fitness studio called Shred415 told *Crain's Chicago Business.* "You sweat and your defense mechanisms come down."[11]

And it doesn't even have to be that extreme. A burgeoning trend is the walking meeting, a practice observed most notably by Facebook founder and CEO Zuckerberg—along with many others. Nilofer Merchant, an author and executive credited with launching more than 100 products, made a passionate case for meeting while walking or hiking in the *Harvard Business Review* in early 2013, under the headline "Sitting is the Smoking of Our Generation."

"When you step outside, you give yourself over to nature, respecting its cycles and unpredictability," she writes. "It keeps me more awake to what is happening around me by experiencing the extreme heats of summer, or the frigid power of winter."[12]

Merchant also said it helped her solve the problem of trading productivity for exercise because she can effectively combine the two. She approaches scheduling them with a business-like rigor, blocking off windows for walking meetings before sitting meetings. The walking meetings set a different tone. It's much harder to check one's mobile device and even the different proximity has an effect. "I can actually listen better when I am walking next to someone than when I'm across from them in some coffee shop," she writes. "There's something about being side-by-side that puts the problem or ideas before us, and us working on it together."

At CEO Challenges, Kennedy is creating a new line of business around that very concept. Called Learn to Tri, the program involves a company asking its executives, and some of their clients, to train and complete a triathlon.

---

[11] Brigid Sweeney, "Exercise + Networking = Sweatworking," *Crain's Chicago Business,* March 11, 2013, www.chicagobusiness.com/article/20130309/ISSUE01/303099976/exercise-networking-sweatworking.

[12] Nilofer Merchant, "Sitting Is the Smoking of Our Generation," *Harvard Business Review,* January 14, 2013, https://hbr.org/2013/01/sitting-is-the-smoking-of-our-generation.

Among the first companies to try it was JLL, a Chicago real estate firm. In May 2014, Kennedy paired 15 JLL brokers with 15 customers and together they began a 12-week training program, culminating in the Chicago triathlon. "You can invite the CEO to a Bears game," Kennedy says. "They may or may not show up, may or may not be engaged."

This group couldn't help but be engaged, given that they were publicly committed to a race, with colleagues. "I've never had a more focused group," he says, the week after more than 80 percent of those who signed up completed the race, some at the sprint distance, and many at the longer, Olympic distance. "I think we're onto something."

He's also launched a program called Fitness Incorporated, which aims to get employees to complete their first 5-K race in eight weeks. And he's not abandoning the CEO set. Kennedy has plans for 2016 for Microsoft Challenge at the NYC Triathlon, where he expects 50 CEOs to participate, as well as the Workday CEO Challenge at the Chicago Triathlon.

One of his earliest customers—former Motorola president Zafirovski—is still more than hanging around the endurance world. After Motorola, he became the CEO of Nortel, the Canadian telecom giant, commuting from his Chicago home. He now runs his own consulting firm, the Zaf Group, from Chicago and serves as executive advisor to Blackstone Group, the investment firm run by Stephen Schwarzman. He commits to at least 10 hours of fitness activity a week, with one big "event" each year, which he's mapped out through 2018. They include a 50-mile run that starts in the Moroccan desert, the U.S. senior swimming championships, and, potentially, a return to the Ironman in 2018, in Kona.

In the fall of 2014, Zafirovski ran the Chicago Marathon, mostly as a training run. That November, he flew to Tempe, Arizona to complete his second full Ironman (in the intervening decade-plus, he finished a handful of half-Ironmans and marathons).

Now 61, he planned to compete alongside his two grown sons, but both pulled out a few months before the race—one for a new job on Wall Street, the other in the throes of his first year of business school. There was also the matter of a bike crash four months before the race, which injured Zafirovski's shoulder to the point that swimming freestyle—the most efficient stroke—was impossible.

He completed the 2.4-mile swim using the much-slower breast stroke, and the bike and the run went off without a hitch. He crossed the line more than 25 minutes faster than his 2001 time.

He shows no signs of slowing down, and anyone who works for him going forward might do well to mention his or her interest in endurance endeavors. Fortunately for Zafirovski, Zelnick, and others, there are more and more races to choose from.

CHAPTER 9

Mary's Merry Marathons

Halfway up Heartbreak Hill—the most famous incline along the route of the world's most prestigious footrace—a local resident held a handwritten sign that said, "Go Mary Wittenberg!"

While many of her fellow runners overlooked that particular encouragement, more than a few marathoners knew exactly who Mary was. As the director of the world's largest marathon, Wittenberg was arguably the most famous recreational runner on that course.

Sometime in the late morning on April 21, 2014, Wittenberg crested Heartbreak Hill, looking forward to the last 10 kilometers of the Boston Marathon. She crossed the finish line at 3:32:55, in the top third of the field, the seventy-seventh woman in her age group. She learned that her friend Meb Keflezighi—an elite runner she'd helped cultivate by inviting him repeatedly to run the New York City marathon, which he'd won in 2009—had crossed the line in 2:08:37 to win the race, the first American man to win Boston since 1983. She'd helped Keflezighi become simply Meb. So like thousands of others, Wittenberg needed only two words to capture the ecstasy and import of his victory that year in Boston: "Meb won."

A few hours earlier, at the starting line in the hamlet of Hopkinton, where each April the 300-year-old town of about 15,000 residents teems with tens of thousands of runners, volunteers, and spectators, Keflezighi and Wittenberg stood, a few thousand people nervously waiting between them.

For the 118th time, runners gathered there for a 26.2 mile footrace to the heart of Boston, past stoic New Englanders sipping coffee, drunken and screaming college students, and Red Sox fans watching the annual Patriots Day late-morning baseball game at Fenway Park.

The Boston Marathon—just Boston to anyone in the marathon world—stands alone in the world of distance running, especially for amateurs. Because of its strict qualifying standards, only a small percentage of those who complete a marathon have a time good enough to make it to the starting line.

What pulsed through the streets in and around Boston that day wasn't just an athletic marvel. It was also an economic juggernaut. The race's organizers estimated that runners, their friends, and family pumped $181 million into the local economy. Obvious beneficiaries included Italian restaurants in Boston's famed North End, where runners and their entourages flocked for Sunday night pre-race pasta dinners, lining the narrow, winding streets clad in sneakers and emitting nervous energy. Hotels across the city were sold out, with some runners making reservations months in advance (some within days of finishing the previous year's race).

Each runner paid $175 just for the privilege of lining up in Hopkinton, quite literally the cost of entry; international racers paid $225. Tack on marathon merchandise, lodging, food, and tours of the city for families abandoned by their resting-their-legs runners and you start to get a sense that this is big business. By contrast, hosting the World Series in 2013 brought about $23 million to St. Louis; the All-Star Game the following year brought Minneapolis about $75 million. (As befits its status as the uber-event, the Super Bowl is worth about $500 million to its host city.)

The 53-year old Wittenberg, at the time of her first Boston run that year, was the CEO of New York Road Runners (NYRR), the largest nonprofit community running organization in the world. That perch made her one of the single most influential figures in the world of running, present and future. NYRR's signature event is the New York City Marathon, the biggest marathon in the world. Throughout the year, the group puts on dozens of other races, including a popular half-marathon series with a race in each of New York's five boroughs.

Her mission: Make it possible for people to "run for life," a motto she adopted for her entire organization, which is headquartered in a sublet beehive of offices in midtown Manhattan, just a couple doors down from Carnegie Hall. (In a nod to the organization's work, workspaces and offices are identified by race bibs with the occupant's name instead of traditional nameplates.)

In 1970, 127 runners suited up to run the first New York Marathon—four consecutive loops of Central Park Drive, the paved road that circumnavigates New York's iconic park (55 people finished). Thirty-five years later, in 2015, about 50,000 runners snaked from Staten Island to the finish line in Central Park, touching each of the five boroughs. It's a massive, sprawling, annual autumn happening, bringing athletes from all over the world to test themselves on the largest stage in this particular sport.

That translates to massive economic power, mostly by virtue of bringing big-spending visitors to cities, often for weekends when the city is otherwise without a convention or other major event. Economic impact often totals tens of millions for a marathon host city, and into the hundreds of millions for the largest races. It starts with the entry fee, which effectively ensures an affluent field.

The New York marathon, arguably the best-known marathon due in part to its location and rich history, and the largest by number of runners (a record 50,530 in 2014), charges $255 for a non-New York Road Runners member (members, who aren't guaranteed entry without completing a prescribed number of other NYRR races and volunteering for another, pay $216). Foreign-based runners pay $347. The marathon has to operate a lottery for entries, owing to the massive number of entries. The high fees clearly aren't scaring anyone off.

That's in part because of the race's participants. The average annual income for a participant in the New York City Marathon is reportedly $130,000.[1] Put another way, that's well north of double the median income of an American household (roughly $51,000).

An economist would point out that the price for the New York City Marathon (and many others) is inelastic. That is, demand doesn't markedly change even when the price changes, in this case dramatically over a period of just a few years. (The nonmember rate was $196 in 2011. New York Road Runners increased it to $255 for the 2012 race, citing the need to pay more of its share of the traffic management costs.)[2]

New York's marathon is credited with an economic impact of about $340 million, a figure from a 2010 study that was cited around the initial decision to hold the 2012 race, even after Superstorm Sandy ravaged the region. The storm depleted public resources and set up a situation where the foot-race would divert men and women from cleaning up and piecing life back together for the region's residents. The race was eventually canceled.

---

[1] Laura Vanderkam, "What's behind Career Achievers' Love of Marathons?" Fortune.com, December 11, 2012, http://management.fortune.cnn.com/2012/12/11/overachievers-marathons-endurance-sports/.
[2] Brett Smiley, "New York City Marathon Significantly Raises Entry Fee," NYmag.com, January 2, 2012, http://nymag.com/daily/intelligencer/2012/01/nyc-marathon-raises-entry-fee.html.

At least one writer has said the actual economic impact was less than half of that. Writing on Forbes.com, Patrick Rishe took issue with the figure, and made his own calculation of $144 million, including the runners and spectators.[3] While significantly less, I'd still argue that's a lot of money generated by a bunch of people running through the streets of New York while 2 million of their friends and family cheer them on. A more recent NYRR study pegged the marathon's impact at $415 million.

Anecdotally, a marathon is a festive weekend where happy runners gladly shell out hard-earned money. For several years, I opted to skip the lottery and race-day hassle of the New York City Marathon (getting from the northern suburbs where I live to Staten Island was a brutal way to start a day whose focus was a 26.2 mile run) in favor of running the Philadelphia Marathon. My own economic impact was roughly: train ticket ($150 round trip), hotel ($175), dinner ($40), taxis ($40), post-race cheesesteak ($10). And that doesn't include the traditional post-post-race visit to the Taco Bell/KFC combo on the way home from the Stamford Amtrak station, because, well, I just ran a marathon.

Since the mid-1990s, long-distance running pivoted from the fringe to the mainstream. The major marathons remain in the hands of local non-profits that nurtured the races from infancy over decades and in at least one case (Boston), more than a century. Beyond those handful (which also includes New York and London), a thriving for-profit business of races is growing.

Turning races into a business feels like a somewhat obvious opportunity, if only for the demographics. You have a large, captive audience of mostly affluent people who've demonstrated their willingness to pay not insignificant sums for the privilege of punishing themselves over a period of many miles and several hours. Once you have them signed up, they're more than willing to fork out more for a T-shirt, sweatshirt, or sticker to remind themselves, their family, and friends of their accomplishment.

Wittenberg, who in 2015 left NYRR to head a new sport company for billionaire Richard Branson, was among the first to truly recognize the marathon's economic and social power. She is fiercely enthusiastic, and famously indefatigable in running circles, omnipresent at start and finish lines, a cheerleader for newbies and elites alike. She has marathon bona fides, winning a Marine Corps Marathon in 2:44 in 1987, good enough for a spot in the 1988

---

[3] Patrick Rishe, "Inflated Economic Impact Predictions Complicated New York City Marathon Decision," Forbes.com, November 2, 2012, www.forbes.com/sites/prishe/2012/11/02/inflated-economic-impact-claims-complicated-the-decision-to-cancel-new-york-city-marathon/.

Olympic Trials (though she dropped out of the trials due to injury). She's still a regular runner and does many interviews and meetings while on a run.

Her tenure at NYRR began in 1998, and she served as a deputy to then-CEO Allan Steinfeld, and then as CEO, beginning in 2005, charted a key period of growth in running. She's watched both New Yorkers and others, of all ages, pour into the sport and presided over growth in her own organization that's hailed by many and criticized by others as expanding far beyond its stated mission as a local club.

Here is the crux of the debate in New York, which speaks to one of the challenges of being the de facto leader of a high-growth sport on the biggest stage: Locals who loved it as a small club where they could run with their friends deplore its ever-expanding reach, not just throughout the United States, but the world, where Wittenberg traveled to woo the best runners to New York. She's also an advocate for the sport for the young, as well as the underprivileged, believing that the simplicity and low cost of running make it an ideal weapon against poor health.

Her tenure was marred, if only temporarily, by the decision to cancel the 2013 race in the wake of Superstorm Sandy, which knocked out power across swaths of Long Island and Staten Island and drove many from their destroyed homes. Wittenberg took intense heat from runners and others for the timing and presentation of the decision. That controversy came weeks after a profile of Wittenberg in the *New York Times* illustrated, at great length, her difficult tightrope act of maintaining a running club's local flavor in the world's most famous city that happens to be the host of a giant marathon that runners globally are desperate to take part in.

Wittenberg and I first met, by accident, after overlapping runs in the Rockefeller State Park Preserve in Westchester County, just north of New York City. She'd come up from her home in Manhattan to run the trails that frequently host Olympic hopefuls, college cross-country teams from Fordham University to West Point, and hundreds of eager amateurs. In the high school parking lot where runners gather for weekend group runs, she chatted a couple of us up, and we all marveled at the beauty of the place. (Ben Cheever, a dean of our local running cohort, subsequently wrote a paean to the park for *Runner's World.*)

We met later that year again, at a Bloomberg-hosted conference on the business of sports. She was grouped with the chief executive of the World Triathlon Corp., which puts on the Ironman, and the head of U.S. Pro Cycling Challenge.

Almost a year after that, we finally officially got together in her office. Her corner setup illustrated the nature of her job. She kept a standing desk that blends into a conference table; a nod, I imagined to how often she has to gather consensus from the various stakeholders cutting across government officials, runners, sponsors, and colleagues.

Wittenberg came to running competitively by accident, in college. She made good on a late-night dare to run a race the following morning and won (the bet and the race). She continued to run, including through law school at Notre Dame, and then as a young lawyer in Richmond, Virginia at Hunton & Williams. While working there, she won the Marine Corps Marathon up the road in Washington.

Running eventually evolved from avocation to vocation and she joined New York Road Runners in 1998, taking a 2/3 pay cut to pursue what she called a dream job that also allowed her to start a family and live what would theoretically be a less frenetic life.

It's undeniable that the New York City Marathon, already famous when she took the NYRR helm, has only grown in stature. Wittenberg was among the architects of the World Marathon Majors, which grouped New York with Boston, London, Berlin, and Chicago. Through a point system, the top male and female professional marathon runners can each earn a separate title and $500,000 for winning the overall crown. The designation helped further cement the big five marathons in a class by themselves.

Wittenberg similarly pushed New York into previously untapped sponsorship relationships and, again owing to the race's prominence, set the standard by which most other marathons are judged.

ING in 2003 became the first title sponsor of a marathon, negotiating its name into the race itself. What was known for more than 20 years as the New York City Marathon became the ING New York City Marathon. A Dutch financial services company, ING went all in on marathons, notching not just New York, but also races in Georgia and Miami. Its bright orange branding was integrated into the New York marathon's color scheme.

The pre- and post-Sandy criticisms of Wittenberg came at a sensitive time. ING had decided not to renew its deal, so she was in pursuit of a new title sponsor. After months of meetings, she ended up not too far away, in one sense. Tata Consulting Services, known as TCS, already was a sponsor of the marathon. The India-based information technology company provided services related to the logistics of the race, including the ability to track runners in real time.

Wittenberg effectively upsold TCS into a role that was bigger in scope than ING's title deal. Not only would the November event become the TCS New York City Marathon, Tata would lend its name to other NYRR races and programs.

While TCS wasn't new, its deepening involvement signaled a shift in the sponsorship landscape, Wittenberg says. Once limited to what she called endemic sponsors, the pool of interested parties expanded. The endemics included shoe sponsors (Asics, in the case of New York, Adidas for Boston) and financial services firms (ING) that often advertise at sporting events with an affluent audience (think JPMorgan Chase and the tennis U.S. Open, and practically every bank in one form or another at many golf tournaments).

Now the roster of marathon sponsors has evolved, as its popularity has grown and the pool is somewhat more diverse. United Airlines is a "Foundation Partner," making it the title sponsor for the New York City Half Marathon, as well as tagging its brand onto the marathon's full title: "TCS New York City Marathon, presented by United Airlines." Perhaps Wittenberg's most interesting win in 2014 was the addition of Airbnb, the Internet-based service that allows people to rent out their houses, extra rooms (or couches) to visitors.

The deal was a fascinating one, especially as it signaled a change in runner demographics and attitudes. It was a nod to runners who said they wanted to travel to New York in part to be with other runners, especially the locals who might play host to them in a room rental, rather than hotel, set up. Like TCS and United, Airbnb signed on as a year-round sponsor, "to engage with us from events to training to youth programs," Wittenberg says. In late 2015, her NYRR successors signed New Balance to a similar deal. "It's a lifestyle connection, not just a one-day race."

As Airbnb and other efforts illustrated, Wittenberg leaned hard into the young cohort that helps define New York City, beyond running. There's the younger set—the Millennials who are increasingly filling up races, often in their familiar packs and who represent the surge of women into the sport—and then there's the actual youth, the kids. There, Wittenberg and NYRR have poured time and resources. The organization's annual report is filled with pictures and statistics about the youth programs, which help upwards of 130,000 kids in and outside of New York.[4]

NYRR's also welcoming when it comes to other races and activities, seeing them as additive rather than subtractive to her ultimate cause of getting everyone who possibly can to run. "Free fitness, classes—all of it builds to people being fit for events," Wittenberg says. "People will stay fitter longer,

---

[4] Juliet Macur, and Ken Belson, "Under Mary Wittenberg, The New York City Marathon Is Thriving. So What's the Problem?" *New York Times,* October 13, 2012, www.nytimes .com/2012/10/14/sports/under-mary-wittenberg-the-new-york-city-marathon-is-thriving-so-whats-the-problem.html.

and it mitigates some injury risk." For Wittenberg, running sits unquestion-ably at the center of the modern fitness boom. Its simplicity is its best asset. You don't have to show up anywhere special or really invest much beyond a pair of shoes.

Maybe most importantly, running is beautifully efficient in the nexus of time and effort. A 20-minute run, especially outdoors, is often enough to take the edge off, to take you just enough outside yourself to feel some mental and physical benefit.

What Wittenberg and her successors at New York Road Runners have is New York itself. While the race is not technically difficult—the biggest inclines and declines are the long bridges between Staten Island and Brooklyn, and Queens and Manhattan—the necessity to touch all five boroughs requires logistical gymnastics that are hard on runners.

Runners spend the least running time, but the most sedentary time, on Staten Island. Since few stay on the island the previous night, the first order of business is getting out there, by bus or ferry from Manhattan. Then it's a waiting game, punctuated by standing in line for port-o-johns. The scene is surreal, made more so by the setting of a former fort built for protection from Atlantic Ocean–borne invaders: Tens of thousands of jittery runners, some sprawled out reading newspapers, others jogging nervously to keep warm and keep the pre-race nerves in check.

The sheer numbers also provide challenges. The New York City Marathon is the second-largest annual footrace in the United States, trail-ing only the Peachtree Road Race in Atlanta, a 10-K held every July 4, according to statistics compiled by Running USA. It's the only marathon in the top five. The differences between the Boston and New York marathons stand as extensions of the cities themselves. New York is big and flashy, often pulling in celebrities by virtue of its location and prominence. Back in 2003 no less than Diddy (aka Puff Daddy, aka Puffy, aka P Diddy) ran New York, complete with an entourage and motorcycle escort, in the middle of the field. He even branded it: "Diddy Runs the City." More recently, in his post-Tour de France doping denial period, Lance Armstrong ran New York, breaking three hours by a whisker the first time, in 2006 (with a half marathon as his longest training run, he reportedly called it one of the hardest things he'd ever done), then knocked 13 minutes off his time the following year. Each November, it seems, some celebrity or another lines up in Staten Island.

For runners with big plans for a bucket-list race, New York is the most popular race to aspire to run. The race draws thousands of first-timers each year, many of them one-timers who want to check that box.

What New York lays claim to in flash, Boston counters in longevity and elitism. It's the oldest marathon in the United States, dating back to the nineteenth century. And then there's the qualifying.

While New York is singular as a city, Boston's marathon stands alone. There is no single word that inspires more fear, aspiration, and envy for the serious long-distance runner. It's become the touchstone for the 26.2 mile distance, the test that you must pass to consider yourself a serious marathon runner.

After the 2013 race, Boston became that much more important, owing to the bombings. The marathon that year became a where-were-you-when moment for runners and those who know them. I was thousands of miles away, sitting in a hotel ballroom in Sao Paulo. The private equity conference I was attending was mostly in Portuguese and I'd taken a break from the translation headset to idly peruse my Twitter feed.

As the details began to emerge, in 140-character bursts, I looked around to find an audience of oblivious mostly non-Americans. At a break, I sought out fellow New Yorkers, who had as few details as I did. One thing was clear that day: Like many others—some Boston veterans, others would-be qualifiers—I vowed to be on the starting line the following year.

It wasn't a sure thing. Despite having a qualifying time, Boston hopefuls faced a new, more complicated process, made more complex by the fact that the 2013 race was stopped before a substantial number of people finished.

The upshot for the 2014 race, having nothing to do with the bombings, was that it was already harder to get in. Facing a race that filled up within hours, Boston dropped qualifying times across the board by almost 6 minutes. For a 40-year-old male like me, what had been a standard of 3:20:59 dropped to 3:15 flat. For a woman the same age, it dropped to 3:45 from 3:50:59.

The next change was how Boston rewarded those who exceeded their qualifying time by 5 minutes or more. Here's how it worked: The race first opened to those who beat their time by 20 minutes or more. A few days later it was 10 minutes, then 5 minutes. Then, assuming there were still spots left, those within 5 minutes of their time could apply. Those registrants would then be ranked by fastest to slowest.

I fretted. My qualifying time was roughly 3 minutes faster than my qualifier. Boston had expanded the field for 2014, mostly to make room for those who'd passed the halfway mark in 2013 and were therefore guaranteed entry if they so desired. I watched and waited for the numbers to come out from the Boston Athletic Association (the BAA to most runners).

When the time came for me to enter, I realized I would be in a meeting so I neurotically asked my wife to submit my electronic entry. (Though I knew they would take them all in and rank them, what if you somehow got points for being one of the first to submit?) She gamely went to the website and sent me the confirmation of entry. I waited. Days passed. My two closest running friends were already in, by dint of being fast enough for early entry. They sent me encouraging texts.

Walking back from a lunch meeting on a sunny late September day, I checked email on my iPhone. There it was. I was in. Standing on a traffic island halfway across Park Avenue in Manhattan, I threw my hands in the air and whooped, figuring no self-respecting New Yorker would think twice about some idiot screaming for no apparent reason.

I found out later how lucky I was. Because of the demand for the 2014 race—all of us who vowed to show up in solidarity for the victims of the previous year—not everyone who qualified got in. When all was calculated, the effective qualifying time was a minute and 38 seconds faster than the standard (e.g., 3:13:22 for my age cohort). Even with the extra room, 2,976 runners who crossed a finish line sometime in the previous 18 months with a coveted Boston qualifying time (also known as BQ) were denied entry.

Getting into Boston brings the same fleeting joy as getting a really difficult new job. There's a thrill, and then you realize you have to actually do it, and more important in the case of the marathon, train for it. And for anyone who lives and trains in the northeast United States, Boston makes you work for it all over again.

Training for the New York City Marathon is a relative pleasure. Summers in and around New York are relatively mild (especially from the perspective of a native Southerner). The days are blissfully long, so even 5:15 a.m. runs happen in natural light. Temperatures moderate even more as fall arrives. Long runs double as foliage tours and, once the chill really sets in, the race is upon you.

Boston training is an entirely different matter. Most training plans stretch over 14 to 16 weeks, so work begins just after the first of the year, also known as the period in the north where you question your life choices. Winter in New York, and certainly Boston, stretches out through March, when snowstorms aren't rare. Darkness is a given. Those long days of summer translate to brutally short days in January and February. And it's usually cold.

The winter of 2014 was a soul-crushing ordeal. Record snowfalls, polar vortexes, and plunging temperatures made training even more daunting than usual. My running partner Wendy and I ran more than once when it was four degrees, much to the chagrin and pity of family and friends who wondered if we'd been apprised of the invention of the treadmill or had lost our minds altogether. I slipped and fell several times on icy roads. The Adidas poster that I got at the Boston Marathon a few years earlier read "Boston With Swagger;" it hung in my basement and seemed to mock me every morning as I put on layer after layer and checked the batteries in my headlamp. I was swagger-less.

April finally arrived. I navigated the additional security, marveling at the oddity and sadness of going through a metal detector to run 26.2 miles. Even with local police and imported law enforcement everywhere, with bomb-sniffing dogs and strict rules about checking bags—or perhaps because of all that—the morning was electric.

We made the long walk from the high school grounds that once a year become the staging ground for tens of thousands of jittery runners. I stood at the starting line in Hopkinton and listened to a rendition of the national anthem that meant more to everyone that morning. And then race director Dave McGillivray gave us our instructions. "Our job today is to take back the finish line," he told the assembled runners. It was on.

Here's the thing about the Boston Marathon: It's really hard. You work your butt off to get there in the first place and then the Boston Athletic Association presents you with what has to be one of the most technically challenging courses out there, certainly of the major, popular races.

Part of the challenge is that the first half is distinctively not hard. It's actually shockingly easy, because most of it is downhill. Hardly anyone can resist going out a little too fast. Others blow it out completely. The second half comes with a relentless set of hills, culminating with Heartbreak Hill. The course then turns sharply downhill, and your quads, having been tortured through the inclines, scream. It is somewhere in that next couple of miles, as the outlying neighborhoods give way to Boston proper, as the Citgo sign sits tantalizingly out of reach at Fenway Park, that most of us ask the question of ourselves: What the hell am I doing here? The exhaustion, mental and physical, is acute.

In Boston the answer comes, finally, on Boylston Street, the final stretch. Twenty-six miles behind you, point-two to go. As there were every other year for decades, the throngs of spectators were 5 to 10 people deep in 2014. I crossed the finish line and spent the next 20 minutes hugging and thanking, and being hugged and thanked. My buddy Billy and I—stinky and fit-for-a-marathon thin—posed for a picture with a couple of beefy Boston police officers. It hangs on my fridge to this day; all four of us are grinning like idiots.

It was true that our very presence there, the full-throated, eager, 36,000 of us who endured the long winter, the qualifying drama, and heightened security was a bold statement against the previous year's horror. But the real show was the classic American response: spending money.

The center of commercial activity for the marathon economy is the race expo, where lean, hungry, amped-up runners show up to collect their race numbers, free T-shirt, and whatever else the sponsors have shoved into the goodie bag. But that's just the beginning.

The Boston Marathon expo stands as the cathedral of running commercialism. Its icon is the Boston jacket.

No one I've met who's run at least one Boston Marathon doesn't have at least one Boston jacket. It's the status symbol that says to your running friends, "Check." It's not an attractive piece of clothing, but a glorified wind-breaker made by official sponsor Adidas with the marathon logo embroidered on the back and the left breast. It has stripes down the side. Buying one is totally awesome and completely worth the $125 they cost at the 2014 race.

But the jacket is only the beginning. In the Adidas area alone, where runners are funneled first (lead sponsorship has its privileges), there were T-shirts (my favorite, which I bought for each of my three sons, read "My dad is faster than your dad"), pint glasses, flip-flops, sweatshirts, and more.

The Adidas section, while the biggest, is just the beginning. Once through that checkout, the expo becomes a bazaar of booths hawking everything from shoes to energy gels to self-massage devices (some of which look and act like medieval torture devices).

Runners are ferocious spenders, many by virtue of simply having the dis-posable income to shell out. Like tourists turned out of a bus on New York's Fifth Avenue, many runners show up ready to throw down cash or credit for a variety of goods that will make them even a little bit faster. (I once spent $20 on a wristband that promised to help me harness my energy; I ran a PR—runners' abbreviation for "personal record"—the next day, so couldn't totally dismiss it.)

Figures on how much people spend at expos are difficult to nail down, but I spotted a thread on a *Runner's World* message board populated ahead of the 2014 Boston Marathon. The question was simple: "How much money do you think you'll spend?" Among the several dozen responses were some expo estimates. The low end was $50, but several admitted that they expected to spend $100 or $200, with at least one person conceding they would drop $500. Another commenter, fearful of his own weakness, said he planned to "lock up his wallet."

Outside of New York and Boston, there are upwards of 750 marathons every year in the United States and Canada, the vast majority of which are smaller. (The 10 biggest races comprise roughly two-thirds of the total participants.) While the biggies slug it out for dominance, a just-as-interesting competitive set lurks one level down.

Patrice Matamoros revived Pittsburgh's Three Rivers Marathon in 2009 after the race was dormant for five years. Five years after the resurrection, the race was among the fastest growing in the country. It's a study in how it all comes together, and the challenges and opportunities inherent in the rest of the races.

Pittsburgh is an old-school American city in many ways. Once a dominant economic force owing to its steel mills and other heavy industry, it slumped through much of the late twentieth century. During the early part of the twenty-first, though, it pivoted right into a new urban trend that favors a lower cost of living, work–life balance, and advanced, information-economy jobs. Pittsburgh has a slate of high-profile colleges and universities, notably the University of Pittsburgh and Carnegie Mellon University, the latter of which is well-known for producing high-earning, sought-after engineers. Fitness fits in nicely.

That's what Matamoros thought back in 2008, when the entire staff of the revived Three Rivers Marathon consisted of her. She's a former star high school and college runner, sidelined in her thirties by injuries. She gets the running thing. When she was approached about the marathon job, Matamoros was a transplanted, very successful local fundraiser. She immediately fell in love with the marathon.

The race had essentially faded away. But Matamoros found a city still ready to back it, both municipally and commercially. "In the beginning it was me going in and selling the dream," she says. "With the thought of bringing back, it was more nostalgia. People really didn't know what it could be."

Her approach was to shoot the moon. She told her board of directors she could pull in 5,000 runners; they asked to publicly aim for 3,500. In its re-inaugural year, the race drew about 10,500.

Like other organizers, she found a radically changed customer base that was less die-hard. She cited statistics around the increasing average finish times—"The average was 2:52 back in the 80s, now it's 4:52." (While slightly exaggerated, the numbers aren't far off.) There are a lot of people able, and willing to run that speed, and putting on a race became largely about "making it easy and fun," she says.

Matamoros was competing in a crowded market, aiming to grab a chunk of the spring marathoners. Pittsburgh sits in the midst of the spring marathon calendar, the same weekend as the Cincinnati Flying Pig and a week removed from Cleveland, both within driving distance. Matamoros's answer was to appeal to the Millennials and women in her backyard and beyond.

What Matamoros found was that Millennials favored a buffet approach to their lives, at work and at play. They wanted the opportunity to sample lots of different things. Social media allowed them to dabble, and to have a slice of this experience or that. With them in mind, Pittsburgh quickly moved past just offering the marathon distance to include a half marathon (now the biggest of the weekend's events), as well as a relay option and a 5-K.

The Generation X crowd was similar, but distinct. Extending the restaurant metaphor, this group prefers to order a la carte, having done lots of homework about their best options. "They're very particular about what they pick and choose," Matamoros says. "They like the VIP experience; they want the option to switch races." (Unlike some other events, Pittsburgh allows changes among distances up to and including race weekend, and processes roughly 1,000 such switches every year, for a $20 fee.)

While Millennials were the most popular demo, Generation X had set it in the public consciousness, she says. "Gen X was the self-help generation. This was a way to be empowered, to make yourself belong by showing power and self-confidence. It became a way of showing they're taking their lives back, grieving through a loss or getting over a divorce," she tells me.

Like many of her fellow race directors, Matamoros came to appreciate women participants, who comprise 60 percent of her runners. "We love them because they commit early," she says. "They bring their friends." Often four or five women will register together, creating a tighter connection to the event.

Going forward, Matamoros said she's focused on several strategies including making the experience last even longer. With Pittsburgh teed up to an Olympic qualifier for the 2016 Olympic Trials, she created a "Game On Pittsburgh" program that hooked runners from sign-up. "From the moment you register with us, you're connected," she says. The runners, already connected with many of their fellow racers through social media, will become a more formal part of a race-created ecosystem.

Like Wittenberg, she's looking to leverage the enthusiasm of nontraditional races like Tough Mudder and The Color Run by converting their newbie athletes into runners. "I love them," she says. "People who didn't think they were runners, it converts them. It's playing a vital role in the marketplace, I just have to make sure the next step is with me."

Matamoros and Wittenberg both noted that while being not-for-profit has advantages and drawbacks, much of it is on the margin, and few participants make much of a distinction among various races' business models.

"It's a business for all of us," Matamoros says. "What we're talking about is a classification. My job is to show how we're different."

It's that competitive aspect, both on the course and behind the scenes that eventually led to what may have seemed inevitable or obvious—turning racing into a big, money-making business.

Taking the local club to the world was Wittenberg's mission at New York Road Runners. She says she always wondered what it would be like to have an even bigger canvas to paint. For that, she needed a singular individual—someone like Richard Branson.

Wittenberg claims she wasn't looking for a new job when the Virgin billionaire's reps came calling. Her first signal was a whisper from a head-hunter who, without naming names, said there was a notable individual with a deep interest in the area who saw an opportunity to get people moving. With a little more details attached, she thought to herself, "Oh, that's Virgin, that makes sense," she says. "And I didn't think about it again." A few months later came a more expansive approach, this time with the Virgin name attached. In the spring of 2015, she met Branson and accepted the job. NYRR effectively split her job between two of her lieutenants. Michael Capiraso became the President and CEO of the organization; Peter Ciaccia was named President of Events and the race director of the marathon.

"I always wanted to take this idea of community-based running and fitness on the road," she says. "To take people from the bucket list and keep it going."

We're sitting in the southwest corner of Central Park, a few blocks from Wittenberg's old NYRR office, but uptown from her new Greenwich Village Virgin digs. She's in the neighborhood because it's three days before the New York Marathon, the first one in about two decades when she won't be some sort of race official. But the same quasi-celebrity status in the running world that made her stand out in Boston is at work here. After seeing me, she's headed to see Paula Radcliffe at a marathon hall of fame event.

Virgin Sport, her new project, is short on specifics but big on vision, the way Branson ideas usually start out. He's deeply into wellness and fitness overall already, through a corporate service called Virgin Pulse and a gym business. Virgin Sport, in theory, is a way to tap into the community-building aspect that's building around running, cycling, and other participatory sports. The opportunity, she says, is in the "gray area of fitness."

"It's the day-to-day," she says. "Everyone can get up for the big race, but how do you weave it in to your life? I believe we're all better together, with others. Connection with others is key to bringing the fun and play to sport, and getting us out the door."

Wittenberg's initial answer is local clubs powered by the trademark Virgin customer experience—something anyone who's ever flown on one of

Branson's airlines knows well. It's a cheeky, winking experience that reflects simultaneously the whimsy and purpose of its founder. That experience, she surmises, is especially important to the up-and-coming generation of fitness fanatics, the Millennials who will drive the communities she aims to build. "A sense of purpose is going to remain important," Wittenberg says. "This is a generation that says, 'We care about who we shop with and who we support,'" she says.

It's also a generation that appreciates blending purpose with profit, and the members of the fitness economy are willing to pay for brands and services they believe in. That's in part what makes Wittenberg's transition from noble nonprofit to a more capitalistic enterprise possible. Virgin, after all, is a for-profit company, funded initially by the Branson family, but with an eye toward bringing on additional investors down the line. Its success will hinge on Wittenberg's ability to wow the paying customers.

"The Virgin brand is about what's amazing for the participant, and the community," Wittenberg says. Making it amazing will be that much more important as she enters a market that seems to get more crowded with competitors each day. Along with her former colleagues and friends at the big-ticket marathons, there's an ever-growing pack of entrepreneurs aiming to please that same pool of athletes.

CHAPTER 10

Money on the Run

The Boston Marathon celebrated its hundredth running in 1996 with much fanfare. Its organizers expanded the field to a record size and celebrated right through Patriots' Day.

A year later, a small company based in La Jolla, California, took out an ad in *Runner's World*. "You missed the first Boston," it read. "Don't miss the first Rock 'n' Roll."

In 1998, almost 20,000 runners, the largest number to ever participate in a first-time marathon, moved 26.2 miles through the streets of San Diego, listening to a band at every mile. The field started more than half an hour late after an argument with the local police. Most of the runners were from out of town. Half of them were women.

The race marked the dawn of a new era in distance running. The 1998 Rock 'n' Roll Marathon would change the way races were organized and promoted, who participated, and what they did before and after running. The event also ushered in a new era of investment in running and fitness, creating a key piece of the fitness ecosystem by providing a focal point beyond local, nonprofit races for a lot more spending and sponsorship.

An organized running race sometimes has the feel of a barn raising. Especially on the small side, a race comprises a group of like-minded folks who mostly know each other, and want to put a little formality around what would otherwise be a regular group run. Sometimes, they just want to see who's really the fastest among them.

The barn-raising aspect comes from the need for dozens, if not hundreds or thousands, of volunteers to stand along the race course for hours, guarding a turn, pointing out potholes, or handing out water and energy drinks to occasionally grateful runners. All for a dose of civic pride and a free T-shirt.

The civic pride element shouldn't be understated. Races are a showcase for communities large and small. At their most prominent, major marathons (and the occasional 10-K like Atlanta's Peachtree Road Race) have grown into signature events for some of the world's iconic cities. The races have become icons in their own right.

Still, the established races had the field mostly to themselves for a long time. When the Rock 'n' Roll Marathon debuted in 1998, it had been 13 years since a major U.S. marathon was born. Bill Burke organized the first LA Marathon, notable for its for-profit model, in 1985 to leverage the athletic attention and infrastructure in the wake of the 1984 Summer Olympics held in that city.

Why did it take 13 years? Mainly because it's an expensive, complicated proposition, to the tune of somewhere between $750,000 to $1 million for a major race to get everyone started and finished. Beyond the majors and local races, the demand through the late 1980s and through most of the 1990s wasn't apparent.

Tracy Sundlun was an irascible running coach in New York who'd navigated a Zelig-like career through the nascent track-and-field and endurance running worlds. The son of businessman and former Rhode Island governor Bruce Sundlun, he attended Philips Exeter and notably decided he wanted to be a coach at the age of 12. He served as an assistant track coach at Georgetown University in the early 1970s. Asked to mentor a young runner who moved east, Sundlun found himself the youngest Olympic coach at the 1972 Summer Games in Munich. (Those Olympics, of course, were where Frank Shorter ignited a stateside distance-running boom with his marathon victory.)

Sundlun went on to become a fixture in the New York running scene, coaching the Warren Street Social and Athletic Club, one of the defining running clubs of the 1980s. By virtue of that association, and an apparent penchant for needing to cause trouble, he agitated—in practice and through the court system—for a more rational system for paying runners who win races, as well as scholarships for women in the wake of the passage and adoption of Title IX.

The national running community was small at the time and most people were connected by a couple of degrees at most. Across the country, Tim Murphy, president and founder of Elite Racing, was a southern California fitness and running entrepreneur whose signature event back in the 1990s was the Carlsbad 5000, an annual 5-K race held in the picturesque town that sits just north of San Diego.

The two men connected in the small world of racing, swapping favors around runner invitations and advice. Murphy was interested in further developing his youth program, called Junior Carlsbad, at his annual 5-K. Knowing Sundlun's experience with youth development in New York, he hired him as a consultant in 1994. Sundlun, who lived and worked in La Jolla as a coach in the late 1970s, was happy to spend a week a month back in Southern California.

The two men clicked further as Sundlun dug into Elite's expanding mission. Murphy, who was already putting on the only major for-profit race other than the LA Marathon, had aspirations for a 26.2 of his own. Given the existing franchises, they pushed for new and different ideas to get both runners and spectators to participate. Boston had Patriot's Day—a school's-out holiday that most companies also close for. New York had a start timed to push runners through the five boroughs at times when people would come out to watch. The most popular viewing area is First Avenue in Manhattan, which comes more than halfway into the race.

A San Diego marathon would have to begin early in the morning. What would entice runners and their supporters? Music. Murphy imagined a course that featured 26 small concerts. The working name was the Rock 'n' Roll Marathon. Sundlun recalls: "Some of us thought it was a dumb-ass name. I did. We had three meetings to come up with better ideas and never had a better one, and thank God."

The bands contributed to an overall festive atmosphere, one much different from a typical race. It pushed the whole marathon experience away from the grim determination of its early, gaunt, hollowed-cheeked die-hards and toward something more palatable to the everyday athlete. "When we started this thing, people ran 90 miles a week, tried to break three [hours], and the courses closed at four hours," Sundlun says. "There were no Porta Potties on the course. They were these lean, mean, type-A male running machines."

The Rock 'n' Roll target market from the beginning was less serious. Many would be more likely to finish in five or more hours. Some would walk most or all of the way. They needed portable toilets along the route—"more Porta Potties than exist in some states on a single course," Sundlun says.

But how slow? Looking at New York finish times, Sundlun decided that seven hours should be sufficient time to keep the course open. At that point, the handful of remaining runners could move to the sidewalk to finish. (In fact, more than 1,500 participants ended up on the course at the seven-hour market, forcing organizers to keep the streets closed—"There isn't a sidewalk in the world big enough to accommodate that many people," he says.)

The first race was fraught with challenges from—yes—start to finish. Just getting people registered was the first challenge. Back in 1998, the Internet was nascent for much of the world and what passed for e-commerce was clunky. But if this was going to be the new model for modern marathons, online registration was a must. The organizers figured they'd get a couple hundred folks to sign up through the web.

One major problem: the initial site didn't make it clear when a registration was completed. Many people unwittingly submitted duplicate entries, including one man who registered upwards of 40 times, Sundlun says. A number of especially enthusiastic would-be runners entered online, by fax, and by mail, leading to a backlog of entries that had to be sorted by humans.

By the time registration closed, about 6,700 people registered online.

The experiment proved a point borne out in areas beyond just registration, according to Sundlun: "We were made by the Internet. Initially, we were screwed by the Internet too."

The Rock 'n' Roll Marathon set out to break the record for an inaugural marathon set by Los Angeles back in 1985. Its goal was 8,500 people. More than 19,000 ended up starting the 1998 San Diego race. In part because of the size and its newness, it was fraught. An overzealous police officer delayed the start by 38 minutes because there were cars parked on streets that were supposed to be cleared.

The stories the following day, in the newspapers, were glowing, Sundlun says.

But the Internet wasn't quite so kind. Grumpy marathoners shot off emails complaining about various elements of race day. Sundlun and his crew did what race directors had done from time immemorial with complaint letters. They gathered them up, figured out what the most common gripes were and, a few days later, sent out a form email apologizing and promising to do better. Too little, too late. "We got crushed," Sundlun says, referring to message boards and complaints about the lack of responsiveness to the original complaints. It was a harbinger of the new interactive, instant early century to come. "Now with social media, you have to have an answer in five seconds."

The huge turnout was a boon to many, including the city of San Diego, which pegged the economic impact of the weekend at $35 million. Team in Training, which had signed on as the exclusive national charity and registered 4,500 runners, raised $15.6 million. I ask Sundlun how Elite Racing made out. He laughs. For a while.

"We lost a million bucks," he says.

While making other people lots of money was a surprise, losing money in its first year of the race wasn't a shock to the Elite team. Part of what kept people out of the business was an unwillingness to invest for a couple years without turning a profit, Sundlun says. Investing meant aggressive advertising and direct mail pieces sent widely to touch a broad audience.

This was the plan: They created the event as a separate company to isolate it from the rest of the business and raised money from investors to cover what they figured to be about $450,000 in costs. Sundlun and Murphy worked their contacts, pulling in $10,000 and $15,000 commitments from other coaches and business contacts; Wilt Chamberlain, who retired to Southern California, was among the original backers.

As registrations poured in, Elite hit another snag, with its local bank. Fees were meant to provide much-needed working capital, but the flood of small deposits set off compliance issues with the bank, Sundlun recalls. The bank told Murphy it would hold all the deposits until the event happened, and wouldn't budge despite desperate pleas. Elite was forced to open a new account, at a different local bank, for new registration fees and wait to get the money held hostage.

The registration process had yielded other, more positive, but unexpected insights. Murphy himself combed through entry forms, noting registrants' locations and occupations. Always on the hunt for sponsors, he'd call up and ask registered runners if their companies wanted to sign up. A call to a pair of Nashville-based record company executives didn't lead to sponsorship, but did open up an entirely new opportunity.

The Tennesseans were excited about the race and demurred sponsoring when Murphy called. But they did have a comment: Why was this company putting on a music-themed event in a city, San Diego, not known for being any sort of music hub. Why not a race in Nashville?

Elite executives were intrigued. They invited the pair out to La Jolla, where they hatched plans to put on what became the Country Music Marathon. That race, held in March of 1999, marked another first: the first time a race organizer had put together a race outside of their home city.

Elite planned the Nashville race armed with lessons learned at the inaugural Rock 'n' Roll. Country Music was another distinct company, with a roster of investors meant to cover the costs. March was warm enough in Nashville to hold a race and it didn't interfere with any other marathons (there would be little overlap with the very serious Boston racers and a presumed batch of newbies down South).

How much distance running's key demographic had changed manifested itself, Sundlun says. Based on San Diego's success in drawing nearly 20,000 runners, Elite set a cap of 15,000 for Nashville. The race drew half that, ending up with roughly 7,500 runners.

It turns out the new, broader class of runners wasn't quite as hearty as the never-say-die, don't-miss-a-workout athletes Sundlun had coached. "People told us, 'It's too cold to be running during the winter. We don't really start running 'til March,'" he says. "In essence, they just weren't ready to run a marathon. It was a different audience."

Even at the lower participation level, Country Music still ranked as one of the five biggest inaugural marathons. Taking another lesson from San Diego, the group sold a $700,000 stake to investors. And still it lost a million dollars the first year.

They remained confident that they could spend their way to profitability over several years, race by race. Elite was tweaking the template to put on a successful race, learning each time how to best attract an audience, how to partner with a city, how to woo sponsors. The next leap forward for Competitor Group came from another, even smaller southern city.

Virginia Beach had an image problem, at least around Labor Day. The three-day weekend at the end of the summer had earned a reputation as a destination for college students who crammed by the dozen into hotel rooms up and down the beach. They drank and frolicked and acted like college students.

Local officials figured they needed to make an end-run around the bacchanal by counterprogramming an event that would bring a different crowd to the area. A marathon seemed like a good idea.

Competitor Group was a natural call. With the Rock 'n' Roll Marathon in San Diego and Country Music Marathon in Nashville established, the company had proved it could put on a race, even in a city far from its home. Competitor sent a team of executives to scope it out.

They found that the town and infrastructure wouldn't support a full marathon. The timing was also difficult, given the roster of established races slated for the fall. Chicago, Washington, New York, and Philadelphia all had firm slots on the calendar. Adding a presumably hot-weather, brand new marathon at the end of the summer, or beginning of the fall racing season, wasn't going to work.

Competitor proposed something that at the time was radical—a standalone half marathon. They'd sell and market it with the same aggressive methods they did their marathons, only with a different tagline: "Half the distance, twice the fun. And you're alive to enjoy it at the finish line."

While Virginia Beach had little to lose, skeptics abounded, Tracy Sunlund recalls. The previous record for an inaugural half marathon had been roughly 2,900 participants, he said. Competitor estimated they could pull in 12,000, maybe as many as 15,000. "They thought we were nuts," he says.

Runner's World doubted Competitor to the point it bet a full-page ad, worth roughly $40,000. Team in Training, the charity that had benefited mightily in the first two San Diego races, opted not to participate. Competitor started its own charity for the race to pull in the do-good-while-running element.

Competitor ultimately got its free, full-page *Runner's World* ad. The race sold out by July and was, Sundlun says, "a rollicking success." Beyond the told-you-so smugness, Competitor made several discoveries that would change how it operated and programmed going forward.

There had been a fear that adding a race shorter than a marathon would dilute a key selling point to cities that Competitor was targeting—the ability to bring in out-of-towners who spent more money than locals at restaurants and hotels. With Virginia Beach, the numbers held. Armed with that knowledge, Competitor began adding half marathons to its existing marathons, giving would-be participants a choice.

More important, the Virginia Beach experience was a harbinger for a dramatic shift in the distance-running landscape: the emergence of the half marathon as a hugely popular distance that drew new runners and kept them in the sport. Almost every running expert I spoke to noted the meteoric rise of the half marathon in popularity. From 2003 until 2013, it was the fastest-growing standard distance in U.S. racing as measured by finishers, rising at an average annual rate of 12.5 percent, according to Running USA.

The same study—a special report on the half marathon released in mid-2014—showed that the number of half-marathon finishers quadrupled since 2000, hitting nearly 2 million in 2013. Since 2010, the half was the second-most popular distance, trailing only the 5-K.

The half marathon is the Goldilocks of distance racing—not too short, and not too long. Not too easy, and not too hard. Unwittingly echoing Sundlun, Mary Wittenberg says, "You don't feel like you're going to die at the end."

The half marathon requires enough of a commitment that it can bring the runner noticeable benefits, mentally and physically. Most training plans call for a long training run of at least 10 miles, a distance that few can hop out of bed and run without some level of conditioning.

It's also enough of a commitment that participants feel okay making a trip of it, either by pulling their family along to a destination, or building a boys' or girls' weekend around it.

A big chunk of the participants are women who pull together a group of friends to train and run. The second-largest half marathon overall in 2013 was the Nike Women's event in San Francisco, with 26,406, according to Running USA. That same year saw the debut of the Nike Women's half marathon in Washington DC—the biggest inaugural half marathon in history, with 14,478 finishers.

Overall, women comprised 61 percent of half marathon finishers in 2013, up from 49 percent in 2004. That number was boosted by a number of women-only races; in addition to the Nike series, there were dude-free races in Chicago and elsewhere that year.

As is the case with Pittsburgh's marathon weekend, for many races, the marathon isn't the main draw. The half is. (There was a nascent movement to change the description of the race from half, to break any assumption that people should pursue a full. Though saying, "I just ran a 13.1" doesn't quite have a ring to it.)

Organizers have added shorter distances, like Philadelphia's 8-K, held the day before the half and full marathons. Competitor, too, got deeper into the expansion act in 2014, with a twist. The innovation began, as many in the entertainment business do, at Disney World.

Disney saw the distance running trend early, and leaned in hard. The first Disney Marathon took place in 1999, the year after Rock 'n' Roll's debut. As the half marathon gained popularity, Disney added a half marathon, but set it for the day previous to the marathon. Looking to draw the hard-core distance runners, Disney offered an option it called the Goofy—run both races, on back-to-back days. In 2014 the World's Happiest Place added another dimension, a Friday 10-K. All three constitutes a Dopey.

A huge part of the appeal of the Goofy and Dopey and even just finishing one race, it turns out, is getting a medal. The hard-core runners of yore were content with, at best, a flimsy cotton T-shirt. Competitor Group, starting with the inaugural Rock 'n' Roll, decided to make the medal a big deal, creating it as a displayable keepsake.

Competitor in 2013 started its Heavy Medal program, which encourages completion of multiple events to earn distinct hardware. Starting with Rock Encore (two events in a year), runners earn special medals all the way up to finishing 10 or more events in a year, which earns you a Rock Idol medal. Competitor said roughly 30 to 50 people a year qualify for that status—conservatively, figuring early registration, such a feat would cost at least $1,000 in entry fees alone.

A huge part of Competitor's success and importance comes from this reach, which is where its owners come in. What began as Tim Murphy's brainchild and expanded amid a ferocious appetite for endurance events grew into a massive enterprise when big money entered the mix. A New York private equity firm called Falconhead Capital saw what Murphy was doing and provided the financial muscle to accelerate its growth and reach.

David Moross, the founder of Falconhead, was in the process of raising money in the mid-2000s. An investor mentioned she just ran a marathon and mentioned Elite Racing, then a small but growing outfit out in the San Diego area that put on three races a year.

Moross was aware of Elite. In his work analyzing trends, he asked a sports statistician named Rich Luger to dig into the fastest-growing participatory sports. Number three was soccer, no shock to any middle-class parent who's spent hours of their weekend on sprawling complexes of suburban fields. The overwhelming No. 1 was walking, "but how the heck does one make money in walking?" Moross says.

And then there was No. 2—running—and Elite was deeply in the middle of it. With roughly $3 million in profit, it was squarely in the sights of investment bankers and investors who wanted to buy it and catch the broader fitness wave. "Six guys like me had already been there," Moross says. He needed an edge, a fresh take to convince Murphy to sell.

He turned to Peter Englehart, an operating partner at the firm with deep experience in sports media and operations. An Emmy-winning producer at ABC Sports and ESPN, Englehart also created the Outdoor Life Network, one experience that gave him deep insights into participatory sports. Moross and Englehart conceived an idea to marry Elite's races with media, including magazines aimed at the triathlete and the competitive athlete.

In 2007, Competitor Group was born, a combination of the media properties and the races. Moross and Englehart set about growing the company rapidly. By the time Falconhead sold Competitor in 2012, it managed more than 80 events. The firm picked up a registration company called Race It and a couple of smaller acquisitions along the way.

Moross and Competitor's breakthrough was to identify, exploit, and encourage broader participation in the sport of running. "This is about the true mass audience," Moross says. While a subset, a small subset, is focused on checking one of the major marathons like New York or Chicago off their list, and an even smaller subset focuses on qualifying for Boston, "Ninety percent of all people running aren't going to do the majors," Moross says.

For the broader audience it's largely about the experience. That's how Competitor ended up putting on a marathon in Las Vegas, after dark, on the iconic Strip.

Vegas is a situation where Competitor saw an opportunity to professionalize and commercialize activities typically left to local organizers or much smaller groups. Clarke County, Nevada had been taken advantage of by a less-than-honest organizer who failed to live up to his financial commitments. Seeing an opportunity to put on a race in a popular tourism destination, Competitor stepped in to take over the race.

What was traditionally a regular old marathon was transformed to be firmly in the Vegas ethos. Dubbed Strip at Night, the annual marathon and half marathon turned into one of Competitor's biggest events. The weekend, which also features a post-race concert that draws nearly 100,000 people, generates $280 million in economic impact for Las Vegas, Moross says.

Falconhead sold Competitor in 2012, after conducting an auction of interested buyers. Given the private equity business model—buy, fix and/or grow, sell at a profit, distribute money, repeat—some sort of so-called exit is necessary. Falconhead sold the company to Calera Capital, another private equity firm.

The price tag was about $250 million, according to *Street & Smith's Sports Business Daily*. The auction illustrated the growing appetite for assets in fitness. The nine-month process drew 32 initial bids, which were narrowed down to six and then two.[1]

Under Calera's ownership, Competitor continues to nurse its ambition, going so far as to get into the New York City market. The company threw its inaugural half marathon in the city's five boroughs in 2015, drawing 17,500 runners to Brooklyn. Competitor has hit some bumps along the way. It drew an outcry from the hard-core running set in 2013, when it announced it was cutting appearance fees for elite athletes (while still covering some travel and lodging costs). The move was seen as private equity slaughtering a sacred cow of the race circuit, threatening to deprive everyday runners chances to line up alongside, or at least near, their marathon heroes.

Within six months, Competitor reinstated the appearance fees, citing the protests from across the running community. "Who we're dealing with is the priority," Sundlun said. "If it costs a few extra dollars? So what? You've got to do the right thing, and we believe that runners and general fans will like the general features of this."[2]

Moross continues to analyze and invest in fitness and wellness, which he says he believes to be a long-term trend. Like others, he sees evidence everywhere. On a business trip to London, he gazed out from his treadmill over Hyde Park at scores of runners. Fifteen years ago, the park was largely empty, he said. "Now, it's similar to New York City. There are simply runners everywhere."

---

[1] Daniel Kaplan, "Competitor Group Reportedly Selling for $250M to Calera Capital," *Street & Smith's Sports Business Daily*, November 30, 2012, www.sportsbusinessdaily.com/Daily/Issues/2012/11/30/Finance/Competitor.aspx.

[2] Mary Pilon, "Organizer Says It Will Reinstate Appearance Fees for Top Racers," *New York Times*, January 22, 2014, www.nytimes.com/2014/01/23/sports/organizer-of-top-running-events-to-reinstate-appearance-fees.html.

Moross remains convinced of the megatrend, especially around running. He notes a direct correlation between emerging markets and improved fitness and health, as demographics shift toward a relatively wealthier population. "Running is usually the first thing the new moneymakers move toward," he says. "Running is the core, it's the real essence."

Marathon money roams far. One of the richest marathons in the world by almost any measure is another of the few for-profit endeavors: The Dubai Marathon, held each winter in the wealthy Middle Eastern emirate.

Dubai isn't built for outdoor athletes, by climate or design. It's brutally hot much of the year, reaching 120 degrees Fahrenheit at the height of summer.

When you can run or bike, it's treacherous in much of the city. An Australian triathlete was struck and killed during a group bike ride in early 2014. Another athlete, a Lebanese expatriate, was killed during a run. Dubai, a Middle Eastern hub that sprung from the desert in the late 1990s in a frenzy of construction, favors cars and trucks over pedestrians.

Dubai is famous for its luxury and many have compared its opulence to that of Las Vegas, owing in part to its role as a playground for Arabs whose more conservative home countries frown upon the excesses Dubai embraces. The emirate is home to the world's tallest building, vast malls teeming with free-spending tourists and locals, and near-constant construction (after a brief, Great Recession-induced pause).

Dubai has nothing if not ambition and strives mightily to be part of the latest trends. And so as fitness gains a stronger foothold in the global consciousness, Dubai shifts with the times.

It's still hot in October—hot enough that a walk outside in midday can soak a dress shirt—and it's on just such a day that I duck into a hotel restaurant in Dubai's Media City section to meet the men behind the Dubai Marathon.

Peter Connerton, the founder and director of the race, isn't a runner and doesn't look like one. He's a genial expat who first came to the region almost three decades ago, after his family's Ireland-based textile company shifted production from India to Sharjah, another of the United Arab Emirates that's adjacent to Dubai. He eventually moved to Dubai attracted, as many Europeans are, by the low cost of living (heightened by a lack of income tax).

He was a businessman in a burgeoning expat community and a friend asked him to raise sponsorship for a 10-K race back in November 1998. The following year, the group decided to add a marathon—the first in the United Arab Emirates—spurred in part by the growing popularity of races that distance in the United States and Europe. The inaugural marathon, with

Connerton as event director, happened in January 2000, with about 120 runners going the full distance, and another 300 or so opting for the 10-K.

The launch was fortuitously timed to Dubai's widening ambitions as a global city, and Connerton grew the race organically alongside the emirate's burgeoning popularity. The field comprised almost exclusively expatriates— locals, known as Emiratis, showed little interest.

Many of those expatriates worked in financial services. Dubai in 2004 created the Dubai International Financial Centre, a zone where foreign banks could set up shop under specially designed rules distinct from federal Emirati law. Soon, most major international banks staked a claim, wooed by Dubai's location as a friendly gateway to the Gulf's riches.

One of those banks was the UK's Standard Chartered, which already had its Middle East headquarters in Dubai and moved into the DIFC. Connerton, taking a cue from the other big marathons, contracted the bank as the title sponsor, adding Dubai to a list of races the bank backed. Flush with new promotional dollars, Connerton marketed the race aggressively overseas.

By 2007, Dubai was pushing deeper into the global consciousness by virtue of audacious development. Rumors abounded that a third of the world's cranes were at work in the city. Emirates Airlines became the most talked about in-air experience for the discerning business traveler, a set similarly impressed by the Burj Al Arab, a seven-star hotel resembling a full sail, situated on a man-made peninsula jutting into the Persian Gulf.

In that spirit, Dubai's ruler—Sheikh Mohammed bin Rashid Al Maktoum —asked how to put Dubai's marathon into the international conversation. The answer: money. Dubai in 2007 offered a tax-free purse of $1 million, including $250,000 for the men's and women's winner. The ruler then went a step further. He pledged an additional $1 million if a world record was set on the course. (To date, it hasn't happened, but remains on offer).

Connerton is a savvy marketer, and with his friend and PR man Alan Ewens—a fellow long-time Dubai expat who represented a number of Dubai's similarly audacious sporting events, including massive golf tournaments—went to the Mecca of marathons to (sort of) quietly announce the big prize.

The two choreographed that announcement beautifully at the 2007 Boston Marathon. Given Boston's stature in the distance-racing world, most everyone was there, especially the complement of journalists needed to write the relevant stories. After the Boston press conference, Connerton began side conversations with the various reporters and soon the story ricocheted around the running community.

Next, Dubai needed a star runner to headline its marathon. Connerton decided on two-time Olympic gold medalist Haile Gebrselassie and set about wooing him. He sealed the deal a week after his Boston announcement, at the London Marathon. After a decade of turbocharged growth as a tourism and financial hub, Dubai had found a way to wedge itself into the global marathon conversation.

Connerton has in some ways the best of both worlds. While enjoying the largesse of the local and federal governments, his marathon is actually his. That is, he owns the race through his company, putting him in the small company of Competitor Group and the Los Angeles Marathon, also privately held. Unhampered by any nonprofit strings, Connerton is a pure entrepreneur, making decisions almost solely based on whether it's good for business.

One of those elements is the course, which has never been the same twice. Dubai as a city is constantly changing (I visit there every year or so for work and am continually amazed to find entire new sections that were sand on my previous trip) and part of the marathon's mission is to advertise the emirate's wares to visitors who increasingly make it a destination marathon. The architecture of Dubai is startling and exotic, a kaleidoscope of buildings of various shapes, most soaring. And the course has to be fast—easier to pull off in the flat desert—to keep the million bucks tantalizingly close.

The collision of money and ambition isn't limited to the Middle East. That cocktail's been made for a century out in Los Angeles, where one of the country's marquee marathons signed up a new title sponsor for its 2016 race—a name that's come hard, fast, and suddenly into the conversation around high-end fitness.

When shoe-giant Asics opted not to renew, LA ended up going local, and taking as its title sponsor Skechers Performance. The Manhattan Beach, California-based shoemaker—long best known for light-up shoes and butt-toning footwear—capped an unlikely jump into the distance-running spotlight with the LA deal.

As has happened with Skechers a lot lately, the timing was impeccable. The 2016 marathon weekend would not only be the debut of its title sponsorship, but also feature the two best-known American marathoners, competing for spots on the U.S. Olympic team. The road to that sort of prominence was long, and owed much to Boston's 2014 edition and its unlikely hero.

CHAPTER 11

The Man Makes the Shoe

Merhawi Keflezighi was apprehensive as he walked out of the Fairmont Copley Hotel on April 21, 2014, toward the finish line of the Boston Marathon. The lead runners were in the final few miles of the race and officials, following their standard practice, brought the family and representatives of those runners to watch the end of the race.

Keflezighi, who goes by "Hawi," fits both categories. His brother, Meb, was also his star client—and he was winning.

At the same time, Rick Higgins stood among his colleagues at Skechers' headquarters in Manhattan Beach, California, before normal business hours and spoke with his boss, Skechers' founder and CEO Robert Greenberg. Higgins put Greenberg on speakerphone.

Greenberg was at home, but he and Higgins and a couple dozen other colleagues who arrived early were all watching the same thing on television. A little more than 3,000 miles away, an almost impossible thing was happening—Meb Keflezighi, wearing a pair of Skechers shoes, was six miles away from winning the Boston Marathon, becoming the first American man to do so in more than three decades.

"Is it possible that he's going to win this?" Greenberg asked Higgins.

Meb turned onto Boylston Street for the final stretch. He'd led since the fifth mile and his comfortable lead was evaporating. Anyone watching on TV had the sense his nearest rival was about to overtake him. As Meb drew closer to downtown Boston, the thickening crowds showered him with "U–S–A" chants. He glanced down at his race number, which he annotated with the names of the victims of the previous year's finish-line bombings. As Keflezighi pushed to the finish, where a year earlier two bombs had killed four and injured dozens more, Greenberg kept calling Higgins back. Even as Keflezighi's lead shrank, Greenberg shifted from asking the question to stating it as fact: He's going to win this.

In the VIP stands, a small clutch of Skechers executives in Boston to tend to Meb and his shoes, screamed and clapped to the point of almost falling off the bleachers. As Keflezighi—who simply became Meb that day—crossed the finish line, the group at Skechers erupted in cheers, hugs, and tears. Almost two years later, Higgins has a hard time describing the scene, owing to the emotion.

The emotion that morning in Boston was raw and real. Meb stood on the starting line as McGillivray gave his simple instruction to reclaim Boylston Street.

The win lit up social media as the winner's @runmeb handle gained thousands of followers and congratulatory Tweets. Beyond the virtual world, the win went viral on the course, rippling through the waves of runners, aided by spectators along the route who'd gotten texts or news alerts. Near mile 17, an industrious fan broke the news to the runners streaming by with a hastily hand-drawn sign: "MEB WON."

The days after the Boston win threw Meb and Skechers into an entirely different light. The significance of this guy winning this race this year was a story few outlets could ignore. Meb made the rounds of national television shows. Daily newspapers used to making passing mention of the Boston Marathon winner deep in the sports section, pulled him to the front of the section, if not the entire paper. He visited with the staff of the New York Road Runners, where he is an elite member, and watched a recap of the race with them, a surreal and delightful experience.

Part of the appeal of the storyline is Meb himself. He's a slight, gentle, gracious guy whose personal history resonates. Born in Eritrea, he immigrated with his family at a young age to Southern California, speaking virtually no English on arrival. One of 11 children, he fell into running by accident, as a way to fit in, and ultimately stand out. Running, he says, was more appealing than soccer, a naturally political sport, on the field and off. "I can control my own destiny," he says of running. "When I don't win or finish in the top 10, there's no one else to blame."

His prowess on the track and on the cross-country trail earned a scholarship to UCLA. He became a naturalized U.S. citizen in 1998, and earned a spot on the U.S. Olympic team.

Just out of college, he signed with Nike, adding his name to a brand synonymous with global athletes, and deeply rooted in running, back to the legendary waffle iron-created running shoes. From the start, Meb was savvy about his brand, and ambitious. He wanted shoes, an energy bar, a drink, and a car. "Right out of college, it was a struggle," he says.

The struggle became, and remains, part of his brand, both he and Hawi say. Meb gained stature by being incredibly consistent, but unable to win a big major race. But he kept showing up and benefited from a long-term relationship with New York Road Runners, widely considered the best-known club of its kind. He signed to run with the club as an elite athlete in 2002, and "I gave them all I had," he says. When Mary Wittenberg took over the top job in 2005, Meb's long, steady ascent was accelerating. While the 2004 Olympic medal was an important moment, winning the New York Marathon in 2009, "that was when my brand started," Meb says.

"New York made me famous," he says. "Going on David Letterman, being in the Thanksgiving Day Parade." Wittenberg and her organization embraced him, in part as a symbol of New York—a foreign-born American champion, achieving something no American man had done since the early 1980s.

The win seemingly only validated Nike's longstanding relationship with Meb, dating back to the late 1990s. As he was graduating from UCLA, Meb was courted by the legendary shoemaker, and wooed them back. He sent a letter to Alberto Salazar at Nike, writing: "I hope Nike can help me reach my goal of becoming one of the top distance runners in the world. I think I would be a great addition to your company because I have good character and versatile athletic ability. In the near future I am confident I will make a positive contribution to U.S. distance running in the 5,000m, 10,000m, road race and marathon."[1]

For a decade the relationship worked, and Meb was a Nike athlete when he crossed the finish line first in New York. Without another major win over the next two years, and moving through the back half of his thirties, Meb's contract with Nike wasn't renewed. He was devastated, knowing he had more he wanted to, and could, achieve. He turned to his brother to help him work on his sponsorships.

Hawi, four years younger than Meb, became his agent a year after the 2004 Olympics. Meb decided then he needed U.S.-based representation, in part to cultivate American sponsorship opportunities as he became an increasingly important figure in an increasingly popular and lucrative sport.

---

[1] Meb Keflezighi, "Letter to Nike," www.scribd.com/doc/22622402/1998-Letter-to-Nike.

At the time, Hawi was in his second year of law school at UCLA, working toward a career in sports management, but with an eye toward representing basketball players. As an undergraduate at the school, he was a student manager of the Bruins basketball team, assiduously developing relationships around the sport.

As a lawyer in training, and Meb's trusted confidant, he reviewed Meb's contracts and knew them intimately, a role that became more important as they searched for new, full-time representation. Talks with a potential agent stalled over financial terms, owing in part to the fact that Meb already had his key deal, with Nike, in place. Hawi offered his services to the agent, as an apprentice of sorts who would work on the Meb account and learn the business. The agent turned that idea down.

"At this point I said, 'Meb, I see your Nike deal, I've seen your deal with NYRR. You're in the peak of your career. I think I could help you,'" Hawi says. "I wrote out a proposal to him in the middle of the night and sent it to him."

Ever deliberate, Meb considered the proposal by making lists of pros and cons and seeking advice from third parties about hiring his brother. Weeks passed, during which Hawi assumed it was a no. Two months after Hawi's Jerry Maguire-esque, insomniac memo to his brother, Meb hired him. "I'm so glad it happened that way," Hawi says of the long consideration period. "It was healthy."

Timing was critical. Hawi says now that Meb's established brand made his hiring possible. "All I could give him was that he could trust me, and I'd have his best interest in mind," he says. "Nike would have to deal with me, even though they didn't know who I was. If Meb was just starting his career, we probably wouldn't be working together. We would both be start-ups."

Still in school, Hawi identified what he could and couldn't do. He linked up with a marketing agency to develop collateral for Meb, seizing on his post-Olympic notoriety. They identified 200 potential sponsors and sent out brochures touting Meb. One-hundred-ninety-nine of them went unnoticed, or unremarked upon. But one drew the attention of Mastercard's agency, which had considered another marathoner, then-world-record-holder Paul Tergat. Mastercard signed Meb.

The three-day shoot, Meb's first non-Nike national ad, earned him as much as the shoemaker paid him for a year. Six months in, Hawi was impressing his older brother.

When Nike ultimately opted out, Hawi had his biggest task yet. He had put together enough sponsorship revenue to keep Meb employed as a professional runner. They assembled a roster of sponsors ranging from the traditional (Powerbar) to the offbeat (Generation UCAN, a nutrition energy drink). But a runner's most important deal is for shoes.

Nothing emerged immediately. The traditional players, all with the caveat of how much they respected Meb, worried aloud about his age (mid-30s), and carrying the burden of a post-Nike athlete, in terms of the cost as well as the notion of rebranding an athlete long associated with the Swoosh.

Hawi turned again to his network of marketing agencies for help, and pulled an unlikely thread. An intern at one New York agency was the son of a senior Skechers executive in charge of what was then known as the Fitness division, and now called Performance. Once he learned about the familial connection, and lacking much traction with larger, better-known running shoe brands, Hawi said, "How about Skechers?" The California company was best known for a couple things that made them an unlikely backer—kids' shoes that lit up, and shoes that claimed to make your butt look better. The latter led to lawsuits and eventually a settlement.

As a Southern Californian for most of his life—Meb grew up there and did his collegiate running at UCLA—paying a visit to the Manhattan Beach headquarters was not a big ask, but it was all Skechers needed in early 2011. "Half the battle was getting someone to come in," Higgins says. "Here's Skechers, this lifestyle brand. And we're talking to an elite Olympic medalist. We needed to get him through the front door. That was the power of him seeing what we do."

Meb is hands-on and reacted immediately to the intimacy of the Skechers team and not only their willingness, but insistence, that he create something of a feedback loop for their shoe development. "We all just hit it off," Higgins says. Even before signing, Meb ran hundreds of miles in existing and prototype shoes. "I would call up and say, 'I ran 20 miles in these shoes, and this is what I think,'" Meb says. "We put all of our brains together."

The courtship lasted for much of 2011, as the Skechers team built shoes based in part on his feedback. "I was a guinea pig," Meb says. By August of that year, he was sold and signed with Skechers. The company best known for light-up shoes had a marquee marathon spokesman. Higgins says both sides took a calculated risk, Skechers on an athlete who was at best pushing up against the back end of his career, and Meb on a brand that had effectively zero association with high performance of any sort.

"Meb took a lot of ridicule, that he was just coming here for the money," Higgins says. "We're kind of used to ridicule. But both of us took a lot of risk."

The risk was calculated. During the talks, Meb told Skechers he was certain he had another personal best in him, in both the half marathon and marathon, times that would be fast enough to win major titles.

The only problem with the timing was New York. Meb was scheduled to run the New York City Marathon—the premier marathon, in the world's most important media market, 12 weeks after signing.

Skechers scrambled to create, tweak, and finalize a custom shoe. Meb, at age 36, posted his fastest marathon ever.

The concept proven, Skechers took the winter to spend even more time with Meb and develop shoes just for him, all the while learning what it took for a high-performance shoe. Meb posted two more personal bests, including at the U.S. Olympic Trials, which he won, earning a trip to the London games. There, he finished fourth in a gutsy effort, moving up from seventeenth place at the halfway mark. He spoke openly at that point of retiring.

Meb and Hawi used the success to their business advantage. As part of the reported mid-six-figure annual deal, they pressed for, and got, a more favorable arrangement than the typical endorsement. Skechers agreed that Meb could wear corporate logos beyond Skechers. The company also agreed to pay the full fee, regardless of performance; traditionally, sponsors were able to cut payments if athletes didn't achieve certain results.[2]

The latter proved unnecessary, given Meb's performance, which kept improving. Skechers developed a wide-ranging marketing campaign using Meb as its spokesman. Higgins and his team also used less traditional means, sending samples to running bloggers. The hope was to get some good word of mouth going among running groups, who tend to talk among themselves—often obsessively—about their gear.

With Meb in the family, Higgins began courting another elite runner, Kara Goucher, who had emerged as the best known American woman runner. She also recently ended her association with Nike, and was looking for something different. Like Meb, the wooing was a long process. Goucher's husband, Adam, a former elite runner in his own right, is also her manager.

The discussions with the Gouchers ramped up in the months leading up to the 2014 Boston race, where Kara Goucher also was competing. During that time, she remained interested, but uncommitted. Hours after Meb won, Higgins texted Adam Goucher: "Convinced yet? Let's announce today." Later, Kara Goucher admitted the win was the deciding factor, but she was hesitant to do anything that detracted from Meb's post-race glow.

---

[2] Sara Germano, "Skechers Sets New Pace on Sponsors," *Wall Street Journal*, April 24, 2012, www.wsj.com/articles/SB10001424052702303592404577363691089413680?alg=y.

Within two months, Goucher signed. Higgins extended his custom approach from the shoes to the deal. Kara Goucher had already agreed to an apparel sponsorship with Oiselle, a start-up clothing company founded by a friend. Unlike Meb, who agreed to a so-called head-to-toe contract, Goucher just wanted the shoes.

Now Skechers had, by most accounts, the best-known male and female marathon runners wearing its new line of shoes.

Such high-profile endorsements, coupled with Meb's win, validated those scores of runners who'd taken a chance and bought a pair of Skechers, Higgins says. Rather suddenly, Skechers were legitimate in the eyes of a notably discerning crowd. Higgins points to Meb's Boston win as critical to his piece of Skechers. "That day is the tipping point for the Performance division," he says.

A year after the Meb victory and the Goucher signing, I met Higgins in person during a trip to New York where he was entertaining buyers in a sprawling series of rooms Skechers keeps in Manhattan for just this purpose. The crowd was in town for an annual sportswear convention. Offering high-end food and drink in one area, Skechers executives mingled and chatted across the various lines of its products.

One of the larger rooms had a wall devoted to the Performance division, and separate life-sized grinning cutouts of Meb and Goucher clad in their respective Skechers gear.

The mood was ebullient, reflecting the general consensus around Skechers. The Meb boost was one part of a tailwind benefiting the entire company. Higgins had also nabbed a high-profile golfer—Matt Kuchar—for his own line of shoes. Kuchar, a Georgia Tech-educated member of the PGA Tour, was engaged in his product in a Meb-like way, offering feedback and suggestions. The golf line proved a near-immediate hit, especially with older golfers already familiar with the Skechers brand. Higgins seized on that, signing up Champions Tour golfers Colin Montgomerie and Billy Andrade to endorse Skechers Performance.

Skechers Performance's success came as Skechers overall was enjoying broader success. The company in 2011 endured a business and public relations debacle around its Shape-up shoes, which promised to help users stay trim and tone their backsides. Skechers ended up with excess inventory of the shoes, and ultimately paid the U.S. Federal Trade Commission $40 million to settle charges it misled customers.

The company has since seen sales grow for its shoes aimed at walking, kids, and even work shoes, as well as the Performance unit. Skechers saw its market cap increase to more than $8 billion, from less than $600 million at the end of 2011 as it retooled its processes to avoid another Shape-up disaster.[3] After achieving those new heights, the stock tumbled again in late 2015, as quarterly sales missed analysts' estimates for the first time in two years. Still, the market cap remained around $4 billion in early 2016.

The world of running shoes is a complicated one. A full history would comprise an entire book of its own. Shoes are, after all, the only real piece of specialized equipment a runner needs. Given that prominence, magazines devote pages and pages to reviews and ads of the newest shoes. Runners tend to experiment with the latest and greatest model, constantly seeking an edge or a way to fend off running injuries.

Fueled largely by the 2009 breakaway bestseller *Born to Run* by Christopher MacDougall, the market for minimal shoes—meant to mimic barefoot running—boomed. A former war correspondent, MacDougall told the amazing true story of a Mexican tribe who mastered the art of running incredible distances with little more than pieces of rubber strapped crudely to their feet.

In the course of the book, MacDougall took dead aim on the modern shoe industry, outlining a strong, coherent argument that companies like Nike and others actually caused running injuries by outfitting us with shoes that made us run in a less-than-natural way. "[B]y arguing that the human body is in fact evolutionarily designed for long-distance running—i.e., we are 'born to run,' not 'born to have plantar fasciitis' or 'born to develop knee problems'— McDougall shook up the entire running shoe industry," *Trail Runner* magazine wrote in a story catching up with the characters in the book.[4]

(As of early 2015, a movie version of *Born to Run* was reportedly in development, with Matthew McConaughey playing a starring role.)

The minimal shoe craze, at least on a widespread basis, was short-lived.

The boom (and bust) was best characterized by Vibram, maker of the Five Fingers shoe, which slid onto one's feet like a tight rubber glove, with individual spaces for each toe. They looked and felt about as weird as you'd imagine. Having struggled with occasional but annoying plantar fasciitis and Achilles tendinitis, I got a pair one year for Christmas and ran in them a total of three times. My wife, likely with my public reputation, and hers, in mind, sold them on eBay.

For a short period, some especially bold souls (always men) would show up in public with them—I saw one gentleman walking around Walt Disney World in a pair.

---

[3] Ira Boudway, "Skechers' Lesson from a Fad That Flopped," *Bloomberg Businessweek*, August 20, 2015.

[4] "Stranger Than Fiction," *Trail Runner*, April 2014, http://trailrunnermag.com/people/profiles/1253-stranger-than-fiction.

Despite MacDougall's solid evidence that perhaps some or all of us might benefit from losing all the padding in modern shoes, many people weren't willing to take the time to break in their feet. Running barefoot, or close to it, requires a dramatic change in form. Those who didn't follow Vibram's pretty clear instructions to ease very slowly into minimalist running, ran the risk of seriously injuring themselves. Broadcaster Keith Olbermann suffered a stress fracture and publicly chalked it up to running in Vibram shoes.

Vibram's reversal of fortune was swift. Disgruntled customers in 2012 filed a class action lawsuit, claiming that the shoes didn't in fact have the health benefits they claimed to. The company settled the case in 2014, agreeing to pay $3.75 million.

Other companies have more nimbly navigated the need for a new type of shoe that hews to one of MacDougall's key tenets—that many running shoes encourage heel striking (that is, landing first on the back of the foot), which leads to the most common running injuries in the heel and foot.

Newton Running was started in Boulder, Colorado, and managed to break out of the proverbial pack with a blend of science and clever marketing. The company anticipated, and helped propel, one seemingly simple tweak— that runners don't mind their shoes being visually loud. Newtons come in bold colors; the model I ran in for several years had black, orange, and green versions.

My introduction to Newton was born on the trails, through the recommendation from a fellow runner of similar build and pace who suffered some similar overuse injuries. He was running in bright blue and green Newtons— their loudness and his enthusiasm started a conversation that stretched across several weekend runs. I found at the time one of the only retailers in the greater New York area that carried the shoes: Paragon Sports, a Mecca for the sporty crammed into several stories of a building near Union Square in Manhattan.

Newton comes with written instructions and also requires a little bit of care and feeding from a salesperson on the front end. While moving to them from traditional running shoes isn't as extreme as going barefoot, any sort of meaningful change in footfall requires a period of adjustment to avoid injury. Newtons are designed to effectively force the runner to run so that the foot touches first near the front, rather than the heel.

I followed the instructions and, like my running buddy, became a convert. This is what companies like Newton not only want, but need in order to achieve anything resembling success. It's a variation on the same challenge Skechers faced. Unlike Skechers, which some had likely heard of, but not in the context the company wanted, Newton had to start from scratch. No one knew the shoes even existed. (There is a benefit to having that blank slate. Newton had no Skechers-esque brand baggage to explain and could focus squarely on a pure segment of the market.)

Shoes are a segment where technology has fundamentally changed the market. Runners once relied on retail stores to buy shoes. Serious runners favored independent specialty shops where knowledgeable salespeople (usually young runners funding their nascent careers at a place that gave them discounts and an excuse to talk about running all the time) could guide the customer through the various options.

Then came the Internet. The web allowed for a number of innovations. One was simply access to products beyond what local stores or mail-order catalogs could offer. Once you identified a shoe you liked, you could find the best price with amazing efficiency. The Internet also created a platform for seemingly endless numbers of detailed product reviews, for an audience that welcomed the opportunity to give its opinion. While it sometimes took work to sift through all the picks and pans, the expertise of the local running shop was at your fingertips.

With all those people online and active, the smart shoe and apparel companies seized on the opportunity. Now Newton was on something a lot closer to parity with a giant competitor like Nike or Asics in a customer's email box.

Newton wasn't alone. Hoka One One has won its own following, by counterprogramming heavily against the minimalist movement. Hoka One One's shoes are maximalist, providing a level of support that gives them what's been called a "clown shoe" look. Like Newton and Skechers, Hoka One One has sought the blessing of both notable and famous runners, and found its tribe among the ultramarathon set.

Both Newton and Hoka One One have leaned into their alternative status, working the race expo circuit, where runners show up ready to spend money. They played on runners' aforementioned chattiness with fellow amateur athletes, and a collective desire to brag about the latest thing that hopefully no one else had heard of. In an age of plenty, being first to adopt the next big thing carries a lot of credibility. Buying a cool new shoe that makes it big is the equivalent of being able to say you saw the band REM thirty years ago at a tiny club in Athens, Georgia.

Skechers Performance, too, hit the race and expo circuit, especially when its stars were scheduled to appear. A week before the 2015 New York marathon, a Skechers billboard featuring Meb loomed over West 34th Street leading to the Jacob Javits Center, where tens of thousands would descend to pick up their race numbers and buy all matter of race gear. He went on to finish seventh in that race, the top American, and, at 40 years old, set a new American record in the master's category.

Even as he enjoyed a return to winning, Meb and his team were thinking about his post-running future. He gravitated to another Southern California company, Competitor Group, where he also had a history dating back to when it was Elite Racing.

The organizer of the Rock 'n' Roll Marathon series saw an opportunity to bring Meb into its ranks and leverage both his cache and goodwill within the running community. For Meb—the only man in history to win the New York City Marathon, the Boston Marathon, and an Olympic medal—it was a way to extend his brand in an authentic way.

Weeks after his Boston win, as his popularity soared, he agreed to run in the pack rather than the front, providing truly amateur runners with a chance to say they ran with Meb. Those bragging rights are more widespread than one might think, his brother says. Meb—slight and graceful—is hard to miss on the trails. He regularly encounters civilians on training runs and, if he's cooling down or warming up, welcomes them to join him.

"They say, 'Are you Meb?' and I point to my shoes," he tells me, laughing. "Since 2011, I've never worn anything but Skechers. I'm in 110 percent."

CHAPTER 12

The Money in Color

Travis Snyder stood on a Paris sidewalk in April 2014 and took it all in.

Eight years earlier, he and his wife had scraped together enough money to come to the City of Lights for the first time and do the American tourist-on-a-tight-budget tour. During that visit he thought what it would be like to stage an event here, in the shadow of the Eiffel Tower. "I remember seeing a Susan G. Komen poster in the subway," he says. "And I thought, 'What would that be like to have an event come over here?' Seemed like a crazy dream."

But here he was on the aforementioned April Sunday, watching 15,000 Parisians and visitors wind through the heart of Paris for five kilometers, from the Cathedral of Notre Dame, past the Louvre, and to the Eiffel Tower, stopping every kilometer for an explosion of colorful paint.

The single most popular run series in the world—with 2 million participants in 2014—isn't timed and it isn't long. It's popular with kids and grandparents and everyone in between. It involves voluntarily getting sprayed with paint made from cornstarch. It's called The Color Run. There has almost certainly been one in your town, or nearby.

This latest evolution in the fitness craze mirrors the evolution of the founder himself, who spent more than a decade putting on triathlons, running races, and rock-climbing events. Snyder now presides over a global empire of races whose motto reads: "Be happy, be healthy, be you." The Color Run bills itself as "The Happiest 5k on the Planet."

The Color Run strips the need to move and be together down to its essence. Snyder leverages the endurance fitness craze, in a postmodern way, with a creation that requires essentially no endurance and little fitness. For Snyder, it's both the antidote and answer to his previous career putting on triathlons. During that period, his wife asked him how she should describe what he did to her friends. His response: "I'm in mid-life crisis management."

That's a pretty good business, and one that through the early part of this century set Snyder up well enough to fund what initially seemed like a much more radical idea.

What became The Color Run was initially met by would-be backers with a mix of amusement and derision—on the face of it, the concept sounds ridiculous. People pay for the privilege to run several miles, untimed, and are covered in paint in the process. The end. The Color Run put on 300 events in more than 50 countries in 2014.

The counterprogramming to the endurance craze is stark. Snyder says: "When you're at the starting line of a competitive 5-K, you're looking at people's legs, their shoes, how much they weigh. You're figuring out if you can beat them. Everyone is a relative measuring stick."

At the start of a The Color Run, you're taking a selfie.

The fastest growing single segment of the broadly defined running industry in 2013 was what Running USA and Active.com called the MOB category. It stands for mud, obstacle, and beer, and is a catch-all term for everything that's not a straight-ahead, ready-set-go, run to the finish line on a road kind of race. This is the business of regular people paying money for the privilege of crawling through mud, under barbed wire, sometimes through cold water with live electrical wires hanging down. Sometimes it's running in your underwear (the Undies Run).

However you define it, it's catching on. The nontraditional category counted 4 million people among its participants in 2013, easily surpassing the 2.5 million finishers (also a record) in the marathon and half marathon combined, according to Running USA.

Why the surge? Beyond the aforementioned newness, the same factors driving participation in more traditional fitness activities took hold in the alternatives—a cultural shift toward health and wellness, accelerated by the broad interest by affluent Millennials and companies that deftly used social media to spread the word about their events, instantly. In its report on the events, Running USA cited "these wow-factor photos and videos" as major contributors to the growth.[1]

"When I was training and doing intervals on the track and puking because I went too hard, that was a beautiful thing," Snyder says. "But running and being active and being social doesn't have to be that all the time."

---

[1] Running USA, "State of the Sport—Part I: Non-Traditional Running Events," April 27, 2014, www.runningusa.org/non-traditional-running-events-special-report.

Snyder has athletic bona fides. In high school, he fell in with a crowd of sport climbers. He took it up competitively and later organized climbing events. As a kid, he also watched *Magnum PI*, the TV series starring Tom Selleck as a Hawaii-based detective. In one episode, Magnum solved a case while competing in an Ironman. The young Snyder vowed to complete his own, and did in 1997.

"I went hard at it, and became a pretty serious endurance athlete," he says. He added triathlons to his repertoire of existing rock-climbing gatherings, feeding his innate affection for putting on shows. "I enjoyed the crash of it—it's a high and it's exciting," he says of organizing a race or a climb.

The growing seriousness prompted his whimsical side to emerge and he entertained competitors with little stunts, like presenting pineapples for trophies, or having a helicopter drop prizes in the triathlon transition area, distracting the super-intense guys intently changing clothes and equipment for the next leg of the race. Part of it was to separate his events from the pack.

What Snyder saw was that these sorts of events, while lucrative and successful, drew a narrow slice of the population—the mid-life crisis demographic he was only half-jokingly referring to in his job description to his wife. His admittedly high-minded goal was a physical activity that would appeal to literally everyone. After selling his existing traditional race-event businesses, he consulted with a handful of companies while mulling this fun-first approach.

The Color Run idea was germinating and he put together a business plan and set out to raise some seed money. More than a couple of people literally laughed at him. While the fitness boom was in full swing, who in the world really wanted to scramble around for 45 minutes and have paint thrown on them? He finally raised a bit of seed money, from an investor willing to take something of a flyer on a rather kooky idea.

Snyder's ambitions were initially modest. He read that Tough Mudder put on eight events during its first year, so he figured he'd put on 12, roughly one a month. The business plan called for two thousand participants in each race.

By the spring of 2011, the first race was set, for late January the following year in Arizona. He activated the registration site and did some modest advertising. Because he wanted to personally track the entries—and because there would presumably be so few—he set it up so he'd get an email each time a new person registered. Basic information: Bob Smith from Tempe, T-shirt size, XL.

Like many races, he set an early-bird discount, which expired on October 31, 2011. He set out that night to take his sons trick or treating. Throughout the evening, the buzzing in his pocket, signaling a new email, increased to a near-constant rate. At first, he checked it, then he let just let it go. While he was trick-or-treating, 900 people signed up.

Even after the early bird expired, registrations poured in as participants spread the word and wittingly or unwittingly recruited friends, family, and neighbors. By the time the event happened, 6,000 people lined up for the inaugural Color Run. That year, instead of putting on a dozen events, Snyder organized 60, for a total of 600,000 people. He had a juggernaut.

While amazingly successful, it was logistically brutal. Snyder had to refile permits, and radically increase the amount of staff to handle the influx. "It's a little terrifying," he says. "To be honest, there have been sides of me that wish it had been on a slower trajectory."

Why did it work? As is often the case, the answer is pretty simple. The people who did it really liked it, and they told everyone so—with pictures.

Technology was a boon. He insisted on high-quality photography on the website to illustrate what's a decidedly vibrant experience. Since they weren't timed, participants stopped all through the three miles to take photos, which immediately showed up on Facebook, Instagram, and Twitter feeds.

Snyder employed his own technology to encourage sharing. "We decided this will be the most visual experience people can have," he says. He used slow-motion cameras to create effects similar to the bullet dodging in *The Matrix* movies. The first video, *Be a Color Runner*, posted in May 2012, quickly got a million views on YouTube. By mid-2014, it had in excess of 5 million.

The speed at which images move helped propel overseas growth. The first Singapore Color Run sold out in a matter of hours, prompting a local woman to lament via social media that she was in tears over not getting in; she'd wanted to do a Color Run for so many years. An amused and slightly baffled Snyder read the comment, noting that The Color Run had only existed for 18 months.

Snyder also had created something that captured the imagination of the demographic motherlode: Millennial women. They showed up in packs, armed with the aforementioned social media accounts. At the same time, The Color Run was within reach for an elementary school student and grandparent alike.

The relative ease draws in people who are sensing the same broad cultural movement toward wellness and togetherness, and want to be a part of it, even if they lack the desire, ability, time, or resources to run a marathon or triath-lon, or even a 10-K. Snyder says that while he competes to some extent with other races, he's thinking more broadly.

"We're competing against the movies and the amusement park," he says. "We could be competing against a family reunion."

Snyder even managed to pull in some of the aggressive athletes he'd once courted for his triathlons; usually a wife or girlfriend dragged them in. They reacted, he said, to the utterly different experience and usually gave themselves over to it, like a grumpy businessman who patronizes his kids with a trip to Disney World, only to end up wearing mouse ears and mugging with Mickey by the end of the day.

Snyder himself began building a bigger and bigger organization to keep up with demand. The company has about 70 employees in Los Angeles and Salt Lake City, with additional contractors hired to deploy runs throughout the world. After going to as many events as possible in the early days, he eased back into more strategic appearances, jumping into five or six races a year to get a customer's view of the event.

The schedule, the mission, and intervening choices changed his approach to his own fitness. His three sons—aged 9, 7, and 2—are his main training partners ("Large, medium, and small," he notes). He mainly tries to maintain a level of fitness in order to play with them, "and be able to take the 9-year-old to field grounders and be able to run back and forth across the field without a problem."

Back at the company, he's adjusting to the rapid transition from winging-it entrepreneur to someone expected to consider big decisions about the company's future. "There's a reason I now subscribe to Stanford business school newsletters," he says.

As for the company, anyone who's putting fun in his company's slogan better hire true believers. Snyder says he jokingly calls the events director, to his face, "Event Jesus." Customer service—to sponsors, participants, and host cities—becomes paramount and he and the team pore over post-event surveys as soon as they come back; the head of that team is among the best paid in the company. City managers get personalized Christmas cards to help pave the way for a return trip to their town.

Happiness, Snyder says, takes many forms on event day. For some it means shorter lines for Porta Potties, for others, a medal to commemorate the day.

That approach was on display on a brisk May morning in Queens, New York, at Citi Field, home of the New York Mets. It's the start of the Memorial Day Weekend and 10,000 New Yorkers are up early on a Saturday for the second annual Color Run in this spot.

The guy in charge on this day is Kent Phippen, a Utah native who met Snyder through a neighbor who happened to be Snyder's college roommate.

Now a three-year veteran of The Color Run, Phippen previously worked for Ragnar, the company that puts on 24-hour team relay races, another booming subgenre. In a Ragnar, pre-set teams of friends or colleagues complete a point-to-point race with each participant running multiple legs. Those not running at a particular time relax in a van that moves along the course as a support vehicle. People love them for all the sweaty, delirious bonding they promote. A neighbor of mine coaxed a dozen friends into a Ragnar to celebrate her fortieth birthday.

Ragnars, like marathons, attract a mix of hard-core and newbie athletes. While there's very little hardcore to The Color Run, Phippen knows how to put on a show, which is ultimately what all of these events are.

On race day, Phippen is the choreographer, directing a staff of about 25, a mix of half a dozen full-time Color Run staffers, with the balance a collection of contractors, some of whom are "road warriors," traveling from race to race. Then there are about 100 local volunteers, often drawn from whatever local charity the race is supporting. In the case of Queens, it's a group called Back on My Feet that uses running as a tool to help people cope with, and transition out of, homelessness.

Volunteers get the fun job—throwing paint.

Aside from being ultimately one of the few people covered in paint, I noticed another thing that made me stand out—I was alone. There was almost no one else at the entire Color Run on their own. People showed up in smartphone-wielding packs, or at least with a support crew of family. It's a sharp contrast to the competitive marathons like New York and Boston, where the starting area usually feels like tens of thousands of ships bumping into each other, nervously.

At The Color Run, togetherness is built in. Participants are encouraged to sign up as teams on the website and in Queens there were a lot of matching T-shirts ("Girls run the world") and tutus (the tutu has become a Color Run meme and women of all ages, and the occasional man, show up wearing them).

About an hour before the race begins, half a dozen instructors take the stage for a massive Zumba session. Zumba is something of an exercise phenomenon in its own right. Its ethos sits squarely in line with The Color Run, the workout equivalent of using applesauce in brownie batter to make them healthier. "We are pretty much the most awesome workout ever," the Zumba website brags, noting its 15 million worldwide participants in 180 countries: "Dance to great music, with great people, and burn a ton of calories without even noticing it."

Zumba serves as both warm up and organizing activity, an elegant way to assemble The Color Run group, and gives way to a conga line, led by the signature Runicorn (a person dressed up in a rather elaborate unicorn costume, with running clothes, naturally). Moving people to the starting line is harder for The Color Run because without an official timing element, no one needs to be in any sort of hurry. There are no time-qualification corrals, or any sign of a clock anywhere. It leads to a slightly odd vibe around the festival, with groups talking among themselves ("I guess we should head into the race?" "Let's give the crowd time to thin out"). Staffers ultimately have to herd people toward the starting line, if only because at some point the Mets need their stadium back.

The stadium itself is a big hit on race day. The previous year, runners were content to run around the outside of the ballpark. For the second-annual race, they actually started inside, along the concourse circling the field, eventually making their way down to the field itself. Talk about selfie heaven. I stand with Phippen in the front row of the third base line as he encourages runners to stop and take pictures. He happily takes several himself for groups whose size doesn't make a selfie feasible.

Given the sheer volume of powdered paint involved in a Color Run, the inside-the-park portion is, not surprisingly, color free. One imagines the Mets' groundskeepers wouldn't enjoy cleaning paint out of the pristine outfield grass. The runners return to the parking lot for their series of paint encounters. The paint-throwing portion is a combination of silly and brilliant and ultimately rather low tech. The volunteers have bottles that look like commercial-grade ketchup and mustard dispensers that they fill from giant bins of powdered paint. Then they line up on either side of the runners as they come through the designated area and they throw paint on them. The runners shriek and giggle, and come across the finish line at the end of 5 kilometers with a kaleidoscope of colors.

The post-race party, with music blaring, looks like a preschool finger-painting session gone very wrong, with grown people smiling and laughing and covered in paint, taking pictures all the while. The "finish festival" also features a coordinated color throw, where participants toss the contents of color packets in the air in unison, directed by the emcee on stage.

In Queens, the stain-remover Shout sponsored an area where a couple of guys with leaf blowers form a sort of mini-tunnel to blow off the excess paint. It's a sharp contrast to the end of a marathon, where more than a few faces are scrunched up in pain and runners gingerly walk, often alone, back to a hotel or to their car. The tweets, Instagram, and Facebook posts accelerate through the party, with pictures taken almost constantly, including at a specially made backdrop—a step and repeat in Hollywood terms—where runners can pose like celebrities.

Throughout the morning, I keep checking Twitter for a fresh series of posts, hashtagged to the Citi Field event, and they're near-constant, from excited pre-event messages to dispatches from the race itself, and, of course, the post-party. It's a reminder of how much social media—and our collective compulsive need to tell everyone what we're doing all the time—are fueling the popularity of these types of events.

By about noon, roughly four hours after runners started showing up, it's more or less over. Phippen and his crew engage in a well-orchestrated break-down, including a multistep process to sweep up and vacuum away the paint. Phippen says none of the paint makes it to the sewers, helping The Color Run to meet its goal of having zero environmental impact.

A month later, some of the same crew would return for an installment of a newer Color Run series, a nighttime event in nearby Brooklyn, where the fluorescent paint would light up thousands more souls.

Success breeds knockoffs and The Color Run faces that seemingly every weekend. (Snyder, by all accounts an easy-going guy, makes a point of noting that it's called "The Color Run," with a capital T, in defense of his brand.) Imitators use the same type of language (even the actual words color run) to promote and put on strikingly similar events, albeit at a smaller scale. For two years, my little town in Westchester has put on a color run in a local park, the proceeds of which go toward the school district's extracurricular activities.

As with the big, officially branded color runs, the beauty is in the simplicity and almost total absence of competition (like many other small communities, we also have a running organization that puts on an annual half marathon and 10-K race, which are timed and, for some, serious). The beauty's also in the near absurdity of it: Run and people are going to throw things on you. Then we'll all stand around, take pictures, and marvel at how ridiculous we look. And we'll pay for that privilege.

While Travis Snyder works on our happiness with brightly colored paint, Will Dean is working the equation from a different angle, with a similar goal in mind: Feeling better, together. Either way, you end up needing to wash your clothes.

Dean's company is Tough Mudder, a Brooklyn-based event series of obstacle events designed to test athleticism and willpower, all while getting absolutely filthy. Tough Mudder, Dean says, isn't about selling fitness, or a race. "We actually sell self-esteem," he says during a chat with me at a Bloomberg sports business conference in September 2014. Through personal and written testimonials, Dean's customers have told him doing a Mudder helped them get through a divorce, the loss of a job, or another sort of life obstacle.

Like The Color Run, Tough Mudder's not timed, and obstacles are designed to be conquered as a group, with teammates literally pulling their mates along, or up and over walls. For Dean, this was a key differentiator. His event wasn't meant to be a more difficult version of a marathon. He was trying to counterprogram the entire experience with an event that largely eliminated the competitive aspects.

As a successful marathoner and triathlete, he has been at the starting, and finish lines. Part of the team-focused inspiration came from an experience at a triathlon. He told one interviewer: "The zipper jammed on my wetsuit and I asked another guy in transition to help and he said no because he was focused on his time. Keep in mind this was not an event either of us were about to win! I believe being so focused on time creates unhealthy behavior."[2]

The notion of Tough Mudder was born at Harvard Business School, in the mind of then-student Dean. Prior to going back to school, he had served as a counterterrorism officer at the U.K. Foreign and Commonwealth Office and ultimately tapped contacts in the British Special Forces in designing Tough Mudder. His idea didn't make the finals of a business plan competition. "My professor said this was a terrible idea," Dean says.

Intent on proving him wrong, Dean sought a proof of concept. He announced an event, aiming to get 500 sign-ups. He got 5,000 paying customers and never raised another dollar. Part of the appeal of the business model is the pay-up-front nature, especially helpful in the early days. Dean and his team would collect the entry fees and use that cash to pay for the event.

Dean tells the Mudder story in the practiced manner of a confident entrepreneur who knows he's onto something big and has been questioned by both media and investors more times than he can recall. He's an affable Englishman, clad in chinos and untucked shirt, sporting something between a couple days' growth and a beard.

He talks about how Tough Mudder exploded, fueled by the broader fitness boom and the Millennial desire to do physical things together. Launched in 2010, the company drew more than 2 million participants by the end of 2015 and was worth an estimated $70 million.[3] Its offices span a loft-style space in Brooklyn—the borough most likely to house a hip, youthful, fast-growing company. Kickstarter and Etsy headquarters are within walking

[2] Dan Simon, "Toughing it Out: 5 Business Tips from 'Tough Mudder' CEO Will Dean," Forbes.com, July 13, 2014, www.forbes.com/sites/dansimon/2014/08/13/toughing-it-out-5-business-tips-from-tough-mudder-ceo-will-dean/.

[3] Ibid.

distance. There's fresh food laid out and booths for spontaneous chats along one wall of an office filled with fit, casually dressed young people talking about how to best incorporate new elements that are just challenging enough to keep people showing up to Tough Mudders, coming back, and, perhaps most importantly, telling their friends in person and through social media.

Like The Color Run, part of Tough Mudder's success comes from the ease with which participation can be shared, instantly understood, and appreciated. There's little need for traditional advertising (though Tough Mudder ads do show up now and again in local media ahead of an event in that city) given that its paying participants are its best promoters.

Tough Mudder's demographics run the gamut, though skew obviously toward those in their twenties and thirties. Dean says he knew it would be appealing to a Generation Y dude like himself (he was in his late twenties when he started the company), but was surprised at the broad appeal. In addition to the already-fit set, there are others who spend months training for their first event, opting to debut their newfound fitness at a Mudder instead of a marathon. The company's expansion speaks to continuing that big-tent approach. In 2015, the company launched Urban Mudder ("Tough Mudder's Cousin in the City"), bringing a grittier feel to the experience. That followed the woman-focused Muddarella, a shorter, less macho event meant to draw in a broader crowd.

Barbed wire, live electricity, and freezing wires, not surprisingly, carry risks. As popularity of the obstacle races soared, reports of injuries emerged. One case involved a 28-year-old Maryland man who died during a Tough Mudder event in West Virginia after drowning in an obstacle that involved murky cold water. In reporting on the man's death, the first in Tough Mudder's then three-year history, *Runner's World* noted that to date the events had included 750,000 participants. Marathons have a rate of roughly one death per 100,000 participants.[4]

Tough Mudder, while the largest, is but one of the events appealing to the rougher side. What would seem attractive to only a few has caught fire. (Fire, too, is an element that plays into some obstacle races.) There's also Spartan Race and the Warrior Dash. Competitor Group, owner of the Rock 'n' Roll race series, introduced Muddy Buddy, but ultimately stopped putting them on.

Part of it is primal. There's something supremely satisfying about being dirty, a return-to-childhood simplicity to the experience. Pictures of finishers,

---

[4] Matt McCue, "Witnesses Report Slow Response in Tough Mudder Death," *Runner's World News-wire,* June 6, 2013, www.runnersworld.com/general-interest/witnesses-report-slow-response-in-tough-mudder-death.

especially those on the race organizers' websites, show people covered in mud and smiling like blissed-out fools, often with arms around teammates.

Taken together, several million more people each year participate in obstacle races than marathons. Spartan and Tough Mudder in 2014 were subjects of profiles in *Men's Journal* and *The New Yorker*, respectively. An entire book on the two companies, and their sometimes Coke versus Pepsi–style rivalry, *Off Course,* was written by journalist Erin Beresini and published in 2014. There was something distinctly zeitgeist about the whole pursuit. As participants clamored, so did investors. Spartan was backed by Raptor Consumer Partners, a Boston-based private equity firm.

Tough Mudder and Spartan have different approaches, most notably that Mudders are untimed events while Spartans are competitions. To wit, the *Men's Journal* piece, which noted that comparisons to the better-known Tough Mudder "frosts [Spartan founder Joe] De Sena's kernels," before explaining: "In his opinion, Mudder is a joke, with the race itself designed to appeal only to pasty-white, couch-loving suburbanites in dire need of bragworthy Twitter fodder and not much else."[5] Spartan's De Sena, a former Wall Street trader who started a pool cleaning business as a younger man, left the financial world and moved to Vermont a few years back and eventually started something called the Death Race. The race, which still exists, involves any number of things, including cutting a log and carrying it, running, retrieving a bicycle chain thrown into a pond and putting it on a bike you then have to ride, even eating a substantial number of raw onions. The waiver for the race simply states, "I may die." The race may last 24 hours, or more. De Sena and his team tend to decide while the race is happening.[6]

Spartan is a more approachable version of the Death Race—there's a set course of defined obstacles that are difficult, but conquerable for the hardcore endurance athlete. De Sena has set about to build something of a philosophy around Spartan, including a bestselling book naturally called *Spartan Up.* The company's Twitter feed, with more than 140,000 followers, is active and filled with brusque encouragement to sign up for races and engage in workouts to prepare for them. In 2014, three-quarters of a million racers signed up for 120 events in 17 countries.[7]

De Sena's goals are beyond ambitious. He and his backers firmly believe that obstacle racing (in the vein of Spartan) will one day be an Olympic sport.

---

[5] Eric Hedegaard, "Joe Hardcore: The Spartan Race Founder Tells All," *Men's Journal,* July 2014, www.mensjournal.com/magazine/joe-hardcore-the-spartan-race-founder-tells-all-20140624.
[6] Ibid.
[7] Ibid.

Obstacle courses have hit the mainstream in other ways, including the popular *American Ninja Warrior* television show.

Spartan took a major step forward as a business in January 2013 by signing on Reebok as its global title sponsor (events are now called Reebok Spartan Races, a move akin to the major marathons, which sell naming rights).

The move was seen as an aggressive but necessary move for Reebok, part
of Adidas, as its own fortunes flagged amid heavy competition in its main
shoe business. Like its deal with CrossFit (where it sponsors the annual championships), the Spartan tie-up was part of its push "to change the way people
perceive, experience and define fitness."[8]

As *Bloomberg Businessweek* noted about nine months after the deal was
announced, and Reebok's brand was plastered over every Spartan race around
the world, it was working. The Reebok division's revenue jumped 11 percent
and profit margins widened to a point not reached since its purchase by
Adidas.[9]

Whether the mud and obstacle races have staying power remains an open
question. Key to longevity is a repeat audience. Ted Kennedy, the CEO and
founder of CEO Challenges, gives the edge here to Spartan, largely because
it's a timed race. "The other events are not races," Kennedy says. "You show
up with your buddies, you walk around an obstacle you don't want to do, you
drink beer at the end. With Spartan, you're out to do a better time. That's the
genius of it. It's timed and competitive."

Getting muddy or covered in paint, while the most popular, aren't the
only options. The alternative races helped pave the way for an ever-growing
roster of events, a number of which revel in their absurdity. Some involve
costumes (dressing up like zombies for the Zombie Run) while others go the
other way (the self-explanatory Undies Run).

For the Zombie Run, participants can choose to either be a zombie or
run from them. Those who don't start undead are given health flags, and if
they or their team hold on to just one, they receive a Survivor medal (those
who get nabbed by a zombie are Infected). Another differentiating benefit,
according to the website: "Advanced training for the Zombie Apocalypse."

The Cupid Undies Run is an annual Valentine's Day event held in multiple cities where participants run in their underwear for what the organizers
call a mile-ish. Proceeds from the race, and money raised by participants,

---

[8] Kyle Stock, "Calling on Muddy Spartans to Save Reebok," *Bloomberg Businessweek,* August 9,
2013, www.businessweek.com/articles/2013-08-09/adidas-calls-on-muddy-spartans-to-save-
reebok.

[9] Ibid.

goes to the Children's Tumor Foundation. The organizers collected more than $2.8 million in 2014, and set a $5 million goal for the following year.

All have a common theme: We are gathering at a certain time and place, together, to do something that's physical. It may be difficult, or it may not. But it will be an experience that I can't get sitting behind a desk, or even at a bar, and not in front of a TV or screen.

Snyder's in the primal needs camp, noting that we're looking to satisfy basic desires not met in other aspects of modern life, where the vast majority of us have jobs that don't require us to use our bodies in any meaningful way. And it's fun to post a picture of yourself dressed up as a zombie, or in your underwear, on the Internet.

Among the most difficult things to predict—and an element that has a huge impact on the events' respective business futures—is to what extent the offbeat races draw a repeat crowd. Just how addicted do people get from the physical or emotional feeling of getting dirty, or painted, with friends?

Dean says Tough Mudder finishers returned at a surprisingly high rate— upwards of 50 percent of people return the very next year, versus 8 or 9 percent for a marathon. (He notes that over five years, around 80 percent of people do another marathon, meaning they come back, just not right away.)

To keep his customers happy, Tough Mudder created a permanent obstacle innovation lab in Pennsylvania, where it can try out new and different ways to challenge people. He told the conference audience his team was working on an obstacle involving tear gas (he said, to nervous laughter). Called "Cry Baby," it debuted in 2015.

It seemed to work. Tough Mudder says more than 5,000 people voluntarily have had its logo tattooed on them after completing an event, usually courtesy of an on-site tattoo artist. Taking advantage of that amenity also won you a discount for your next Tough Mudder. Dean notes that a number of people had subsequent Tough Mudder dates added to the original tattoo, a practice that's long been popular with Ironman finishers.

The alternative races and events all seem aware of their own need to innovate, lest they see done to them what they did to the more established activities. The Color Run in 2014 branded its series as the Kaleidoscope Tour, impressing upon new and returning participants how this time was better, cooler, and different. The following year brought the Shine Tour.

The nontraditional space helps push the basic premise of getting out and doing something, usually with other people, deeper into the broader consciousness. With so many options, it became hard to resist. Running's too boring? Try climbing over some stuff and wallowing in some mud. Don't want to compete? We don't even time you or give out prizes. (Unless you really want that, in which case there's another event that will do those things for you.) Want to do something with your elderly parents and kids, maybe at the same time? Bring them along.

Just make sure it's all on your Facebook page and Twitter feed.

Three months after he presided over the 2014 Paris Color Run, Snyder was in Minneapolis. The Major League Baseball All-Star Weekend features a 5-K run as part of the festivities—another way to engage the fans who show up to what's become a four-day festival around the mid-season showcase of the game's top players.

Ahead of the 2014 version, baseball executives were mulling what they might do differently. It turned out The Color Run was on the schedule for a nearby weekend. An initial feeling-out conversation early in the year led to more serious discussions, and eventually a deal was struck to stage The Color Run as part of the festivities, winning billing alongside mainstays like the Home Run Derby.

And so Snyder watched as various professional baseball mascots, along with giant inflated baseballs, careened through the 5 kilometers. Two days later, highlights of the run showed on the Jumbotron during the game itself.

The moment felt significant to Snyder, a lifelong baseball fan who's steeped his three young sons in the Great American Pastime, collecting baseball cards with them and cheering on the Anaheim Angels, their local team. Here was his concept, sharing a big stage of sorts. "It's a healthy reminder that baseball is, at its heart, a fun, 'boys of summer'–type of sport," he says. "And there's Color Run, a funky thing that turns it all on its head."

The Color Run reprised its role at the 2015 All-Star Weekend in Cincinnati. In Paris, the 2015 version drew 23,000 runners (more than 50 percent more than the debut). Snyder sent me pictures of himself on stage revving up the crowd, the Eiffel Tower in view.

While The Color Run won't overtake baseball anytime soon, it's clear Snyder is onto something that resonates in the same way in the category of good, clean fun, for anyone who's interested.

Two million people probably aren't wrong.

CHAPTER 13

The Guts

Rick Stollmeyer wasn't looking to get into the fitness business. Personal fitness is a holdover from training at the U.S. Naval Academy, where he studied to become an engineer on a nuclear submarine. He's an in-shape guy.

Stollmeyer hails from a family of small-business owners and even as he proceeded through a typical post-Navy life, working for a military contractor in San Luis Obispo, California on satellite technology, he was nursing that latent entrepreneurial streak.

Unsatisfied with the track he was on, he began seriously noodling business ideas with a high school friend named Blake Beltram. A programmer, Beltram wrote software that helped Pilates pioneer Mari Winsor manage her studio in Los Angeles. The year was 2000. The high school buddies saw a market well beyond Pilates.

It started as HardBody Software and the market was growing—boutique fitness studios were relying on any number of inefficient ways to run their surprisingly complex operations. Some were running their schedules and payments through personal computers. Others, like Barry and his eponymous bootcamp, used a cumbersome system of index cards to keep track of their members. Most were somewhere in between.

Stollmeyer jumped in. "What I fell in love with was that this was grassroots entrepreneurialism, people following their passion and leaving their corporate jobs," he says. "I come from a small business background. That really resonated with me. We could level the playing field, help them compete with the big boxes."

The pair also saw the megatrend of health and fitness, with multiple generations moving toward wellness in general, and to studios where they could get in shape together. Seeing how consumers, especially Millennials, were thinking about fitness much more holistically, and with an eye toward the mind as well as the body, they dropped the word "hard" and added "mind" in the company's name.

"One of our theories is that technology allows us to be more and more separate, there's a commensurate hunger to have that face-to-face connection," Stollmeyer says.

The hunger is fierce, based on his company's own numbers. Revenue grew at least 50 percent year over year for the seven years ended in 2013, with 2009 standing as the only exception. That year, the depth of the Great Recession, Stollmeyer says "we took our foot off the gas," not knowing how a bleak economy would play through their customers' numbers. In 2014, revenue jumped 43 percent, to $70 million.

The recession was a hardly a blip and, in fact, ended up helping his business. First, the ultimate consumers—customers of Stollmeyers' customers—didn't stop showing up, even as many suffered economically. Second, the small businesses—as Stollmeyer had seen with his own family—figured out a way to stay open because failure wasn't an option.

"These people are committed," he says. "They cashed in 401(k)'s, cut staff, and worked seven days a week. This is my mom and dad running their lighting fixture store. We had that understanding of their mindset."

Armed with that information, Stollmeyer continued to seek outside money to grow the business. In the depth of the recession, talks with the New York-based investment firm Catalyst got serious. What they saw was that once-reluctant, would-be customers listened harder to pitches that could save them money. "People had been comfortable with their clunky systems," he says. "There was now an urgency."

Catalyst put in $5.6 million in 2009 and MindBody continued to grow. Three years later, the company raised an additional $35 million from existing investors and blue-chip firms led by Institutional Venture Partners, a decades-old venture capital and private equity firm with more than $4 billion in assets under management.

Getting the money on board, initially, and even in the later rounds, was largely about convincing backers about the breadth of the opportunity. Stollmeyer preached a story that extended well beyond the neighborhood yoga studio, pointing to the industry statistics, as well as the demographics of the end customers.

Stollmeyer echoes the sentiment that those customers tend to be upper middle income and female. The Baby Boomers are on the front edge, with the time and the money to take care of themselves. They gave birth to the

Millennials, "the most affluent generation ever born," and a group willing to spend money on themselves, he says.

Then there's the need for loads of technology that Millennials—and all of us—take for granted. It starts with scheduling. Because most studios are classes that begin and end at certain times, and not just a series of machines that can be used ad hoc, rosters have to be managed. You have to keep in touch with those students, who may number in the hundreds, or thousands. And they have to be able to pay you, online and in person.

There are the instructors, who themselves have to be scheduled and paid. Those deals vary by studio, and sometimes by instructor within a certain studio, with guaranteed pay per class and then more on a per-head basis.

And most studios are selling merchandise, from water to smoothies to branded T-shirts so there's a point-of-sale component. "You add all that up, it's a beast of a product," he says.

Stollmeyer says he's not worried about certain exercises falling in and out of favor with a fickle product, in part because he's already seen smaller studios pivot to new classes to meet demand. His nephew Darik runs his own boutique in San Luis Obispo called Rev SLO and has broadened to include spin, yoga, and Zumba based on local demand.

And they're not just sticky in terms of staying around—they're numerous. By mid-2014, MindBody had 38,000 customers and no one customer accounted for more than 0.5 percent of the company's revenue, Stollmeyer says.

Now, MindBody is one of those companies that almost anyone who's signed up for a fitness class has encountered, even unwittingly. The purveyors of that fitness are highly aware of MindBody's existence—it's one of the things you sort of have to do in order to not drive yourself crazy doing your own books. Lillian So says it was something of a sign of growing up, even though she initially balked at laying out the monthly cost to be on the platform.

Any lasting economy requires a certain amount of infrastructure, and that's the role that companies like MindBody play in the fitness ecosystem. These also are the sorts of companies that investors seek out in a rapidly expanding market, even as the sexier, consumer-facing companies draw headlines and eye-popping valuations.

The power lies, in part, in how entrenched and necessary such a company can become, especially if it's a leader in its given market, as MindBody is. And given how much time most studio operators want to spend worrying about technology (not much), if MindBody can get in and keep their customers—and their customers' customers—happy, it's likely to have loyal clients.

Other companies have sought to connect consumers with their activities, including Active Networks, whose Active.com online sign-up service is familiar to most people who've signed up for a race on the Internet.

While MindBody and Active improve efficiency and convenience for both businesses and consumers, their impact pales in comparison to that of applications, websites, and platforms that are user-driven.

The dawn, and explosion, of social networks—fueled by the visceral power of still images and video—is among the most powerful influences on the rise in participation sports. It is impossible to imagine many of the companies described in this book thriving, maybe even existing, without the direct or indirect help of social networks. Facebook, Twitter, and Instagram especially allow us to brag, compete, and advertise instantaneously and cheaply, to breathtaking effect.

Today's social media feeds are riddled with references to fitness. Every day, people tweet and retweet, post and Like, and Favorite descriptions and pictures of their workouts and races. Especially committed athletes send out agonizingly long recaps of their races, training and triumph screeds that read like manifestos.

Twitter and Facebook are rife with posts of encouragement, support, and good old-fashioned bragging about exploits in various races, or even just workouts. Friends celebrate and rib each other, one-upping on times or accomplishments. Social networking helped popularize the humblebrag, a long-practiced method of letting people know that you did something interesting or difficult, couched in seemingly low-key or self-deprecating tones. Example (fictional) tweet: "Bad girlfriend for falling asleep at 9 pm. Must've been the 20-miler this morning. #NYCmarathon."

All corners of the sports world have leveraged social media. Nearly every brand has its own Facebook page and Twitter handle, and many have someone (or several someones) whose job it is to populate and update those sites. They follow and tag interesting and influential athletes or participants, Favoriting mentions of the brand or race. Every race of any stature has a hashtag on race day, and encourages participants and fans alike to tweet about their experience.

Social media have a democratizing effect. The presence of athletes on social media only draws them closer to everyday participants, and a win—or even just a finish by Meb Keflezighi or Kara Goucher—elicits hundreds, or thousands, or tens of thousands of social media mentions. Each of them has more than 80,000 followers on Twitter.

Like authors, journalists, and performers, many athletes use social media to cultivate their fan base. That draws them to appearances before races and makes them that much more attractive to sponsors. A social media-savvy athlete brings a built-in audience that's immediately available to market to.

Social media help amplify, sometimes to a painful extent for our friends and families, the narcissism embedded in the pursuit of these sports. Our modern need to over-communicate takes flight in these forums. The beauty and horror of Twitter and Facebook (and Instagram, and Pinterest, and sites not created in time for this book's publication) is that they are unfiltered and ready to be exploited for our own selfish gain. There is nothing stopping any of us from posting all the time about our latest run, ride, swim, or workout.

A positive aspect is the motivation provided by seeing a virtual stream of friends or colleagues note their achievements. Companies are increasingly using social media to motivate their employees to participate. Technology allows for open competition that otherwise might not happen, or be very difficult to initiate and track. *Prevention Magazine* cited a firm called ShapeUp, which found that employees at companies that used social media to run their wellness programs saw at least double the participation rates of a walking program and upwards of four times that of a traditional weight-loss effort.[1]

For runners, cyclists, and other everyday athletes, social media is a way to connect with like-minded individuals, to crowdsource a good workout—through applications like MapMyRun—or read a review of a new pair of shoes on sites like *SlowTwitch* or message boards created by *Runner's World* and other specialty magazines. Tweeting and Facebooking puts us in a conversation.

So even as technology is a great enabler of our athletic pursuits, it's also pushing us in a different way, toward an active life that is more social, where we can actually have real, meaningful, physical human contact.

Running and cycling began as distinctly individual activities, very much apart from the teams many of us grow up on. As kids, we are socialized by our Little League or soccer team. They are a key to learning how to get along with others, how to take direction, how to be gracious in both victory and defeat. And there is something special about being a teammate.

To that end, our reliance on, and obsession with, technology may have an unintended, and happy consequence—at least for those of who believe that exercising makes us happier and healthier people.

---

[1] Laurie Tarkan,. "How Social Media Can Motivate You to Exercise and Work Out," FoxNews. com *via Prevention.com*, March 2012, www.prevention.com/fitness/fitness-tips/how-social-media-can-motivate-you-exercise-and-work-out.

As we became more attached to our devices, it was probably only a matter of time before they became totally attached to us. With the size and cost of electronics shrinking, owing to advances in processing and memory, *wearables* became a word thrown around by executives and investors alike.

The annual gathering once known as the Consumer Electronics Show, and now known simply as CES, is a geek's paradise. Held every winter in Las Vegas, it's a chance for the electronics industry to sniff each other out, and for the rest of us to get a peek at what's next. Its scope usually allows for a bevy of predictions around what the big tech companies and their scrappier start-up counterparts are betting consumers will buy in the coming year or two.

The 2014 version was all about wearables, with a fitness and wellness bent. As online tech bible *CNet* wrote as the show came to a close, "Like 'the cloud' a few years ago, 'wearable tech' was an unavoidable catchphrase, a show floor fever dream, a vague future strategy that nearly every company seemed to toss into their press conference."[2]

The wearable craze in fitness initially blossomed around the ability to make a relatively simple pedometer sexy. Once attractive only to mall-walking retirees looking to satisfy their doctor's request to be more active, person-based activity trackers became a tool for the fitness-obsessed.

And the early versions weren't much more than step-counters. Initial products from Nike, as well as upstarts Fitbit and Jawbone, relied mostly on answering that simple question ("How many steps did I take today?") to get people hooked on their respective wristbands.

Nike was the first band I began to see as useful in any meaningful way. I was startled in early 2013 to see two private equity investors—one London-based, one from New York—sporting their Nike FuelBands during a meeting in Doha. One of them, a guy in his late fifties, bragged that he was a top performer in his gender and age cohort, according to the Nike-compiled statistics.

The FuelBand, in addition to counting steps and stairs climbed, came with its own proprietary measure—"fuel"—that factored in the user's activity to come up with a proscribed number of points per day. Achieving that goal led the band to light up with congratulations.

The ability to feed one's data into a larger set underscores the social exercise theory. Friendly (and sometimes not-so-friendly) competition is a powerful motivator. Strava stands as the most popular in that regard, allowing its users to win what it calls segments. As the (U.K.) *Telegraph* put it in a piece with tips to help Strava users get a leg up on each other, "Strava has forever

[2] Scott Stein,. "Wearable Tech at CES: Many, Many Small Steps," CNet, January 9, 2014, www.cnet.com/news/wearable-tech-at-ces-2014-many-many-small-steps/.

changed cycling, for better or worse . . .Now even a short trip to the super-market has an element of competition."[3]

Offloading some of the motivating pressure from one's self is a powerful tool. Fitbit and others (including Under Armour's Record app, which pulls data from any number of devices, including its own wearables, as well as Fit-bit's) allow users to go head to head, to join up with a group of friends and compete on steps taken or floors climbed.

Competition is a funny thing. The elements have to be just right to moti-vate us to perform better. In their book *Top Dog*, Po Bronson and Ashley Merryman write about studies related to selecting just the right cohort to boost performance. A small group (as is often the case with the curated fitness gangs) can be powerful. They write: "When there are only a few people in the race, we put our foot on the gas, working harder and harder to outpace our competitors. And the competition becomes very personal, a referendum on our own ability." Putting too many people in the mix is dispiriting. "Once the crowd is large enough that we don't feel the element of personal competition, the result doesn't feel like a personal statement of our worth, so we don't try as hard."[4]

By 2014, it was clear that private equity dealmakers and venture capital-ists weren't just slapping the bracelets on their wrists, but also writing huge checks to fund the wearable fitness market. Fitbit in August 2013 raised $43 million in a single round of funding, drawing new money from SAP Ven-tures, Qualcomm Ventures and existing investors led by Softbank Ventures.[5]

Fitbit was only one of the wearable fitness companies drawing attention from the moneyed set. Jawbone, an electronics company selling speakers and headsets as well as the Up and Up 24 fitness bracelets, raised $100 million in equity and debt a month after the Fitbit round was announced.[6]

By May 2014, Jawbone's ambitions, and coffers, were even bigger. It was in the midst of raising somewhere between $250 million and $300 million, according to published reports. One of those quoted CEO Hosain Rahman validating the broader wearables thesis, namely that it was about collect-ing lots and lots of data: "Tomorrow is all about more information, more

---

[3] Matthew Sparkes, "Top 10 Strava Tips And Tricks," *The Telegraph*, www.telegraph.co.uk/men/active/recreational-cycling/10170185/Top-10-Strava-tips-and-tricks.html.

[4] Po Bronson and Ashley Merryman, *Top Dog: The Science of Winning and Losing* (New York: Grand Central Publishing, 2014), 35.

[5] Dan Primack, "Fitbit Raises $43 Million in New Funding," Fortune.com, August 13, 2013, http://finance.fortune.cnn.com/2013/08/13/fitbit-raises-43-million-in-new-funding/.

[6] Dan Primack, "Exclusive: Jawbone Raises More than $100 Million," Fortune.com, Septem-ber 12, 2013, http://finance.fortune.cnn.com/2013/09/12/jawbone-100-million/.

signals, more understanding of yourself, but then taking all of that and really crunching it," he said. "Taking all that data, contextualizing it for the use and turning it that into understanding which leads to data [is the goal]."[7]

While his logic appears circular at first (Go get some data, do stuff with it, and then turn it into more data), it gets right to the heart of why companies and investors piled so heavily into the business of tracking fitness. All of us seem quite willing to share an excruciating amount of detail about our lives. Some of it, on its face, seems absurdly useless (see: the vast majority of Facebook posts, especially those involving descriptions and pictures of food consumed at restaurants). And yet even that nonsense has some use, when put together with lots of similar data. (Our posts tell would-be advertisers things we may not even realize about ourselves and our habits).

It's even easier to see why data about our health and bodies and habits would be that much more useful. Most of us are generally fiercely protective of our medical records; strong state and federal laws prevent the sharing and dissemination of our health history, lest we be discriminated against for a new job or made to pay more for health insurance.

There is a dark side to all of this, raised eloquently by the activist magazine *Mother Jones* in a January 2014 article. The piece reviews the privacy policies, which they deem insufficient to really protect the user who is voluntarily (and happily) entering in data such as blood pressure and glucose levels. The article quotes the executive director of the Center for Digital Democracy: "When companies promise that they aren't selling your data, that's because they haven't developed a business model to do so yet."[8]

The ability to measure appeals to a certain type of professional person who is used to taking stock (sometimes literally) in their everyday lives. In the information economy, the person with the most robust spreadsheet is king. So why not apply the same metric-driven rigor to one's personal life? (I'm reminded of a senior private equity executive I interviewed, who voluntarily used all the performance metrics applied to companies his firm acquired to himself, measuring his productivity at work and at home.)

Data gathering plays to our own modern self-involvement, too. The satirist David Sedaris, who has long eschewed exercise, wrote in *The New Yorker* about falling into the throes of obsession with his Fitbit. "At the end of my

---

[7] Leena Rao, "Jawbone's Newest Investor is Rizvi Traverse," Techcrunch.com, http://techcrunch.com/2014/05/09/jawbones-newest-investor-is-rizvi-traverse/.

[8] Dana Liebelson, "Are Fitbit, Nike, and Garmin Planning to Sell Your Personal Fitness Data?," MotherJones.com, January 31, 2014, www.motherjones.com/politics/2014/01/are-fitbit-nike-and-garmin-selling-your-personal-fitness-data.

first sixty-thousand-step day, I staggered home with my flashlight knowing that I'd advance to sixty-five thousand, and that there will be no end to it until my feet snap off at the ankles. Then it'll just be my jagged bones stabbing into the soft ground. Why is it some people can manage a thing like a Fitbit, while others go off the rails and allow it to rule, and perhaps even ruin, their lives?"[9]

Falconhead's David Moross says that while many wearable users get excited, even addicted, only to drop the device within weeks or months, the broader movement stands, especially for the more serious among the every-day athletes increasingly accustomed to information close at hand, all the time. "Being able to go back to your computer after a workout and see things instantly is the future, it's where it's going," he says. "Everyone wants instant data to help performance."

My own experiments with the fitness bracelets stoked something of an attachment. I first bought a Fitbit Force, which I found mildly useful. It tracked my steps and gave me a general idea of the distance covered (general in the sense that it usually varied, sometimes substantially, from my Garmin running watch, which uses GPS.)

The breakthrough for me, oddly, was the silent alarm on both the Fitbit, and later, the Jawbone Up. Through the app, I was able to set the bracelet to gently buzz me awake in the morning. I'm among those who wake up before most of humanity to exercise, so the ability to set an alarm that didn't wake up my wife with a loud alarm was a huge boon. I honestly would pay the $100+ price tag for this feature alone.

In early 2014, the Fitbit Force was recalled. The company cited a number of wrist rashes apparently caused by wearing the Force and offered full refunds, including shipping, no questions asked. I didn't have a rash, but sent it back anyway, mainly to try a different wearable.

The Jawbone Up is funnier looking and lacks the digital display of the Fitbit, which was a bummer. I'm not a big jewelry guy, and the Jawbone from a distance appears to be a somewhat bulky bracelet with no function. But, the app is sleek and I concede to easily falling into its sway; I liked looking at the various charts of my activity and sleep.

After going through a couple of Jawbones (both companies are good about replacing them, quickly and free, when something breaks) I went back to the Fitbit, mainly because the model I prefer has a screen that shows the time when I flick my wrist in a certain way or press the button on the side. But mostly, I'm in it for the numbers.

---

[9] David Sedaris, "Stepping Out," *The New Yorker,* June 30, 2014, www.newyorker.com/magazine/2014/06/30/stepping-out-3.

The data are useful in aggregate and to look at patterns. Some of them are obvious—I, like most modern American working parents, don't get enough sleep. I also remain surprised at how much effort it takes to hit certain step goals. The U.S. government, through the Centers for Disease Control, recommends that people partake in moderate exercise for at least 150 minutes a week, as well as "muscle-strengthening activities" two days a week. For reasons of history, ease, and simple numbers, 10,000 steps has caught on as a standard measure of daily good health. By virtue of that, Fitbit and Jawbone set that as their step goal defaults. That many steps is the equivalent of almost five miles of walking and I have a hard time imagining how most Americans—especially those outside of urban centers with desk jobs at offices they drive to—come anywhere close to that. Ditto the 150 minutes, and certainly the muscle activities.

That's largely based on extrapolating from my personal experience. Given my penchant for running almost daily—which is good for 8,000 or so steps alone—I set my Fitbit and Jawbone goals at 15,000 (in part to prove, if to no one else other than me, that I'm above average) and check it most days. On days when I hit the 15,000, it buzzes happily and flashes, and sends me a notification on my phone. I confess to feeling a small flush of satisfaction when this happens.

But that goal takes a certain amount of work. I'm fortunate to have a step-heavy commute, living and working within walking distance of the commuter train stations at either end. I prefer to walk whenever I can, and certainly feel somewhat compelled to do so, in order to get my steps in. But on those days when I don't run in the morning and drop any walking segments of my commute, I fall well short of not just my own 15,000-step goal, but even the 10,000 government-prescribed steps. When I think back to my days in Atlanta, where I drove to and from the office, I realized there was no way I'd get halfway to the goal without extraordinary effort. If 10,000 steps is really what we need, many, many people are failing that test.

There's also the question of using steps as the main measure. During a lively fitness challenge at Bloomberg one summer, we used the Under Armour Record app to compare and compete, logging workouts manually and steps automatically through our devices. Not surprisingly, the runners reigned supreme in any version of the contest based on steps. I liked that, but understood my colleagues' dismay. My swim workouts, which were as intense and seemingly worthwhile as my runs, didn't contribute to my step count and couldn't be measured in any meaningful way (my Fitbit isn't waterproof, nor are any of the basic wearable models, though that element was promised in later versions).

So the incomplete or insufficient data simply leaves at least some of us wanting more, better, and more comprehensive information that we can, at least theoretically, leverage into higher performance.

Runners and cyclists are especially susceptible to the data trap, poring over a recent run or ride, picking apart power exerted, heart rates, and per-mile pace to judge the quality of the workout. Entire books have been written by running coaches featuring formulae to make a mathematician blush. Among the volumes on my shelf is *Daniels' Running Formula* (second edition) by Jack Daniels, PhD, who *Runner's World* magazine (as noted on the cover of the book) dubbed the World's Best Running Coach.

Daniels' major contribution is the use of VDOT, a measure of exertion that a subset of serious runners and their coaches use to build their training plans. The VDOT phenomenon illustrates the absurdity as well as the utility of the personal deep data dive. In-depth training plans, especially those that use lots of math, are wildly appealing to the category of amateur athletes who dissect companies or securities for a living. *Wait, there's a way that I can use a spreadsheet in my personal life to slice and dice each and every workout, track my progress, and achieve a goal? Yes, please.*

(The obsessive runners' relationship to technology and tracking is nothing compared to cyclists, who can spend hours and thousands of dollars, sometimes tens of thousands, on gadgets that track their speed and effort).

What was clear at CES in 2014 (and 2015, and 2016) was that wearables and personal measurement were appealing beyond just the crazies. While Fitbit and Jawbone—along with the Nike FuelBand product—had pioneered the industry, the show demonstrated that the world's biggest consumer electronics companies were putting real research and money into the trend.

Samsung, the Korean mobile phone giant, showed off a wrist-based device called the Gear Fit, a band that promised to play well with Samsung's ever-growing line of smartphones. Another mobile phone behemoth, LG, talked about a similar product.

And then there was Apple, which had hinted repeatedly at a smartwatch that many expected would be the proverbial category killer, keying off the company's historical design savvy and the undeniable popularity of the iPod and iPhone. The Apple Watch debuted in 2015.

Apple's interest, along with Samsung and the other big electronics makers, signaled the tipping point for the wearables movement.

Calling a winner in 2016 is hard to do in this space, though there's consensus that the Apple Watch was not the Fitbit and Jawbone killer that many, including some inside those companies, feared it would be. At least not yet. Apple Watch sales during its debut year were lower than expected, and there wasn't the expected uptake from the fitness community, even for the Apple model aimed squarely at that set. Among the major missing elements, amid the hundreds of apps, was a reliable GPS tracking method—critical to convincing runners to ditch their Garmin.

And so the temporary winner was Fitbit, which survived the Apple storm and proceeded with its initial public offering on the New York Stock Exchange. Investors valued the company at $4 billion in a transaction that raised $732 million for the company and some of its investors. The stock doubled in its first three months of trading and even after some late-year turbulence, was trading at a market capitalization of more than $6 billion at the end of 2015. The market's appetite for the stock was hearty. During the week of the IPO, Fitbit raised the price range and expanded the size of the offering, and a day after that, said it sold more stock than it expected. That boosted the total by $254 million beyond what the company had previously set out to collect.

The IPO of Fitbit was notable for its segment of the economy of mind and body, and taken in the larger context of three other offerings—MindBody, Planet Fitness, and SoulCycle—an indication that something substantial is indeed going on.

MindBody debuted in the summer of 2015, just ahead of several months of broader market volatility. The stock jumped around amid that market commotion, and settled in by the end of the year around its $14 IPO price. Planet Fitness followed in August, debuting at $16 a share, where it hovered during its first few months of being a public company. SoulCycle was expected to begin trading in 2016.

While private equity investment signals something meaningful for a group of companies, so too does a slate of initial public offerings, especially if they lead to well-performing, sustainable public companies. At the risk of oversimplifying the matter, that signals maturity, or at least a road to it.

That's for several reasons. First, it encourages more early investment by venture capital and private equity firms because they see a path to making profits for themselves and for their investors. With the aforementioned stocks trading above their IPO prices, some well above, early investors were headed for healthy gains.

Second, if they are the previously mentioned well-performing, sustainable companies that signals something about the overall market for their goods and services. A company's stock price is, at its core, a reflection of its investors' view of its future earnings potential. That's why one of the most tried and true ways of valuing a stock is its so-called P/E multiple, the ratio of its stock price per share to its future earnings per share.

And finally, this lifecycle for companies—from idea to investment to profits and going public and becoming its own form of investor and acquirer—begets the sort of ecosystem described at the beginning of this book. The Aarti Kapoors, Brian Smiths, and Brian Woods find they are jockeying for deals amid a much larger set of competitors, as the potential pie for profits, and associated fees, gets ever larger.

There's always the potential for a bust, as shown by the history of market manias runs from tulips centuries ago to, more recently, dot-coms. Here, the fundamentals seem more likely to create a long-term upward trend.

The body is only going to be a bigger business.

CONCLUSION

Early in fall 2015, the ads started showing up in the corridors and cars of the New York City subway, on bus shelters, and via YouTube: "Host a Runner: Meet the World."

The ads were for Airbnb, reprising its role as the official community hospitality sponsor of the New York marathon, now formally known as the TCS New York City Marathon. Here, in one ad, was running, community, technology, and money, colliding once again, right in front of me.

Since signing on officially—Airbnb hosts were housing runners for several years before that, this just made it more formal—the company and all that it represents has only become more influential. Airbnb epitomized what the pundits in Silicon Valley called unicorns—private tech companies with valuations exceeding a billion dollars. Airbnb, by mid-2015, was worth a reported $25 billion.

Airbnb deepened its relationship with the marathon in 2015, signing up to sponsor—some might say, naturally—the Brooklyn Half Marathon. While based in San Francisco, Millennial-saturated Brooklyn is the company's spiritual home on the East Coast.

Airbnb is a major player in the so-called sharing economy that marries technology to community in its own right. While not a part of the fitness economy, its presence as a significant marathon sponsor underscores how deeply these activities are entrenched in modern life. The overlap in customers is clear—the Airbnb crowd is young, active, tech-savvy, and relatively affluent.

Once I started looking for evidence of the new economy of mind and body, it was everywhere. New events, ads on trains and in magazines, plotlines in TV shows and movies; Twitter and Facebook feeds filled with humblebrags and pictures.

The challenge of this book wasn't getting people to talk. It was getting them to shut up. Everyone, it seems, has a story of a race, or a workout, or sometimes a frustration with a partner or spouse who became obsessed with their own fitness to the detriment of relationships with friends and family. It often took little, if any, prompting to get people going.

And they are evangelists preaching with the fervor of the converted. Technology, especially in the form of social media, is a megaphone to spread the gospel and validate their fellow congregants with positive reinforcement splashed across the Internet.

Their persistent enthusiasm, married to consumption of a wide range of goods and services dedicated to fitness, is ultimately what will sustain this new economy. The challenge for the entrepreneurs and investors is figuring out, in one venture capitalist's phrasing, what's a cheeseburger and what's a cupcake.

It's a funny metaphor, especially when talking about the obsession around fit minds and bodies. Alan Taetle's an old friend of mine and the dean of the venture capital community in Atlanta. When he's not investing in tech start-ups, he's an avid fitness guy and, like many, can't help but see those activities through his investing lens.

He leaves me a voicemail at one point laying out the theory, in short. A good burger joint, he says, is forever. Despite fad diets and the whims of the consumer, a great cheeseburger will always inspire loyalty. Cupcakes, on the other hand, were the essence of fad. Spurred by the likes of Magnolia Bakery (and thanks to that New York shop's cameo on *Sex and the City*), cupcakes were a veritable craze that spawned shops seemingly on every block in major cities. And then many of them closed.

In Taetle's assessment, running and yoga are solid cheeseburgers—proven activities experiencing steady, long-term growth. But boutique fitness is a landscape littered with cupcakes, with new entrants arriving practically every month and grabbing the attention of the ever-experimenting Millennial crowd. That's all making it more complicated for the operators looking to expand wisely, and for investors aiming to grab a share of the sweat-driven profits.

In these relatively early days of this new economy, Moelis's Aarti Kapoor says she looks at a number of overlapping elements to assess a company's chances. Being able to distinguish a concept in an increasingly crowded marketplace and to transfer that concept to other markets is critical.

Data is critical to the whole endeavor and the technology to collect and analyze information about users is the Holy Grail for companies in the fitness business and beyond. Happily, consumers seem quite willing to hand over a lot of information about their health and wellness, as well as personal information about where they live and what they earn. All of that's extraordinarily valuable.

All the data make it that much easier to track the members activity (or inactivity), to understand when and how often they show up, which instructors are the most popular, and, in the case of multi-activity gyms, what folks actually use.

"An investor's dream is having a profitable, replicable, and transferable prototype developed," Kapoor says. Brand loyalty, while important, only goes so far. Finally, investors want to see a plan to scale the business, and proof that it works, especially in a variety of scenarios.

Frank Sinatra's axiom notwithstanding, making it in New York or Los Angeles doesn't mean a fitness concept will work anywhere. "The best margins you'll ever get are in New York City," Kapoor says. "You can charge high prices and get high volumes," owing to the concentration of money and fitness fanatics. Finally, there's talent. Balancing the power of personality and the ability to broaden the reach beyond that person's class or product is critical.

Kapoor and her banking compatriots, perhaps in their enlightened self-interest, see an overcrowded market ripe for consolidation. What that will look like is unclear. The larger gym businesses may look to bolt on boutiques as Equinox did with SoulCycle and Pure Yoga, but there aren't a lot of Equinoxes out there, especially with its combination of reach, brand, and real estate.

Raj Kapoor, having gone through a consolidation of his own, sees a future of bigger companies, as well as lots of small businesses. "The industry went from Walmart (e.g., big box gyms) to corner stores (e.g., boutique studios)," he says. "Are we going back to Walmart, with everyone consolidating under major national brands like Orangetheory, SoulCycle, and Barry's? I don't think so. Small businesses with passionate owners that deliver differentiated fitness experiences will continue to flourish."

While the debate over cheeseburgers and cupcakes will persist, the overall trend toward wellness—and fitness as a means of achieving it—is solid. The megatrend is intact. It's hard to imagine a scenario in which we collectively decide that smoking cigarettes and being morbidly obese is awesome after all. For a growing segment of the population, fitness has become a defining lifestyle element, a measure of who we are, not just something we do. It's accelerated over the generations, with Millennials pursuing a fitness-driven lifestyle passionately.

"Past generations viewed fitness as a means to an end," says Equinox CEO Harvey Spevak. "It was just about sustaining life. For Millennials, it's more culturally social and about community. They are fitness-focused, making it a fundamental priority, not an option. It's about eating right and staying active for long-term happiness."

Technology enables constant sharing and monitoring, of ourselves and each other. And the need to occasionally escape that deluge sends us to studios and running trails to reconnect with ourselves.

That's good news for the growing list of bankers, venture capitalists, and private equity managers, and the capital-hungry entrepreneurs with big ideas. Rick Stollmeyer at Mind Body, Harvey Spevak at Equinox, and Barry Jay at his namesake boutique all have to figure out how to defend their turf. Chip Wilson is working to find his next, post-Lulu angle. The boom's a boon for Mary Wittenberg, who's got a billionaire's platform to build a new fitness empire. And Robert Wolfe, who can use all this to help people think about diverting some time and money to worthwhile causes.

The work of those true believers, and their ilk, is everywhere. On a quick morning run through the London neighborhoods of Islington and Shoreditch during a work trip, I encountered two yoga studios, two fitness chains, and a bike and running shop, all within a mile of each other. I nodded to several fellow runners and was nearly run over by three separate giant packs of commuting cyclists (that was on me—I looked the wrong way like a typical American).

Back in the United States, I dropped in to see Rick Higgins at the expo for the New York City Marathon. Since I ran the marathon six years earlier, the field and the associated festivities had grown, necessitating a move into a convention hall several times larger than before. Skechers Performance had taken a big space in the middle of the floor, in part to tout its new partnership with the L.A. marathon. Higgins showed me the line of apparel they designed especially for New York, a sleek black-and-white series, a version that Meb wore in the race.

Since I wasn't running, I resisted the temptation to buy anything, more out of superstition than lack of desire for new running gear. But I saw my tribe, filing into the Javits Center with the haunted, hungry look of racers on the eve of their moment, eager to shell out whatever cash was necessary to remind themselves, and anyone who saw them, that they were among the self-chosen fit.

About the Author

Jason Kelly is the New York Bureau Chief for Bloomberg and the author of *The New Tycoons: Inside the Trillion Dollar Private Equity Industry That Owns Everything,* the product of five years leading Bloomberg's global private equity coverage. During a tenure at Bloomberg spanning more than a dozen years, he's written about everything from the global semiconductor industry to economic development during the war in Afghanistan, as well as managing the company's global conference business. He's a contributor to Bloomberg TV and *Markets* magazine, as well as a frequent speaker and host of conferences around the world. Prior to joining Bloomberg, he was the editor-in-chief of *digitalsouth* magazine, a publication covering technology and venture capital in the southeastern United States. He began his journalism career working for *The Atlanta Journal-Constitution* and *The Atlanta Business Chronicle.* Jason has completed more than a dozen marathons, including races in New York, Boston, and Chicago. A graduate of Georgetown University, he lives in Sleepy Hollow, New York, with his wife, Jennifer, and sons.

Index

Abdul-Jabbar, Kareem, 88
Abercrombie & Fitch, 65
Active.com, 170, 186
Activity-specific food and drink, 73–74
Adidas, 133, 137, 138, 180
Advent International, 62–63, 64
Affluence, and food/drink, 72
AIDS Ride, 97
AIG, 113
Airbnb, 46, 133, 197
Albrecht, Henry, 116–117
Alexander, Craig, 113
All Screens Media, 56–57
All-Star Game, 128
All-Star Weekend, 182
Al Maktoum, Mohammed bin Rashid, 154
Almond milk, 71
ALS Association, 108
Alternative races. *See also* Color Run, The
  defined, 170
  Ragnars, 174
  repeat participants, 181
  Spartan Race, 114, 178, 179–180
  Tough Mudder, 140, 171, 176–178,
    179, 181
  Undies Run, 170, 180–181
  Zombie Run, 180
American Cancer Society, 100
American Foundation for Suicide Preven-
  tion, 100
American History X (film), 93, 94
American Journal of Clinical Nutrition, 72
& Go, 65
Andrade, Billy, 163
Aniston, Jennifer, 84

Anytime Fitness, 17–18
Apparel. *See also* Shoes; *specific companies*
  Bloom, 69
  Lululemon, 61–65, 68–69, 70
  private equity and, 62–63
  sport-specific, 66–67
  triathlon, 66–67
  yoga, 69
Appearance fees for elite athletes, 152
Apple Watch, 193–194
Armstrong, Lance, 104–105, 134
Asics, 133, 155, 166
Athleisure, 61, 69–70
Athleta, 68–69
Athletes:
  appearance fees for elite, 152
  as yoga participants, 87, 88–89
Athletic clothing. *See also* Shoes; *specific*
  companies
  Bloom, 69
  Lululemon, 61–65, 68–69, 70
  private equity and, 62–63
  sport-specific, 66–67
  triathlon, 66–67
  yoga, 69
Atlanta, 134, 144

BAA (Boston Athletic Association), 135, 137.
  See also Boston Marathon
Baby Boomers:
  about, xvi
  demographics, 184
  meaning, looking for, 81–82
Back on My Feet, 174
Bain, Ellen, 88–89

Bally, 14
Banana Republic, 65
Banks, 1, 2–11. *See also specific banks*
Bardoel, Anne, 122
Barn-raising aspect of races, 143–144
Barry's Bootcamp:
    as brand, 36–37, 41
    celebrities and, 30, 32, 95
    challenges, future, 200
    classes, 35–36
    costs, 36
    décor, 29
    food and drink, 29–30
    instructors, 36
    name, 30–31
    North Castle and, 11, 41
    operations, 197
    workouts, 29, 31–33
Baseball, 182
Be a Color Runner, 172
Beltram, Blake, 183
Beresini, Erin, 179
Berk, Lotte, 34, 80
BFX, 26
Bicycling, 68
Biggest Loser, The, 122
Bittman, Mark, 73
Blank gyms, 25
Blanks, Billy, 55
Blau, Jeff, 21–22
Bloomberg, 119
Bloomberg Businessweek, 180
Bloomberg News, 63, 66
Bloomberg Television, 64
Bloom clothing line, 69
BodyArmor, 74
Bombings, Boston Marathon, 135
Boorman, Arthur, 59–60
Born to Run (MacDougall), 164
Boston Athletic Association (BAA), 135, 137.
    See also Boston Marathon
Boston Marathon:
    1996 race, 143
    2007 race, 154
    2013 race, 135
    2014 race, 127, 128, 135–136, 137–138,
        157–158
    bombings, 135
    charity, 103, 104
    commercialism, 138
    Dubai Marathon announcement at, 154
    economic impact, 128
    entry fees, 128
    expo, 138
    jacket, 138
    Patriots' Day and, 145
    qualifying standards, 104, 128, 135, 136
    registration, 135–136
    security for, 137
    technology and, 121
    training for, 136–137
Boston to New York AIDS Ride, 97
Boutique fitness. *See also specific companies*
    business model, 35–36
    classes, charging extra for, 40
    fixed costs, 36
    instructors, 36
    pay-per-visit model, 35–36
    personalities, 36–37
    real estate costs, 36
Brands, gurus as, 56–60
Branson, Richard, 130, 141
Breen, Ed, 109, 110
Brewer, Chris, 105
Broad, William J., 83–84, 86
Bronson, Po, 189
Brooklyn Half Marathon, 152, 197
Bryant, Kobe, 74
Bullivant, Stephen, 77–78
Bundchen, Gisele, 70
Burch, Beryl, 88
Burke, Bill, 144
Business Insider, 119
Business models:
    boutique fitness, 35–36
    ClassPass, 47–48
    fitmob, 46
    gyms, 14–15
    monthly plans, 14–15
    pay-as-you-go, 46
    pay-per-visit, 35–36
    private equity, 152
    sampling, 47–48
Buteau, Michael, 124

Calera Capital, 152
California AIDS ride, 97
Canarick, John, 10–11
Cantor, Eddie, 106
Capiraso, Michael, 141
Carlsbad 5000, 144–145
Cash flow, gym, 15
Catalyst (investment firm), 184
Catterton Partners, 34, 87
Cause Marketing Forum, 101
Celebrities. *See also specific celebrities*
    Barry's Bootcamp and, 30, 32, 95
    charity and, 93–94, 95, 104–105
    New York City Marathon and, 134
    yoga and, 84–85
CEO Challenges, 17, 109, 110, 111–114,
    125–126
CES (Consumer Electronics Show), 188, 193
Challenged Athletes Foundation, 112
Challenges, future, 199–200
Chamberlain, Wilt, 147
Charity:
    Boston Marathon, 103, 104
    celebrities, 93–94, 95, 104–105
    CEO Challenges, 112
    Color Run, The, 174
    CrowdRise, 93–96, 99–100, 102, 108
    Cupid Undies Run, 180–181
    Hessekiel, David, 100–102, 103
    Ice Bucket Challenge, 108
    marathons, 102–104
    New York City Marathon, 103, 104
    Rock 'n' Roll Marathon, 146
    Schaye, Paul, 96–98
    statistics, 100, 101
    Team in Training, 98–99, 101, 102, 103
    technology and, 101–102
    Virginia Beach half marathon, 148–149
    walkathons for, 106–107
Cheeseburger versus cupcake metaphor,
    198–199
Cheever, Ben, 131
Cher, 14
Chestnut Hill Partners, 96
Chicago Triathlon, 126
Children's Tumor Foundation, 180–181
Ciaccia, Peter, 141

Cigarette smoking, 53
Citi Field (Queens, New York),
    173–176
Citigroup, xiii
Civic pride, 143–144
Classes:
    Barry's Bootcamp, 35–36
    boutique fitness, 40
    charging extra for, 40
    loyalty to, 55–56
ClassPass, 47–48
Classtivity, 47
Cleland, Bruce, 98, 99, 104
Cleland, Georgia, 98
Clothing. *See also* Shoes; *specific companies*
    Bloom, 69
    Lululemon, 61–65, 68–69, 70
    private equity and, 62–63
    sport-specific, 66–67
    triathlon, 66–67
    yoga, 69
Cognitive flexibility, 118
Collins, John, 6
Collins, Judy, 6
Color Run, The:
    branded series, 181
    charity, 174
    competitors, 172–173
    discount, early-bird, 171–172
    evolution of, 171–176
    impact of, 140
    innovation, 181
    Major League Baseball All-Star Weekend
        and, 182
    model for, 169–170
    overseas growth, 172
    Paris, 169, 182
    participants, 172
    photography, 172, 175
    Queens, New York, 173–176
    registration, 171–172
    Singapore, 172
    social media, 172, 175–176
    technology and, 172
    video for, 172
    volunteers, 174
    Zumba and, 174

Commercialism:
  Boston Marathon, 138
  yoga, backlash against, 90–91
Community, 48–49, 78
Competitor Group, 10, 148–149, 150,
  151–152, 167
Connerton, Peter, 153–155
Consumer Electronics Show (CES), 188, 193
Cope, Brianna, 70
Copeland, Misty, 70
Core Fusion, 80
CorePower Yoga, 87
Corporate Challenge, 117
Corporate wellness and profitability,
  117–118
Country Music Marathon, 147–148
Course hours, race, 145
Crain's Chicago Business, 125
CrossFit, 26–28, 180
CrowdRise, 93–96, 99–100, 102, 108
Crunch gym, 39
Cupcake versus cheeseburger metaphor,
  198–199
Cupid Undies Run, 180–181
Cycle for Survival, 97
Cycle of Lies: the Fall of Lance Armstrong
  (Macur), 105
Cycling, indoor, 23–25, 37–38, 81

Dalian Wanda Group, 9–10\
Daniels, Jack, 193
Daniloff, Caleb, 52
Darling, Hobey, 124
Day, Christine, 64
DDP Yoga, 58–60
Dean, Will, 176–177, 178, 181
Death by race participants, 178
Death Race, 179
Dederer, Claire, 83
De Sena, Joe, 179
DeVito, Fred, 80–81
Diddy, 134
Differentiation of gyms:
  by price, 18–20
  by quality, 20–23
DiLorenzo, Joe, 66, 96
DiLorenzo, Matt, 66–67
Discounts, early-bird, 171–172

Disney Marathon, 150
Disney World, 150
Disq, 39
Djokavic, Novak, 71
Dopey option (Disney World), 150
Double Triple Bypass, 119
Drinks, energy/sports, 73–74. *See also*
  Food and drink
Dubai International Financial Centre, 154
Du Bey, Jesse, 5–6, 7–8, 9–10
Du Bey Family Foundation, 9

Early-bird discounts, 171–172
Economic impact:
  Boston Marathon, 128
  New York City Marathon, 129–130
  Philadelphia Marathon, 130
  Rock 'n' Roll Marathon, 146
Elite athletes, appearance fees for, 152
Elite Racing, 144–145, 146–147, 148,
  150–151
Ellis, Lincoln, 119–120, 121
Emerson, Ralph Waldo, 78
Employee engagement, 124–125
Energy drinks, 73–74
Energy Gel Central, 74
Engagement, employee, 124–125
Englehart, Peter, 151
Entry fees:
  Boston Marathon, 128
  New York City Marathon, 129
Equinox:
  boutique fitness and, 199
  challenges, future, 200
  clientele, 22
  hotels, branded, 22
  Kapoor, Aarti, and, xiii
  mission, 25
  North Castle and, 11
  private equity and, 21
  quality as differentiating element,
    20–23
  real estate and, 21–23
  Speedball and, 54, 56
Equipment, gym, 15
Escape:
  running as, 79–80
  yoga as, 82

Escape from Alcatraz, 113
Eschbach, Annbeth, 81
exhale studios, 80–81
Expos, 138, 200

Facebook, 186–187, 190
Falconhead Capital, 10, 150–151, 153
Fashion, 65–66
Fed Up, 72
Feinberg, Steve, 53–55, 56–57
Female participants:
    Color Run, 172
    half marathon, 149–150
    marathon, 140
    yoga, 83, 84
Fidelity Investments, 117
*Fit for Consumption: Sociology and the
    Business of Fitness* (Maguire), 89–90
Fitbit, 188–194
Fitmob, 45, 46–47, 48
Fitness centers. *See also specific fitness centers*
    business model, 14–15
    cash flow, 15
    differentiation of, 18–23
    equipment, 15
    evolution of, 14–16, 18
    as lifestyle, 16
    monthly plans, 14–15
    price, differentiation by, 18–20
    private equity and, 16–17, 21
    profitability, 16
    quality, differentiation by, 20–23
    as social center, 15–16
    statistics, 13
Fitness Incorporated, 126
Flexibility, cognitive, 118
Flywheel, xiv, 38
Fonda, Jane, 37
Food and drink:
    activity-specific, 73–74
    affluence and, 72
    Barry's Bootcamp, 29–30
    energy/sports drinks, 73–74
    as fitness economy sector, 71–74
    organic, 71–72
Forbes, 74
Forbes.com, 130
Friendships, work, 123

Furniss, Steve, 66
Future challenges, 199–200
Galter Life Center, 44
Galvin, Christopher, 109, 110
"Game On Pittsburgh" program, 140
Gap Inc., 68, 69
Gebrselassie, Haile, 155
Gels, 74
Generation X:
    about, xvi
    marathon participation by, 140
    meaning, looking for, 82
Golden Bond, 102
Golf, 124, 163
Gonzalez, Joey, 36
Goofy option (Disney World), 150
Goucher, Adam, 162
Goucher, Kara, 162–163, 186
Graham, Brogan, 51–52
Greenberg, Robert, 157, 158
Groupies (Wall Street/athlete archetype), 120
Gurus, as brands, 56–60
Gyms. *See also specific gyms*
    business model, 14–15
    cash flow, 15
    differentiation of, 18–23
    equipment, 15
    evolution of, 14–16, 18
    as lifestyle, 16
    monthly plans, 14–15
    price, differentiation by, 18–20
    private equity and, 16–17, 21
    profitability, 16
    quality, differentiation by, 20–23
    as social center, 15–16
    statistics, 13

Half marathons:
    Brooklyn Half Marathon, 152, 197
    Nike Women's, 149
    Virginia Beach, 148, 149
    women participants, 149–150
Halfpapp, Elizabeth, 80–81
Haller, Gordon, 6
HardBody Software, 183
Harvard Business Review, 117–118, 125
Harvard Business School, 177
Harvie, Robin, 79

Health club industry statistics, 35
Heartbreak Hill, 127, 137
Heavy Medal program, 150
Hessekiel, David, 100–102, 103
Hessler, Chris, 5–6
Heumiller, Peter, 56–57
Higgins, Rick, 157, 158, 161, 162, 163, 200
Hincapie, George, 113
Hira, Nadira, 48–49, 78, 116
Hoit, Roger, xiv
Hoka One One, 166
Hoopfest, 116
Horton, Tony, 45
Hotels, branded, 22
Hours, race course, 145
Howe, Neil, 49

Ice Bucket Challenge, 108
Imperial Capital, 3
Independent Running Retailer Association, 68
Indoor cycling, 23–25, 37–38, 81
ING, 132, 133
ING New York City Marathon, 132. *See also*
    New York City Marathon
Injuries, 178
Instructors:
    Barry's Bootcamp, 36
    boutique fitness, 36
    fitmob, 46–47
    loyalty to, 55–56
InStyle, 70
Investment banks, 1, 2–11. *See also specific*
    banks
IPOs, 194
Ironman. *See also* Triathlons
    about, 6–8, 9–10
    CEO Challenges and, 109, 110, 113

Jacket, Boston Marathon, 138
Jawbone, 188–193
Jay, Barry, 29–33, 36–37, 200. *See also*
    Barry's Bootcamp
JLL (real estate firm), 126
Jobs, Steve, 114
Johnson & Johnson, 117
JP Morgan Corporate Challenge, 117
Junior Carlsbad, 144–145

Kadakia, Payal, 47
Kaleidoscope Tour, 181
Kapoor, Aarti:
    biography, xiii–xv
    boutique fitness, 41
    fitness economy, xvi–xvii
    food sector, 74
    gyms, 13, 14, 19, 25, 26
    investment criteria, 198–199
    private equity, 3–4
Kapoor, Raj, 45–47, 48, 199
Karimloo, Ramin, 30
Keflezighi, Hawi, 157, 159–161, 162, 167
Keflezighi, Meb:
    Boston Marathon, 127, 157–158
    Keflezighi, Hawi, as agent, 159–161
    New York City Marathon, 159, 162, 166
    New York Road Runners and, 158, 159
    Olympics, 159
    personal history, 158–159
    Rock 'n' Roll Marathon, 167
    Skechers and, 157, 158, 161–162, 163,
        166, 167
    sponsorship revenue, 160–161
    Twitter and, 186
    Wittenberg, Mary, and, 127, 158
Kennedy, Ted, 111–112, 125–126, 180
Kickstarter, 94
Kit + Ace, 65, 70–71, 75
Klinger, Jeff, 17
Knudsen, Brent, 2
Kuchar, Matt, 163
Kung fu, 54

"Lace Up Local" campaign, 68
LA Fitness, 16
LA Marathon, 144, 146, 155, 200
Lanman, Fritz, 47
Las Vegas, 151–152
Leadville 100, 17, 111, 114
Learn to Tri, 125–126
Legere, John, 121
Leonard Green & Co., 16–17
Let's Move campaign, 73
Leukemia & Lymphoma Society, 98
Levchin, Max, 121
LG, 193

Lifestyle:
  fitness as, 199–200
  gyms as, 16
Life Time Fitness, 16–17, 111, 114
Lighthouse Triathlon, 119
Limeade (company), 116–117
LinkedIn, 122
Livestrong, 104–105
London, 152, 200
London Marathon, 102
Los Angeles Marathon, 144, 146, 155, 200
Lotte Berk Method, 34, 80–81
Luger, Rich, 151
Lululemon, 61–65, 68–69, 70
Lure of Long Distances, The (Harvie), 79
Luvo, 64
Lyft, 45–46, 48

Maasai Wilderness Conservation Trust, The,
    93, 99, 104
MacDougall, Christopher, 164, 165
Macur, Juliet, 105
Mad Men, 66
Magnum PI, 171
Maguire, Jennifer Smith, 89–90
Major League Baseball All-Star Weekend, 182
Males as yoga participants, 83, 84
Mandaric, Bojan, 51–52
Mantra (Yoga to the People), 90–91
MapMyRun, 187
Marathons. *See also* Boston Marathon; New
    York City Marathon
  charity and, 102–104
  costs, operating, 144, 146–147, 148
  Country Music Marathon, 147–148
  course hours, 145
  death rate among participants, 178
  Disney Marathon, 150
  Dubai Marathon, 153–155
  Generation X participants, 140
  ING New York City Marathon, 132
  LA Marathon, 144, 146, 155, 200
  London Marathon, 102
  Marine Corps Marathon, 130–131, 132
  Millennial participants, 139–140
  Philadelphia Marathon, 130
  registration, online, 145–146

Rock 'n' Roll Marathon, 98, 143, 144,
    145–147
  Strip at Night, 151–152
  TCS New York City Marathon, 132–133,
    197
  Three Rivers Marathon, 139–140
  Virgin Money London Marathon, 102
  women participants, 140
  World Marathon Majors, 132
March for Babies, 107
March of Dimes, 106–107
Marine Corps Marathon, 130–131, 132
Mastercard, 160
Matamoros, Patrice, 139–140
McCann's, 73
McCartney, Kathleen, 6
McGillivray, Dave, 137, 158
Meaning, looking for:
  Baby Boomers, 81–82
  community aspects, 78
  Generation X, 82
  Millennials, 78, 82, 142
  mind-body connection, 77–78
  as recent phenomenon, 89–90
  religion, 77, 78
  running, as escape, 79–80
  running, spiritual benefits of, 78–79
  Seekers (Wall Street/athlete archetype), 120
  spirituality, 78–79
  yoga, 82–89, 90–91
Medals, 150
Meditation, 75
Meetings, walking, 125
Men as yoga participants, 83, 84
Men's Journal, 179
Merchant, Nilofer, 125
Merryman, Asjley, 189
Microsoft Challenge, 126
Millennials:
  about, xvi
  Color Run participation by, 172
  fitness as lifestyle, 186
  marathon participation by, 139–140
  meaning, looking for, 78, 82, 142
  November Project, 52
  peer pressure around wellness, 48–49
  technology and, 185

Millennials (*continued*)
  work, attitude toward, 116
  work friendships, 123
MindBody, 52, 53, 121–122, 184–186, 194
Mind-body connection, 77–78. *See also*
  Meaning, looking for
MindBody Evolve, 122
Minimal shoes, 164–165
Mipham, Sakyong, 78–79
MOB (mud, obstacle, and beer) races. *See*
  also Color Run, The
  defined, 170
  Ragnars, 174
  repeat participants, 181
  Spartan Race, 114, 178, 179–180
  Tough Mudder, 140, 171, 176–178,
    179, 181
  Undies Run, 170, 180–181
  Zombie Run, 180
Models, business:
  boutique fitness, 35–36
  ClassPass, 47–48
  fitmob, 46
  gyms, 14–15
  monthly plans, 14–15
  pay-as-you-go, 46
  pay-per-visit, 35–36
  private equity, 152
  sampling, 47–48
Moelis & Co., xiii, xiv–xv. *See also* Kapoor,
  Aarti
Money prize for Dubai Marathon, 154
Montgomerie, Colin, 163
Monthly plans, 14–15
Moosejaw, 95–96
Moross, David, 10, 150–151, 152–153, 191
Mortensen, Dave, 17
Moss, Julie, 6
Motorola, 109–110
Movember, 100
Mud, obstacle, and beer (MOB) races.
  See also Color Run, The
  defined, 170
  Ragnars, 174
  repeat participants, 181
  Spartan Race, 114, 178, 179–180
  Tough Mudder, 140, 171, 176–178,
    179, 181

  Undies Run, 170, 180–181
  Zombie Run, 180
Muddarella, 178
Mumford, Rachel, 31, 36
Murphy, Tim, 98, 144–145, 147, 150

Nashville, 147–148
National Business Group on Health, 117
National Foundation for Infantile Paralysis, 106
New Balance, 133
Newby-Fraser, Paul, 112
Newton Running, 165–166
New York City:
  American consciousness, role in, 118
  as marathon setting, 134
  margins in, 199
  November Project, 49–52
New York City Marathon:
  2009 race, 159
  2011 race, 162
  2013 race cancellation, 129, 131
  2015 race, 166
  Airbnb and, 197
  celebrity participation in, 134
  charity, 103, 104
  economic impact, 129–130
  entry fees, 129
  expo, 200
  growth of, 128–129
  personality of, 134
  sponsorship relationships, 132–133
  training for, 136
  viewers, 145
New York Equinox hotel, 22
New Yorker, 179
New York Road Runners (NYRR). *See also*
  New York City Marathon
  charity runners, 104
  economic impact of marathon, 130
  executives, current, 141
  JP Morgan Corporate Challenge, 117
  Keflezighi, Meb, and, 158, 159
  races, 103
  Wittenberg, Mary, as CEO, 128, 131,
    132–134, 159
  youth programs, 133
New York Times, 131
New York Times Magazine, 57, 59

Nike, 105, 159, 160, 161, 188, 193
Nike FuelBand, 188, 193
Nike Women's half marathon, 149
Nontraditional races. *See also* Color Run, The
 defined, 170
 Ragnars, 174
 repeat participants, 181
 Spartan Race, 114, 178, 179–180
 Tough Mudder, 140, 171, 176–178, 179,
  181
 Undies Run, 170, 180–181
 Zombie Run, 180
Nordstrom, 66
North Castle, 10–11, 21, 41
Norton, Edward, 93, 94, 99, 102, 104
November Project, 49–52
Novy-Williams, Eben, 124
NYC Triathlon, 126
NYRR (New York Road Runners). *See also*
 New York City Marathon
 charity runners, 104
 economic impact of marathon, 130
 executives, current, 141
 JP Morgan Corporate Challenge, 117
 Keflezighi, Meb, and, 158, 159
 races, 103
 Wittenberg, Mary, as CEO, 128, 131,
  132–134, 159
 youth programs, 133

O2 Fitness, 40
Oatmeal, 73
Obama, Michelle, 73
Obesity, 72
Off Course (Beresini), 179
Oiselle, 163
Olander, Michael, Jr., 39–41
Olbermann, Keith, 165
Oldenburg, Ray, 2
Olympics, 144, 159
Olympic Trials, 130–131, 140, 162
Online registration, 145–146
Online shopping, 166
Organic food, 71–72
Organic Trade Association, 72
Orkila Capital, 9
Out of the Darkness Community Walks
 series, 100

Page, Diamond Dallas, 57–60
Pan-Mass Challenge (PMC), 97
Paragon Sports, 165
Paris Color Run, 169, 182
Participants. *See also specific activities and events*
 athletes in yoga, 87, 88–89
 Color Run, The, 172
 death rate among race, 178
 Generation X in marathons, 140
 marathons, 139–140, 178
 men in yoga, 83, 84
 Millennial in marathons, 139–140
 women in Color Run, 172
 women in half marathons, 149–150
 women in marathons, 140
 women in yoga, 83, 84
 yoga, 83, 84, 87, 88–89
Participatory sports, fastest-growing, 151
Partnership Capital Growth, 2–3
Passion, 53
Passport (service), 47–48
Patriots' Day, 143, 145
Paul's Posse, 97
Pay-as-you-go business model, 46
Pay-per-visit business model, 35–36
Peachtree Road Race, 134, 144
Peer pressure:
 around fitness lifestyle, 122
 around wellness, 48–49
Peer-to-Peer Forum, 101
Personalities, in boutique fitness, 36–37
Pew Research Center, 78
Philadelphia Marathon, 130
Philadelphia's 8-K, 150
Phippen, Kent, 173–174, 175, 176
Photography, 172, 175
Pink, Daniel H., 81–82
Piper Jaffray (firm), 2, 3
Pittsburgh, 139–140
Planet Fitness, 18–20
Plenty (firm), 106
PMC (Pan-Mass Challenge), 97
Polio, 106–107
Poser (Dederer), 83
Potdevin, Laurent, 64
Powder Days, 124
Power Yoga (Burch), 88
Prevention Magazine, 187

Price, for differentiating gyms, 18–20
Pride, civic, 143–144
Private equity. *See also specific firms*
   about, 3–5
   athletic clothing and, 62–63
   business model, 152
   gyms and, 16–17, 21
   yoga and, 87
Profitability:
   corporate wellness and, 117–118
   of gyms, 16
   of yoga, 86–87
#TheProgram, 115
Providence Equity Partners, 7, 8, 9
Pump One, 18
Pure Barre, 33–34

Quality, differentiating gyms by, 20–23
Queens, New York, Color Run, 173–176
Queer Eye for the Straight Guy, 65

Race course hours, 145
Race expos, 138, 200
Race It, 151
Race Ready, 74
Radcliffe, Paula, 141
Ragnars, 174
Rahman, Hosain, 189
Raptor Consumer Partners, 179
Ratey, John J., 118
Real estate, 21–23, 36, 126
Reebok, 180
Reebok Spartan Races, 180
Reebok Sports Club NY, 55
Refinery studio, 44
Registration:
   Boston Marathon, 135–136
   Color Run, The, 171–172
   marathons, 145–146
   online, 145–146
Related Companies, 21, 22, 23
Relay for Life, 100
Religion, 77, 78
Resurrection of Jake the Snake, The, 59
Rezabek Dorr, Carrie, 34
Rishe, Patrick, 130
Roberts, Jake "The Snake," 59

Robertson, Gregor, 62
Robertson, Shauna, 93, 94
Rockefeller State Park Preserve, 131
Rock Encore medals, 150
Rock Idol medals, 150
Rock 'n' Roll Marathon, 98–99, 143, 144,
   145–147
Rodale, 68
Roemer, Tracy, 125
Rondeau, Chris, 19–20
Roosevelt, Franklin D., 106–107
Ross, Julie, 119
Ross, Stephen, 21
Runner's World:
   Color Run ad, 143
   Competitor Group and, 148, 149
   consumerism and, 68, 138
   November Project, 50, 52
   as online community, 67, 138
   Rockefeller State Park Preserve, 131
   running as escape, 79
   Tough Mudder, 178
   Virginia Beach half marathon,
      148, 149
Running. *See also specific topics*
   as escape, 79–80
   spiritual benefits of, 78–79
Running Times, 68
Running USA, 134, 149, 170
Running with the Mind of Meditation
   (Mipham), 78–79
Run Walk Ride Fundraising Council, 101
Runyon, Chuck, 17–18
Saidman, Colleen, 84, 85–86
Salazar, Alberto, 159
Sampling, as business model, 47–48
Samsung, 193
San Diego, 143, 144–146, 147
Sandy, Superstorm, 129, 131
San Francisco, 43, 45, 46–47
Schadler, Laura, 89
Schaye, Paul, 66, 96–98
Science of Yoga: The Risks and the Rewards
   (Broad), 83–84
Security for Boston Marathon, 137
Sedaris, David, 190
Seekers (Wall Street/athlete archetype), 120

Seidler Companies, The, 3
September 11, 2001 terrorist attacks, 81
ShapeUp, 187
Shape-up shoes, 161, 163, 164
Sharing economy, 45–46, 48, 197
Shine Tour, 181
Shoes. *See also* Skechers; *specific brands*
    minimal, 164–165
    Shape-up, 161, 163, 164
    technology and, 166
Shopping, online, 166
Shorter, Frank, 144
Shred415, 125
Shuck, Jeff, 106, 107–108
Silicon Valley, 120–122
Silver Bond, 102
Simmons, Richard, 37
Singapore Color Run, 172
Skechers:
    Keflezighi, Meb, and, 157, 158, 161–162, 163, 166, 167
    as LA Marathon sponsor, 155, 200
Skechers Performance, 161, 163, 165, 166
Skullcandy, 124
SlowTwitch.com, 67
Smartphones, 122
Smith, Brian, 2, 10
Smoking, cigarette, 53
Snyder, Travis, 169–170, 176, 181, 182
So, Lillian, 43–45, 48, 55
Soccer, 151
Social lives, 15–16, 51, 123
Social media:
    about, 123
    athletes and, 186–187
    Color Run, The, 172, 175–176
    role of, 186–187
SoFierce, 43, 45
SoFluid, 43, 45
SoulCycle, 23–25, 81
Spark: The Revolutionary New Science of Exercise and the Brain (Ratey), 118
Spartan Race, 114, 178, 179–180
Spartan Up (De Sena), 179
Speedball, 53, 54–55, 56–57
Speedball Media and Merchandise, 57
Spevak, Harvey, 21, 22, 23, 24, 25, 200

Spinning, 23–25, 37–38, 81
Spirituality, 78–79
Sponsors. *See also specific companies*
    Keflezighi, Meb, 160–161
    LA Marathon, 155, 200
    New York City Marathon, 132–133
Sports apparel. *See also* Shoes; *specific companies*
    Bloom, 69
    Lululemon, 61–65, 68–69, 70
    private equity and, 62–63
    sport-specific, 66–67
    triathlon, 66–67
    yoga, 69
Sports Authority, 69
Sports drinks, 73–74
Sport-specific clothing, 66–67
Standard Chartered bank, 154
Statistics:
    charity, 100, 101
    gyms, 13
    health club industry, 35
    yoga, 83
Steps, measurement of, 188–189, 191–192
Sting, 85
Stollmeyer, Rick, 52–53, 122, 183–185
Stop & Shop, 72
Strava, 188–189
Street & Smith's Sports Business Daily, 152
Strip at Night, 151–152
Sunlun, Tracy:
    appearance fees for elite athletes, 152
    biography, 144
    charity, 98, 99
    Murphy, Tim, and, 144–145
    Rock 'n' Roll Marathon, 98, 99, 145, 146–147
    Virginia Beach half marathon, 148, 149
Super Bowl, 128
Superfood, 73
Superstorm Sandy, 129, 131
Sweatworking, as term, 125
Sweeney, Allison, 122

Tae Bo, 55
Taetle, Alan, 198
Take-Two Interactive, 115
Tata Consulting Services (TCS), 132–133

Tattoos, 7, 17, 181
TCS (Tata Consulting Services), 132–133
TCS New York City Marathon, 132–133,
    197. *See also* New York City Marathon
Team in Training (TNT):
    Hessekiel, David, and, 101
    Rock 'n' Roll Marathon and, 98–99, 146
    team aspect, 102, 103
    Virginia Beach half marathon and, 148–149
Technology:
    Boston Marathon and, 121
    charity and, 101–102
    Color Run and, 172
    companies specializing in, 120–121
    gear/apparel and, 67–68
    role of, 1–2, 184, 186
    shoes and, 166
    socializing effect of, 187
Tergat, Paul, 160
#TheProgram, 115
Thomson Reuters, 63
Thoreau, Henry David, 78
Three Rivers Marathon, 139–140
TNT (Team in Training):
    Hessekiel, David, and, 101
    Rock 'n' Roll Marathon and, 98–99, 146
    team aspect, 102, 103
    Virginia Beach half marathon and, 148–149
TOMS, 64
Top Dog (Bronson and Merryman), 189
TorqBoard, xiv, 38
Tough Mudder, 140, 171, 176–178, 179, 181
Town Sports International, 25–26
TPG Capital, 16–17
Trail Runner, 79, 164
Training:
    Boston Marathon, 136–137
    New York City Marathon, 136
Train with Yoga, 88–89
Trends, 197–200
Triathlete, 68
Triathlon magazine, 68
Triathlons:
    Chicago Triathlon, 126
    clothing, 66–67
    growth of, 8
    Ironman, 6–8, 9–10, 109, 110, 113

Lighthouse Triathlon, 119
    NYC Triathlon, 126
Triple Bypass, 119
Twentieth Century Fox, 115
24-Hour Fitness, xiii
Twitter, 60, 175–176, 186–187
Type-A's (Wall Street/athlete archetype), 120
Tyr, 66–67

Uber, 45–46, 48
UCLA (University of California, Los Angeles),
    160, 161
Under Armour, 70
Undies Run, 170, 180–181
Uniqlo, 119–120
United Airlines, 133
University of California, Los Angeles
    (UCLA), 160, 161
Urban Mudder, 178
Urban Outfitters, 69
USA Triathlon, 8

Vancouver, British Columbia, 62
*VB6: Eat Vegan Before 6:00 to Lose Weight and
    Restore Your Health ... For Good* (Bitt-
    man), 73
VDOT, 193
Veganism, 29–30, 73
Vibram, 164, 165
Videos:
    Color Run, 172
    yoga, 59–60, 85–86
Vigil, Fernando, 5–6
Virginia Beach, 148–149
Virgin Money London Marathon, 102
Virgin Pulse, 141
Virgin Sport, 130, 141–142
Volunteers:
    Color Run, The, 174
    races, organized running, 143–144

Wade, Lisa, 90, 91
WalkAmerica, 107
Walkathons, 106–107
Walking, popularity of, 151
Walking meetings, 125
Wall, Jaime, 33

Wall Street, 118–120
Wall Street Decathlon, 119
Wall Street Journal, 39
Walsh, Patrick, 26
Wanda Group, 9–10
Warren Street Social and Athletic Club, 144
Wearable technology, 188–194
Websites:
  Active.com, 170
  Forbes.com, 130
  SlowTwitch.com, 67
  whil.com, 75
Wellness. *See also specific topics*
  market size, xv
  peer pressure around, 48–49
Whelan, Melanie, 24–25
whil.com, 75
WhiteWave, 71
Whole Foods, 71–72
Whole New Mind, A (Pink), 81–82
Williamson, Charles, 113
Wilson, Chip, 61–65, 70–71, 75, 186
Wilson, Fred, 94
Wilson, JJ, 65, 70
Wilson, Shannon, 65, 70
Winfrey, Oprah, 84–85
Winsor, Mari, 183
Without Walls, 69
Wittenberg, Mary:
  challenges, future, 200
  half marathons, 149
  Keflezighi, Meb, and, 127, 158
  marathon as business, 140
  as marathon participant, 127, 130–131, 158
  as NYRR CEO, 128, 131, 132–134, 159
  as Virgin Sport head, 130, 141–142
WJ Partners, 33, 34
Wolfe, Jeffrey, 93
Wolfe, Robert, 93–94, 95–96, 99–100, 108, 200
Wolfe, Tom, 89–90
Women participants:
  Color Run, 172
  half marathon, 149–150
  marathon, 140
  yoga, 83, 84
Wood, Brian, 3, 35

Work and working out:
  CEO Challenges, 17, 109, 110, 111–114, 125–126
  corporate wellness and profitability, 117–118
  employee engagement, 124–125
  fitness companies, 121–122
  friendships at work, 123
  Silicon Valley, 120–121, 121–122
  social lives, 123
  Wall Street, 118–120
  Zafirovski, Mike, 109–111, 126
  Zelnick, Strauss, 115, 116, 124
Workday CEO Challenge, 126
Work friendships, 123
World Marathon Majors, 132
World Series, 128
World's Fittest CEO, 111
World Triathlon Corp. (WTC), 9–10, 111, 113
World Wrestling Entertainment (WWE), 59
Wrestling, professional, 57, 58, 59
WTC (World Triathlon Corp.), 9–10, 111, 113
WWE (World Wrestling Entertainment), 59

Yee, Rodney, 84, 85–86
Yoga:
  appeal of, 82–84
  athlete participants, 87, 88–89
  celebrities and, 84–85
  clothing for, 69
  commercialization, backlash against, 90–91
  CorePower Yoga, 87
  DDP Yoga, 58–60
  as escape, 82
  as intimidating, 83
  meaning, looking for, 82–89, 90–91
  men participants, 83, 84
  personal versus communal aspects, 85, 87
  private equity and, 87
  profitability of, 86–87
  So, Lillian, and, 44
  statistics, 83
  Train with Yoga, 88–89
  videos, 59–60, 85–86
  women participants, 83, 84

Yoga For Regular Guys: The Best Damn Work-out on the Planet! (Page), 58–59
Yoga Journal, 68, 83
Yoga Shanti, 86
Yoga to the People, 90–91
Young Presidents Organization, 113
Youth programs:
　Junior Carlsbad, 144–145
　New York Road Runners, 133

YouTube, 59–60
Yu, Steve, 59

Zafirovski, Mike, 109–111, 126
Zelnick, Strauss, 115, 116, 124
Zelnick Media Capital, 115
Zombie, Rob, 58
Zombie Run, 180
Zuckerberg, Mark, 114, 125
Zumba, 174